Benjamin Shambaugh
and the Intellectual Foundations
of Public History

BENJAMIN SHAMBAUGH

and the Intellectual Foundations of Public History

by Rebecca Conard

University of Iowa Press · Iowa City

University of Iowa Press, Iowa City 52242
Printed in the United States of America

Design by Omega Clay

http://www.uiowa.edu/~uipress

The State Historical Society, Inc., and the University of Iowa Foundation
generously subsidized the publication of this work.

Printed on acid-free paper

Library of Congress Cataloging-in-Publication Data
Conard, Rebecca.
   Benjamin Shambaugh and the intellectual foundations of public history /
by Rebecca Conard.
       p.   cm.
   Includes bibliographical references and index.
   ISBN 0-87745-789-1
   1. Shambaugh, Benjamin Franklin, 1871–1940. 2. Historians—United
States—Biography. 3. Historians—Iowa—Biography. 4. Public history—
United States. 5. Public history—Iowa. 6. United States—Historiography.
7. Iowa—Historiography. I. Title.

E175.5.S43 C66 2002
973'.07'202—dc21
[B]   2001027986

02 03 04 05 06 C 5 4 3 2 1

FRONTISPIECE. Benjamin F. Shambaugh. *Courtesy State Historical Society of
Iowa, Iowa City.*

Dedicated to

the memory of Jacob A. Swisher

Contents

Foreword and Acknowledgments

BENJAMIN FRANKLIN SHAMBAUGH (1871–1940), superintendent of the State Historical Society of Iowa and chair of the Department of Political Science at the University of Iowa, was one of the first "pioneers" to be discovered in the early days of the modern public history movement. In 1980, while compiling an annotated bibliography of public works and environmental history, a staff member at the Public Works Historical Society (PWHS) stumbled across the six-volume Iowa Applied History Series and was "shock[ed] to discover that the concept of 'public historian' was being successfully applied nearly seventy years ago." Alan M. Schroder, then an editor at the State Historical Society of Iowa (SHSI), subsequently wrote an article on Shambaugh and the Applied History Series for the *Public Works Historical Society Newsletter*, noting that the series provided an "excellent example of the practical operation of the principles of 'the new history.'"[1] Peter Stearns and Joel Tarr quickly perceived in the Applied History Series a precursor to the goals of the Applied History and Social Science Program at Carnegie-Mellon University.[2] Stanley Ridgeway cited the Commonwealth Conference, a series of policy forums Shambaugh conceived and convened at Iowa City during the 1920s, as a model for later university-based think tanks. Ridgeway, however, interpreted the conference as a pioneering instance of "applied social science," a term that fails to capture Shambaugh's full intent when the Commonwealth Conference is viewed within his entire career.[3]

In any case, two of Shambaugh's major contributions, the Applied History Series and the Commonwealth Conference, have been recognized in recent years. For me, this raised questions about how these two notable achievements should be measured in relation to the entire output of Shambaugh's career, how Shambaugh viewed himself as a professional

ix

historian and political scientist, what he thought about the value of history to society, and how his concept of applied history squared with the modern public history movement. Over the years, as I kept discovering more about his achievements in Iowa and his involvement in the major historical and political science organizations, these questions became more intriguing. I began to sense that Shambaugh's career would somehow speak to those who believe in the power of history to engage and inspire local audiences as well as to those who believe that historians should apply their knowledge and methods outside the academy in pursuit of greater public good.

Shambaugh's papers, however, present something of a challenge to answering these questions because he made little distinction between the personal and professional aspects of his life. This might have been an asset, except that many of his papers are intertwined with those of his wife, Bertha Horack, a writer and photographer in her own right. Thus, to separate a portion of his life for critical examination, even though that portion captures the dominant aspects of his intellectual training and his professional career, necessarily leaves much untouched. Moreover, to write about Benjamin's professional career without including Bertha's role would be unthinkable, yet to portray her as the true partner she was in his career would have obscured his critical role in laying the foundations of public history.

Fortunately, some of the sifting and sorting had already been done, as I discovered with the help of Mary Bennett, special collections coordinator at the SHSI. One summer day a few years ago, while I was simultaneously working on another research project in the manuscripts room at the SHSI and visiting with Mary, a long-time colleague, we got to talking about the Shambaughs' combined legacy.[4] As we talked, Mary asked if I had ever looked through an unpublished biography of Benjamin written sometime in the 1940s by one of his protégés, Jacob Swisher. I had not, so she retrieved it. One thing led to another, and we were soon brainstorming a book project that would examine the lives of this extraordinary Iowa couple by integrating Swisher's manuscript with Bertha Shambaugh's photographs. The more we thought about this idea, however, the more unwieldy it became, and eventually we abandoned a joint project as unfeasible. In the meantime, I read Swisher's manuscript for insight into what made Benjamin Shambaugh tick, and as I did so my questions about the meaning of his career for the modern public history movement became more compelling. So, Mary handed me an SHSI publication, Alan Schroder's report of an institutional self-study the historical society undertook in 1978–1979. This provided me with an invaluable framework for understanding Benjamin Shambaugh's immense contributions to the society's development.[5]

Thus was this book project launched, and in some respects it is about Jacob Swisher as well as Benjamin Shambaugh. Chapters 2 through 6 are based on Swisher's unpublished biography, which I have used much like a diary in constructing an interwoven narrative. These chapters follow Shambaugh's career from the time he entered the University of Iowa in 1888 until his death in 1940. They trace the forces and choices that shaped his intellectual development during his undergraduate and graduate training and the early years of his career, his administration of the SHSI, his development of applied history and commonwealth history in the 1910s and 1920s, and the transformations in his thinking and his career during the 1930s. The prologue and chapter 1 contextualize Shambaugh's professional development within the development of the historical profession as a whole in the late nineteenth and early twentieth centuries. Chapter 7, the concluding chapter, attempts to assess Shambaugh's career within the post–World War II emergence of the modern public history movement.

For chapters 2 through 6, I chose an interwoven narrative style for several reasons. In the first place, Swisher laid his manuscript aside unpolished, and I suspect deliberately so. Editorial notes on early drafts, written by Bertha when she was a widow, suggest that she was devotedly protective of her husband's legacy, so much so that she rewrote at least one chapter, and a third party, Ethan P. Allen, rewrote the same chapter yet again. Trying to read between the lines, I began to wonder if the question of editorial control eventually reached a point of irreconcilability: Swisher could no longer claim sole authorship, and he could not bring himself to ease Bertha out of the process. But this is pure speculation, since Swisher left no explanation as to why he never took the manuscript to publication.[6] In any case, the manuscript reads more like hagiography than biography, no doubt a reflection of Swisher's close relationship with both Shambaughs, and he never returned to the manuscript in his own later years to take a more distanced view. Additionally, the manuscript in its entirety includes treatments of Shambaugh's youth, his extracurricular academic life, his public speaking and community life, and the Sham-

Jacob Swisher. *Courtesy State Historical Society of Iowa, Iowa City.*

baughs at home. From a biographical perspective, these are important aspects of the whole person, but they are less important for my limited examination of Shambaugh's professional career. I therefore excerpted text from only a dozen of twenty-one chapters. As I delved into Swisher's manuscript, I discovered more disorganization and rhetorical redundancy than had been apparent at first. Consequently, anyone who bothers to check the original manuscript against the passages from Swisher that appear here will find that I have taken considerable liberty in rearranging text and eliminating excessive verbiage. And because his manuscript never received the benefit of copyediting for publication, I have made stylistic corrections as well as renumbered his notes, clarified them when possible, and incorporated them into the overall chapter notes. Swisher's notes tend toward brevity, as one might expect in a draft manuscript, and occasionally the original source could not be located, in which case an explanatory comment appears in the note.

Swisher was not one of Shambaugh's stars who went on to a distinguished career elsewhere. Rather, I suspect that Shambaugh probably considered him an industrious, persevering student and a well-trained, utterly reliable research associate. Swisher entered the University of Iowa as a student in 1914, when he was thirty years old and had been married for four years, a "nontraditional student" at a time when the category did not exist. There he earned his B.A. and M.A. before returning to his native state, Illinois, to take a law degree from the University of Illinois, although it is unclear whether he ever practiced law. He came back to Iowa City in 1922 where he worked part-time at the SHSI while continuing graduate studies at the university. In 1927 he received a Ph.D. in political science. These must have been lean years in the Swisher household since he and his first wife, Nora May Anthony, had several children. After he finished his doctorate, Swisher became a full-time research associate at the SHSI, and he remained there until he retired in 1950. As a research associate, Swisher's job was, simply, to research and write books, articles, and reports, although he also was called upon to edit the work of others. By the time he retired in 1950, he had written more than a hundred articles for the society's various serial publications and authored several books, including *Leonard Fletcher Parker* (1927), *The American Legion in Iowa* (1929), *Some Historic Sites in Iowa* (n.d.), *Robert Gordon Cousins* (1938), *Iowa—Land of Many Mills* (1940), and *Iowa—In Times of War* (1943).[7]

Thus, for most of the years between 1914 and 1940 Swisher was Shambaugh's student or his employee or both. Swisher's professional home was the SHSI, and he no doubt owed his career to Shambaugh, inasmuch as Shambaugh's correspondence with former students indicates that he almost always welcomed them back to the society and created research positions for them whenever he could. Since Swisher and Shambaugh worked in close proximity from 1922 on, there is no correspondence between the two men that might provide clues about the character of their personal relationship, but it is obvious from Swisher's manuscript that he revered his mentor and boss. Nor was he alone in his measure of respect. Upon Shambaugh's death in April of 1940, so great was the outpouring of letters, telegrams, resolutions, editorials, and eulogies from across Iowa and the nation that SHSI senior staff put aside other projects to compile a memorial volume to their departed "Chief." *Benjamin Franklin Shambaugh As Iowa Remembers Him: In Memoriam* can only be described as a true labor of love. It is the kind of tribute rarely given, but Shambaugh always was more than just an esteemed colleague, a highly respected college professor, or a distinguished leader. Shambaugh's name, as John Ely Briggs phrased it in the introduction, "became synonymous with Iowa history and ideals. His achievements were widely known and cherished."[8] The sense of loss was both widespread and deep.

Swisher was unable to distance himself enough, probably incapable of distancing himself, from his subject to write objectively, and his manuscript is no more publishable now, as is, than it was in the mid 1940s. Still, his words exude an unrefined, palpable veneration that could only come from one who knew Shambaugh personally, and it seemed that this quality of the manuscript deserved an audience. After flirting with annotating the manuscript, I abandoned the idea because Swisher left out too much important material. I also disregarded suggestions that I just start over, in part because it seemed a bit unfair and in part because I was drawn to the intimacy of Swisher's manuscript, which provides an almost tangible link to the subject himself. It was only when one of my own former students, Christy Davis, suggested I treat the manuscript as a diary that I began to conceptualize a workable narrative. Thus the structure that emerged is a weaving of passages from Swisher's manuscript and my own annotations and additions, which are sometimes lengthy. To provide narrative flow yet keep the texts distinguishable, Swisher's text is set off by rules and appears in a sans serif typeface.

The resulting work is something Jacob Swisher could not possibly have entertained, but I hope that I have done justice to the spirit in which he wrote his biography and that I have succeeded in giving proper voice to his words within the context of my own interpretation. In addition to Mary Bennett, I also thank the following people for their assistance, support, or suggestions along the way: Marv Bergman, Mike Carrier, Holly Carver, Andrew Gulliford, Dave Hudson, Steve Kettering, Andy Kravschaar, David McCartney, Lorne McWatters, Tom Morain, Howard (Dick) Miller, Jan Nash, Mae Pan, Matt Schaefer, Ginalie Swaim, Lori Vermass, and Lonn Wiegel. I offer a special thank you to the graduate students whom I subjected to reading the unexpurgated Swisher manuscript and the earliest draft of this book: Tony Brusca and Christy Davis, graduates of Wichita State University, and, at Middle Tennessee State University, Tammy Allison, Perky Beisel, Stephanie Chalifoux, Rob DeHart, Laura Finger, Andrea Gales, Mary Allison Haynie, Monty Hedstrom, Stan Hutson, Nathan Kinser, John Lodl, Andrew Quist, Ed Salo, Jen Stoecker, and Stacy Weber.

Arnita Jones, Patricia Melvin-Mooney, and Ramon Powers read the manuscript in its entirety and offered many thoughtful comments. Each, however, had rather different comments concerning the structure and organization of material, and as a result I found myself relying more heavily on one set of comments as I revised the manuscript. This no doubt will be apparent to them, so I hasten to add that I gave equal consideration to the comments of each. Robert Burchfield's superb editing coaxed me into one more stimulating engagement with the material, and for this gift, "thank you" is not enough. The exchange of notes we affixed to and interleaved with the manuscript pages constituted a running dialogue that kept me attentive and without question enhanced the printed book in ways both subtle and substantive. Any remaining errors, omissions, misstatements, and irregular stylistic conventions are entirely my own.

Finally, many thanks to Middle Tennessee State University for a summer research grant that enabled me to devote three months to writing in 1999 and to the State Historical Society, Inc., for generously subsidizing the publication of this work.

Prologue: The Last Dance

AT THE HEIGHT of the Gilded Age, in December of 1897, the members of the American Historical Association (AHA) and the American Economic Association met jointly in Cleveland, mostly, it seems, to celebrate the holiday season. Senator Mark Hanna entertained a select group of AHA officers in his home. Three other prominent Cleveland couples hosted social receptions in their "handsome" homes. Highlighting the evening events were "two dancing parties at The Stillman [Hotel], which gave the learned historians and economists a double chance to see the beauty and chivalry of Cleveland," and late hours were given over to "pleasant reunion[s] of old friends at The Stillman or at some well-known club." AHA Secretary Herbert Baxter Adams later summed up the proceedings by noting that "the most striking feature of the Cleveland convention was its social success. . . . [A] series of receptions and luncheons . . . far excelled the regular sessions."[1]

This was the last AHA conference where social receptions and dancing parties would take precedence in the reporting over scholarly matters and the profession's business. Indeed, thereafter all references to dancing parties disappear from the published proceedings, replaced by minutes of increasingly serious business. It is to be much regretted that historians gave up dancing in order to accommodate evermore sessions, committee meetings, and committee reports. It is also fitting, however, that Herbert Baxter Adams recorded this inadvertent rite of passage. The Cleveland convention, as it turned out, more or less coincided with the passing of the village community theory of history, or the Teutonic germ theory, of which Adams has been labeled its "most zealous American promoter," and the ascendance of Frederick Jackson Turner's frontier thesis as a driving intellectual force.[2]

1

Actually, the reported gaiety of the 1897 meeting masked several new departures in the historical profession. A Committee of Seven, appointed in 1896, arranged sessions devoted to the teaching of history in colleges and secondary schools, the first of several annual discussions on this topic. In 1897 the AHA also began planning to assume sponsorship of the *American Historical Review*, a plan formalized in 1898. The AHA's Historical Manuscripts Commission, charged with editing and publishing manuscript collections of national importance, gave its second annual report. Of particular interest with regard to the role that Benjamin Shambaugh was about to play in Iowa, three distinguished historians—J. Franklin Jameson, Reuben Gold Thwaites, and J. F. Wright—presented papers addressing the organization and functions of state and local historical societies. A year later the AHA would establish a committee to survey the status of state and local historical societies nationwide. Two years later it would form the Public Archives Commission, charged with investigating, and then reforming, the nation's repositories for official records.

Not only was the nature of inquiry changing in the American historical profession, but the profile of historians, as professionals, was undergoing transformation as well. Historians were not unique among scholars in this regard; they were part of a general trend toward university-based professions in the late nineteenth century. Younger scholars in particular increasingly saw a professional role for themselves in the corporate institutional world that emerged with large-scale industrialization.[3] Peter Novick calls this trend, as manifest in the discipline of history, "the professionalization project."[4]

Morey Rothberg has shown that, among historians, J. Franklin Jameson proved to be a highly skilled leader in "the professionalization project." As early as 1891 Jameson advocated that the AHA utilize its quasi-official status with the federal government, which brought access to the Government Printing Office, to publish historical documents of national importance. As the first chair of the AHA's Historical Manuscripts Commission, Jameson began to implement this idea. "It was apparent by the turn of the century," Rothberg writes, "that a career unique in the annals of American scholarship was taking shape." As the AHA's first president to come from academic ranks; as conceptualizer of the Carnegie Institution's Department of Historical Research, which he directed from 1905 to 1928; as editor of the *American Historical Review* from 1895 to 1901 and again from 1905 to 1928; and as the sustaining advocate for federal funding to construct a national archives building, Jameson was the leader in "drawing together virtually all the elements that now constitute the American historical profession."[5]

However, as Laurence Veysey points out, "professionalism" is a vague concept and particularly so in the humanities, where the change was not so much the *creation* of university-based professional identities, as was the case in sociology, economics, and engineering, but "the transition from an older, long existing professional outlook and mentality to newer, more specialized versions of it at the end of the nineteenth century."[6] Moreover, professionalization in the humanities must be viewed within the larger context of related changes in middle-class culture because "the new academic scene did not monopolize humanistic activity." In addition to the emergence of university departments of history, English, philosophy, music, and art, there was a general flowering of humanistic organizations. Museums, archives, and libraries proliferated to take custody of tangible items vested with cultural value. Women's clubs, Chautauquas, patriotic societies, and historical societies promoted cultural uplift in varying degrees and in various ways. Publishers, art societies, opera companies, theaters, and symphony orchestras produced an outpouring of cultural events for the social and educated elite.[7]

The audience for history at the end of the nineteenth century also was changing, but the contours of that change are a bit more difficult to discern. On the one hand, fewer people were buying the weighty volumes produced by "gentleman scholars," thereby exposing a declining appetite for historical disquisition among the elite reading public.[8] On the other, there was greater public interest in history as a means to justify American nationalism. Veysey points out that Congress conferred semiofficial status on the AHA with an act of incorporation in 1889, just one year before the quintessential patriotic society, the Daughters of the American Revolution (DAR), was founded.[9] The DAR was but one of hundreds of women's clubs, local historical societies, and other patriotic societies organized during the 1890s and early 1900s. Their interest in history ran toward marking historic sites (especially battlefields), collecting the reminiscences of "pioneers," and staging historical pageants. In some respects, this rising tide of public interest was much broader, in that literally hundreds of civic and private organizations were making history more visible to the general public. It also was highly decentralized, and the snatches of history placed before the public reflected the specialized or localized interests of sponsoring organizations. If there was any semblance of common purpose, it lay in the fact that historical and patriotic societies often were engaged in a quest for origins or tribal history.[10]

This, then, was the great change taking place in history, as a humanistic endeavor, at the end of the nineteenth century: a new professional outlook closely tied to academic specialization and a doctoral degree as the basic credential for entering the professoriate, juxtaposed with growing public interest in American history to shape and support vague, decentralized nationalistic impulses. Historians expressed this new professional outlook and a new sense of national spirit in at least three general ways. First, they promoted historical awareness as the foundation of a civil society, not just the hallmark of enlightened leaders and thinkers. Second, if history had a role to play in cultivating civil society, it followed that historians also had a duty to preserve the official public records of the nation. Finally, responding to the groundswell of public interest in local and regional history, professional historians felt an obligation to guide such efforts toward a higher purpose.

Within this milieu of change, Benjamin Shambaugh entered what would become a dual career as head of the State Historical Society of Iowa (SHSI) and as a professor of political science at the University of Iowa. In his own way, he was part of "the professionalization project." It profoundly influenced his approach to elevating the preservation and the use of history in the state of Iowa. To this transformation, however, he added his own vision. Rothberg defines the elements of the historical profession that Jameson drew together as "teaching, research and writing, documentary editing, journal editing, institution building, and advocacy."[11] Shambaugh added another element that might be called "serving the commonwealth." The labels Shambaugh himself gave to this element were "applied history" and "commonwealth history," terms he favored at different stages in his career. They meant essentially the same thing: collecting, preserving, publishing, and using history for the greater good of the state.

Highlighting Jameson's central role in professionalizing the discipline of history underscores the gradual nature of the process. Conversely, it also obscures the complexity of the process. By looking a little deeper into the ranks of the discipline, it is possible to see that the professional profile emerging in the early twentieth century was even more multifaceted than the careers of its leading lights would indicate.[12] In this regard, Shambaugh's vision of professional history also retained some of the flavor of what Novick has called "pre-professional" history in that it was "directed outward" at a public audience.[13] But whereas preprofessional historians largely produced written histories that catered to the educated elite, Shambaugh's goal was to present history in many different forms to serve a broader public, still educated but increasingly middle class in station and public-minded in outlook.

Like many professionals of his generation, Shambaugh was caught up in progressivism. Although he never described himself as politically progressive, it is no small coincidence that his career flourished alongside progressive politics in one of the most politically active states during the early twentieth century.[14] Frank Friedel has observed that "Iowa was typical of prosperous, progressive, rural America, with its small towns and cities dotting one of the world's most productive farming areas. It [was] representative of both middle-class and agrarian progressivism."[15] Shambaugh's concepts of "applied" and "commonwealth" history had many facets, but the unifying element was a belief in the efficacy of historical analysis to shape and direct the progress of democratic institutions in the modern age.

Shambaugh also was an early adherent of the New History, an intellectual bent no doubt encouraged by studies under James Harvey Robinson during the two years (1893–1895) he spent at the University of Pennsylvania earning a doctorate and by postdoctoral studies at the universities of Halle, Leipzig, and Berlin. In 1896 he accepted a faculty post at the University of Iowa, where he had earned both his bachelor's and master's degrees; shortly thereafter he was appointed chair of the new Department of Political Science. In 1897 he was elected to the Board of Curators of the SHSI, and ten years later he was named superintendent and editor, a new post that marked the society's transition to professional administration. Shambaugh held these two positions until his death in 1940 and by every account devoted himself fully to the responsibilities of both.

At the beginning of his career, Shambaugh joined the AHA, an affiliation that led him to participate in professional developments at the national level. Shambaugh was a founding and active member of two organizations calved by the AHA: the American Political Science Association (APSA), organized in 1903, and the Mississippi Valley Historical Association (MVHA), organized in 1907. With Albert Bushnell Hart and W. W. Willoughby, he founded the *American Political Science Review* and served on its editorial board from 1906 to 1914. To help establish the MVHA, Shambaugh edited the association's *Proceedings* from 1907 to 1914 and then edited the *Mississippi Valley Historical Review* during the years 1914–1916 and 1927–1930. He served as MVHA president in 1909–1910 and as APSA president in 1930.[16] As an active member of the AHA, Shambaugh also participated in the work of two committees, or sections, that did much to redefine the profession of history in the early twentieth century: the Public Archives Commission, formed in 1900, and the Conference of State and Local Historical Societies, first convened in 1904.

The many initiatives that ultimately made up Shambaugh's "applied" and "commonwealth" history are thoroughly fused with the ideals of the New History as well as the motives that gave life to AHA splinter groups and special interest sections. He transformed the SHSI from an antiquarian club into a research and publications institution. He was the force behind the creation of a professional state archives. During World War I, he spearheaded one of the most successful efforts to collect history as it happened. He not only believed in the value of history for policymaking, he devised practical ways to cultivate a historical perspective among policymakers. Finally, he took bold steps to popularize history in order to reach wider audiences. In retrospect, it is tempting to cast Shambaugh as a man in the forefront of the profession, yet by the 1930s he was curiously out of step with it. Shambaugh's career can only be understood if it is examined within the matrix of intellectual currents and professional affiliations that were part and parcel of his maturation.

1

From the New History to Applied History

The New History

James Harvey Robinson synthesized the canons of the New History in his collection of essays published under the same name in 1912, but the phrase first appeared in 1898, and the intellectual reform movement it signified had been gathering adherents throughout 1890s. Earle W. Dow introduced the term in the pages of the *American Historical Review* in a long discourse on the German historian Karl Lamprecht. Dow noted that scholars drawn to "the new history" sought to integrate social phenomena, economic factors, the "material sides of life," religion, and other aspects of culture into their analyses of historical questions. Political life, while not unimportant, no longer took center stage in historical inquiry. Despite considerable individualism among their works, Dow perceived that, collectively, these scholars were all searching for "evolutional, causal relations."[1]

Edward Eggleston echoed the phrase two years later in a speech written for, but not actually delivered to, the members of the AHA. Eggleston, elected AHA president in 1900, was too ill to attend the annual meeting, but his remarks appeared in the published proceedings.[2] Perhaps it was just as well that he could not attend, for he dismissed as dry and duplicitous much of the work of venerated, but dead, American historians and metaphorically thumbed his nose at most of his aging colleagues. In contrast, he praised the young postgraduates who were writing "township, community and other institutional history" as well as "the humble historians" who were engaged in compiling the annals of towns and cities.[3]

Eggleston defined the New History as comprising four distinct aspects. The first of these he called a "keen modern interest in the little details of life," to be revealed through the localized study of history and institutions.

7

To this central condition he added an ability to treat political life without the adulterant of patriotism and a desire to cultivate militarism out of human nature by focusing scholarly attention on diplomacy rather than on "drum and trumpet history." Finally, the New History proposed that the "main object of teaching history [wa]s to make . . . cultivated and broad men and women," not simply to make intelligent voters, which before the Nineteenth Amendment (1920) included only half of the adult population. Eggleston predicted, correctly, that when the AHA assembled "a hundred years hence" at the close of the twentieth century, there would be "gifted writers" of cultural history, "the real history of men and women."[4]

As it took shape, the New History became a mixed bag. Part of the reform focused on cultivating scientific rigor and objectivity in the intellectual process. Americans who took at least part of their graduate studies in Germany, as many did, absorbed the philosophy and conventions that Leopold von Ranke advocated and then transported them back to American universities, with some modification. German mentors exposed American students to new research techniques that could unlock the secrets of what we now call "material" culture—coins, medals, seals, signets, and inscriptions. The seminar, with its focus on communal scholarship, became the centerpiece of graduate training. Americans diverged, however, from the spirit of historical inquiry cultivated in German universities. They embraced the Rankean school's disciplined approach to investigation but failed to grasp the intuitive nature of analysis that Ranke deemed essential to historical inquiry and interpretation. Americans thus transformed Rankean ideals into a kind of stripped empiricism that rested on the systematic gathering of facts and a detached, neutral approach to analysis and presentation. The result was a retreat from literary history and an increasing tendency among scholars to become immersed in the particulate matter of history.[5]

The New Historians also sought to expand the scope of historical inquiry. In this respect, they drew much of their inspiration from mid-nineteenth-century literary historians in Europe, who had extended the horizon to include the life of the common people. Frederick Jackson Turner, however, largely reshaped the field of inquiry in the United States. Turner's frontier thesis challenged the village community, or germ, theory of history accepted by the historical profession in the 1880s. The germ theory, based in Darwinism, postulated an evolutionary model of democratic and liberal institutions. It held that the seeds of American institutions, particularly the New England town, were to be found in the Teutonic villages of ancient Europe. These institutional seeds, or "Teutonic germs," were carried first to Britain in the fifth and sixth centuries and then to America in the seventeenth.[6] Turner's frontier thesis offered an alternative model, also based in Darwinism but much more dynamic and distinctly homegrown. He argued that the foundation of American democratic institutions lay in the availability of free land and that the process of humans interacting with the environment in successive frontiers as America expanded westward constituted an evolutionary force constantly renewing democracy.[7]

Turner did not see himself as abandoning the village community theory so much as recasting it with geography in mind. What he rejected was its extreme political-institutional bias. Indeed, Turner was drawn to the study of communities and of the common people. He admired Therold Rogers's *Economic Interpretation of History* precisely because it focused on "the fourth estate, the great mass of the people" and because it resonated with his own sense of the issues he believed scholars should address in the modern industrial age: questions of economics and social conditions.[8] A sense of social responsibility motivated Turner to assert that history was, "in truth, the self-consciousness of humanity," a thought that logically led him to an organic concept of historical inquiry: "all the spheres of man's activity must be considered" and considered holistically, for "no one department of social life can be understood in isolation from the others." Moreover, the past was implicit in present-day life, in every age. It therefore followed that "each age must be studied in the light of all the past; local history must be viewed in the light of world history."[9] The study of history was itself an evolutionary process, and no corner of inquiry should be neglected because everything was important to understanding the progress of humankind.

Turner's own research focused on regional, or "sectional," interpretations rather than on local history per se, and later historians have faulted him for overlooking the role of class conflict and for excluding women, American Indians, and other minorities from his vision of American democracy.[10] Additionally, Turner had a tendency to get mired in the details of his organic, evolutionary model, but he nonetheless was the great idea person of his generation. Turner's ideas appealed especially to midwestern historians, who, at the time, thought of themselves as "western" historians. For one thing, it meant that instead of being stuck in the hinterlands of the historical profession they were in the midst of the expanding "field" of historical inquiry. History was, literally, at their doorsteps, and there was a lot of it to be considered. This sudden abundance of historical data close at hand kindled an enthusiasm for harvesting it that was not unlike the renewing force of democracy Turner ascribed to the frontier. Historians in the Mississippi River valley led the way to new standards for the collection and organization of historical material in archival repositories. They also sought to enlist the aid of local historical societies in the task of harvesting, for surely the volume of important material far exceeded the capacity of universities and state historical societies to house it. In addition, Turner's ideas contributed to the emergence of "Americanists" in the historical profession. The ultimate expression of this identity split was the formation of the Mississippi Valley Historical Association (MVHA) in 1907, the parent of the Organization of American Historians.

Leaders among the New Historians also saw the value of using history to explain contemporary issues, to make history relevant to the present. Again, Turner was among the first to advocate the utility of history. More precisely, he advocated the "union of public service and historical study" particularly in the way that Germany and France had done so, by encouraging, if not requiring, that public officials be trained in history and political science.[11] However, Charles Beard, Carl Becker, and James Harvey Robinson wore the "progressive" label more prominently—Beard and Becker because they boldly infused historical inquiry with political ideology and Robinson because he was more insistent about the ability of history to help shape the contours of progressive reform.[12] For Robinson, history not only could but should assist with the "great contemporaneous task of human betterment." He called upon historians to help Americans "develop historical-mindedness upon a far more generous scale than hitherto, for this will add a still deficient element in our intellectual equipment and will promote rational progress as nothing else can do."[13]

The founding motives of those who created the American Political Science Association (APSA) and the MVHA reflect the intellectual as well as the utilitarian ideals of the New History. Its pragmatic dimension gave rise to the APSA, which was organized to provide a forum that would bring together "not only those engaged in academic work, but also the statesman, the jurist, the administrator, and the publicist, and to secure the cooperation of all these forces in the scientific study and discussion of the many important questions in practical and theoretical politics." Pragmatically, the APSA, like the American Economic Association, met concurrently with the AHA so that "members of the different societies [could] attend all the meetings without additional expense in time and money."[14]

The MVHA, conversely, was founded for ideological reasons. Shambaugh's role in defining the rationale for the MVHA is reflected in a brief passage he penned, as editor, for the first volume of the *Proceedings*, later reiterated in a speech delivered at the MVHA's twenty-fifth annual meeting. This new association, wholly independent of the AHA, was, he explained, "the outgrowth of a realization that the history of the Middle West is marked by a unity of development which justifies an organized and unified study, that the activities of the state historical societies and departments of history and of archives need the supplement of a broader work and a closer correlation, and that the history of the United States as a whole can not be justly written without a more adequate study of the forces and events by which the region west of the Alleghanies and east of the Rockies has taken its part in the life of the Nation."[15]

Every aspect of the New History influenced Benjamin Shambaugh, and there can be no doubt that he was particularly impressed, early in his career, by history's utilitarian possibilities. Shambaugh was part of the inner circle of scholars who pushed to expand the intellectual boundaries of history during the progressive era. At the same time, he also was involved in professionalizing the practice of history outside the academy. He worked with the AHA's Public Archives Commission to promote public archives and professional archival standards, and he worked to establish closer ties between the historical profession and state and local historical societies through the AHA's Conference of State and Local Historical Societies.

Public Archives Commission

The 1889 congressional act establishing a legal connection between the federal government and the AHA inherently made the association a quasi-public agency. The AHA leadership had a rather rarified notion of the public responsibility congressional sanction conferred but nonetheless took this responsibility seriously. On the one hand, as J. Franklin Jameson explained it some years later, "the act tended to place an expert body in the position of adviser to the government in historical matters," although few, if any, elected or appointed federal officials ever called upon the AHA for advice. On the other hand, the AHA was seen "to constitute perhaps as satisfactory an instrument as the United States government is likely to develop for the performance of its [the nation's] historical functions." In essence, AHA leaders asserted that the national government had a "historical function," which meant, as the idea took shape, saving historical materials important to the nation from neglect and destruction.[16] On behalf of the national government, then, the AHA set itself up to function more or less as the public guardian of documents important to American history.

This was the basic rationale for establishing, in 1894, the Historical Manuscripts Commission as a standing committee charged with identifying manuscript collections containing the papers of important political figures or official documents, particularly collections held privately, and publishing edited versions of their contents. This, too, was the rationale for the early 1890s' suggestion to have state and local historical societies report to the AHA and to compile bibliographies of their publications and calendars of their holdings.[17] Jameson argued forcefully that the most important work state and local historical societies could do was publish historical documents. It was, in his words, "the work which counts in the long run."[18] State historical societies, however, were moving at a snail's pace in this direction, and local societies seemed hopelessly lost.

By 1900, AHA leaders believed that the efforts of the Historical Manuscripts Commission, while important, would be insufficient to carry out the task. In order to shoulder the burden of public records guardianship, the AHA would have to lay the groundwork for a coordinated network of professionally administered archives. Thus at the turn of the century the AHA formed another standing committee, the Public Archives Commission, "to investigate and report, from the point of view of historical study, upon the character, contents, and functions of our public repositories of manuscript records."[19] To carry out this investigation, the commission sought a $5,000 appropriation from Congress to defray expenses, justifying the request by stating that Congress had a "duty" to support work that was in the interest of "the public welfare." The commission also solicited representatives from each state to survey their respective repositories. The sought-for appropriation did not materialize, but work nonetheless went forward. From state reports obtained the first year, the commission confirmed what everyone more or less knew: that large volumes of records had disappeared, that few states had any system for preserving records, and that many official documents were in the hands of private collectors.[20]

During the first few years, the commission's work consisted principally of publishing the reports submitted by state representatives. Among the twenty-two individuals who responded affirmatively to the commission's initial call for assistance were three men who later played key roles in the Conference of State and Local Historical Societies: Benjamin Shambaugh, Thomas Owen, and Franklin Riley, respectively representing Iowa, Alabama, and Mississippi. Iowa's report was published as one of the initial ten state reports appearing in the commission's 1900 annual report.[21] Mississippi's report appeared with the next group of six published in the 1903 annual report.[22]

In 1904 Owen issued a fervent call for state support of public archives and the professional administration of them, and he held up the recently established Alabama Department of Archives and History as a model for other states to follow. In 1901 the Alabama legislature had created a separate state agency charged specifically with the care and custody of its official archives, to be maintained through annual appropriations from the state's general fund. Alabama was the first state to take this step, and the Mississippi legislature passed a similar act the next year. Owen acknowledged that by this time many states were expending funds for the care of official records. However, state aid, he observed, usually was appropriated as a "sort of subsidy" to historical societies, granted for specific purposes such as publishing state papers or military records or collecting historical documents of an official nature. There was, Owen charged, "a painful lack of organized effort" among historical organizations, learned societies, and educational institutions to force states to assume the duty of caring for their public records.[23]

Perhaps the situation was not as grim as Owen pictured it, but it was disorganized, and successful efforts were episodic. More precisely, fully state-supported archives were just beginning to emerge; Alabama and Mississippi were out in front in terms of recognizing the need for professional administration on par with the administration of other departments of state government. Well into the twentieth century, many states simply left the organization and preservation of public records to the discretion of officials in charge of various agencies and commissions, a practice that cultivated all the horrors of benign neglect.[24]

During the next few years the AHA's Public Archives Commission promoted or supported legislation to establish state-supported public archives whenever the opportunity arose. In 1902 the New York legislature

debated a bill that would have made the state historian also a commissioner of records, but it never came to the floor for a vote. Two successes
came in 1903 when the Pennsylvania legislature created a division of public records under the state library and the North Carolina legislature established a historical commission for the purpose of collecting documents
pertaining to the history of the state.[25] The Public Archives Commission
also was pleased to report that in 1904 the Maryland legislature had established a public records commission to "examine the condition and com-
pleteness" of Maryland's public records and, within two years, make recommendations to the legislature for the custody, arrangement, and
preservation of such records.[26]

Owen did not disparage these efforts, but he did hope to avert a scatter-
shot approach to the problem before it was too late. The heart of his plea
was that the learned members of the AHA recognize not only the need for
state-supported archives but also the need for trained archivists to run
them. "How many librarians are fit to cope with musty archives?" he
asked. "How many are equipped to edit your historical publications? How
many are able to respond to calls for detailed historical or statistical information?" Owen half-apologized for seeming "unfriendly" to librarians before going on to emphasize his point "that our hopes in reference to the
care and preservation of our archives and our historical interests must not
be centered in them. In the past they have been just about as indifferent on
such subjects as other State officials."[27]

The work of the Public Archives Commission received a boost in 1905
when J. Franklin Jameson succeeded Andrew McLaughlin as director of
the Department of Historical Research at the Carnegie Institution in
Washington, D.C. Jameson made it clear from the very beginning that he
would use this post, which he had essentially invented in 1902, to promote
a more organized and systematic approach among institutions at the national, state, and local levels for preserving and publishing important historical documents. In this sense, as Rothberg argues, Jameson set out to
nationalize historical scholarship.[28] His chief aide in this endeavor was
Waldo G. Leland, a former student of his at Brown University who had
gone on to graduate studies at Harvard. As events unfolded, Jameson and
Leland found a task of gargantuan proportions awaiting them in what Leland later called the "archival slums of the national government."[29] Eventually, they would focus their attention on campaigning for a federally
funded archival institution modeled on those of European countries, a

campaign that culminated in 1934 with the establishment of the National Archives.

Meanwhile, by 1907 substantial progress at the state level was evident, as detailed in a summary report compiled by Herman V. Ames, chair of the Public Archives Commission.[30] Two years later, at the 1909 meeting, Ames took pride in recounting a decade of state-by-state progress, which, he boldly asserted, could "be traced either directly or indirectly to the influence of the commission." With this achievement in hand, Ames further declared that it was time to transform the commission into a "conference of archivists" to address matters of more practical importance.[31]

In this manner, archivists began to assume a distinct professional identity, shaped gradually through the efforts of Leland and New York State Historian Victor Paltsits, who increasingly realized that the AHA had little interest in the professional administration of archives. The academicians of the AHA had been primarily interested in saving public records from destruction or neglect; once that crisis seemingly passed, the issue lost cogency. By the early 1920s, the Conference of Archivists had shrunk to a luncheon meeting at the annual AHA conference. However, the establishment of the National Archives set the stage for a serious discussion about the relationship between historians and archivists. In 1936 the Conference of Archivists more or less declared independence from the AHA, forming the Society of American Archivists to address professional issues as an organized body.[32]

In retrospect, it would be fair to say that the AHA's leadership saw the Historical Manuscripts Commission and the Public Archives Commission as the principal agents carrying out the association's "public" function in the early twentieth century. Nevertheless, to a large degree the Conference of State and Local Historical Societies constituted the AHA's major outreach effort to become a more inclusive body of historians. While the work of the Public Archives Commission and the Conference of State and Local Historical Societies overlapped considerably—several AHA members were active in both—each of these two bodies nevertheless had its own set of goals, which ultimately led to different ends.

The Conference of Historical Societies

The AHA was only six years old when members began to take an interest in the work of state and local historical societies, the number of which had been rapidly growing during the 1880s. In 1890 W. P. Trent, professor of history at the University of the South, suggested that state and local bodies report annually to the AHA, and Paul Leicester Ford of Brooklyn, New York, submitted a plan for keeping track of the publications emanating from them. As a result, the AHA annual reports for 1890, 1892, and 1895 contain bibliographies of state and local historical society publications, edited by A. P. C. Griffin. Interest then flagged until Reuben Gold Thwaites, superintendent of the State Historical Society of Wisconsin (SHSW), injected new life into the issue with the paper he delivered at the 1897 annual meeting.[33]

Wisconsin holds a venerable spot in American history as the leader in progressive politics. It is not surprising, then, that by the turn of the century the SHSW had become *the* model of progressivism among state historical societies. Among other innovations, Thwaites promoted closer ties between the society and the University of Wisconsin. When his predecessor, Lyman Draper, turned over his own collection of historical manuscripts to the society in 1891, Thwaites invited Frederick Jackson Turner and his advanced seminar students to research these and other collections. Thwaites also succeeded in promoting the construction of a new building on the campus at Madison to house both the historical society and the university library.[34] Julian P. Boyd, who assessed the status of state and local historical societies in 1934, credited Draper and Thwaites as having "prepared the way for the far-reaching researches of Turner and others." Even more important in Boyd's estimation, "they inaugurated a new conception of the function of a historical society in a republic, that of making history serve a democratic role in the development of the community culture."[35]

In his 1897 talk on the structure and success of the SHSW, Thwaites paid due respect to Draper, who spent thirty-three years building up a reference library of 118,000 books and doggedly pursuing legislators first to pay his salary and then appropriate funds annually to cover the society's operating expenses. By 1897, Thwaites had been at the helm for eleven years, and the state of Wisconsin was in the process of building a new, half-million-dollar home for the society on the University of Wisconsin campus.[36]

"From the outset," Thwaites noted, "[s]tate aid ha[d] substantially shaped the policy of the Wisconsin Society, causing it to adopt methods widely differing from those . . . [of] its older and more conservative sisters in the Eastern States." Thwaites also pointed out that the well-established

James Harvey Robinson, 1895. *Courtesy Columbia University Archives—Columbiana Library.*

Frederick Jackson Turner, 1911. *Courtesy State Historical Society of Wisconsin, WHi (D489) 12333.*

Reuben Gold Thwaites. *Courtesy State Historical Society of Wisconsin, WHi (X3) 31002.*

eastern historical societies to which he referred were privately financed. Funding made all the difference in the world. It was obvious to the founders of the Wisconsin society that "state appropriations could not long be secured for a closed corporation of scholastics," so membership was opened to all, giving the society a "purely popular character." State aid and an open membership led the society to establish a museum and a "historical portrait gallery" because the general public "care[d] little for the library—the chief strength of the society." Thwaites candidly admitted that "in the beginning these were designed chiefly as popular attractions" but nonetheless defended them as part of the society's educational function. The publishing function, an extension of maintaining a library and archive, also had been shaped by state aid. By then, the SHSW had established a solid reputation for publishing historical documents important to the study of frontier history, but the society also published "attractive essays on the local history of the State . . . for the average man of affairs may consider a book devoted exclusively to documentary material, a useless expenditure for the Commonwealth."[37]

Thwaites noted that the SHSW also functioned as something of a public information bureau, supplying local newspapers with articles on local history and routinely answering inquiries from legislators, state agency staff, teachers, and just plain citizens. Another function combined fieldwork and what would today be called field services, soliciting documentary and artifactual material from private citizens, recording the memories of pioneers, and organizing local historical societies as "auxiliaries" to augment the capacity and the ability of the state historical society to preserve the state's history. These functions formed the "fundamental principles" by which Thwaites believed state-supported historical societies must operate. He minced no words. In order for a state-supported institution to survive, "it must perpetually demonstrate its reason for being, by proving useful and inspiring to the public whose support it seeks."[38]

Thwaites's report reflected growing interest among AHA members not only about the ways in which state historical societies were organized and funded but the level at which state and local historical societies, both public and private, were performing their functions. Jameson, appearing on the same panel as Thwaites in 1897, did not give them high marks. In his estimation, their publications were "lamentably out of proportion" to their financial resources; research collections and publications "superabundantly" reflected a lack of scholarly interest in post–Revolutionary

War history; funds were extravagantly misspent to placate genealogical researchers; society members typically were devoted to antiquarianism and parochialism, eschewing the exploration of local history for its "significance with respect to the larger life of the nation"; and college professors were conspicuously absent from the ranks of active members. Jameson further grumped that state and local historical societies had by and large conceded the "true ideals" of historical scholarship to popular demands, had lost faith that the scholarly pursuit of American history would elevate humanity, and had "adjust[ed] themselves with outward cheerfulness to the actual conditions of their life."[39]

A year later, in 1898, AHA members voted to authorize the formation of a committee to assess the status of state and local historical societies in the United States.[40] However, the interest level was not yet very high; nothing of substance happened for five years. Henry E. Bourne, professor of history at Western Reserve University, deserves credit for restarting the initiative in 1903, during which year he also served as chair of the AHA's General Committee. In this effort he sought the aid of Thwaites, which, with hesitation, Thwaites provided.

Bourne revealed in a letter to Thwaites that Lucy Salmon, a professor of history at Vassar College, had some years earlier submitted a proposal to federate local historical societies under the AHA, but her idea went no further. He asked Thwaites whether he thought it would be worthwhile to arrange one or more sessions at the annual meeting on topics pertinent to local historical societies and, if so, what topics would be most appropriate: management, collections, editing? Bourne confessed that, from information he had so far collected, "there would be comparatively few local societies which have sufficient vigor to lead their members to desire conferences" but that perhaps there were enough of them "to justify some effort" on the part of the AHA to bring their representatives together for this purpose.[41]

Thwaites was skeptical of the results but willing to give it a go: "*Entre nous*, I haven't much faith in the result, for I know the local bodies quite thoroughly; but I should be quite willing to join you in seeing if anything might come of it."[42] To Shambaugh, Thwaites later confided similar doubts: "The great trouble [with organizing state and local societies] is, as of course you know as well as I, the apathy and the old fogyism which seem to pervade our societies. Exceedingly few of them are up to the mark."[43]

It was with some lack of enthusiasm, then, that plans began to take shape at the 1903 annual meeting. The program committee decided to devote one session of the next meeting to a conference on the work of local historical societies. Bourne agreed to present the results of his ad hoc inquiries into the organization and work of local and state societies. Jameson, chair of the 1904 program committee, asked Thwaites to organize the conference to be held in Chicago. He agreed to do so but again expressed his reservations. "I sometimes feel rather discouraged over these local historical societies," he responded to Jameson's request, "for the majority of them seem to be run by excessively narrow minded people given over to the dry as dust of antiquarianism . . . . The correspondence which I sometimes get from these institutions, and the questions they ask of us fairly make me weary."[44] In making their plans, the two men agreed on the need to extend special invitations only to those societies located west of the Alleghenies as well as Florida. Thwaites believed that eastern societies were "sufficiently organized on the old-fashioned basis and would derive very little benefit or have very little sympathy with a conference of this character," but they were not excluded from attending.[45]

Bourne passed along discussion topics he had gathered from Shambaugh, Salmon, and several others. With this information and suggestions solicited from among his counterparts in other states, Thwaites pulled the conference together. By late October, Alabama, Iowa, Louisiana, Minnesota, Missouri, Montana, Nebraska, New York, Ohio, Tennessee, and Texas had notified Thwaites that they would send delegates.[46] As it materialized, the conference consisted of a roundtable session, scarcely two hours in length, and a separate report by Bourne on his two-year investigation. However, the Chicago conference yielded more than either Thwaites, or Jameson for that matter, ever thought possible; it laid the basis for an annual conference that convened as part of the AHA annual meeting through 1940, when it reorganized separately as the American Association for State and Local History.

At the Chicago conference, Bourne succinctly summed up the state of American historical organizations: diverse and decentralized. By that time there were more than four hundred organized historical societies in the United States. Broadly speaking, statewide organizations fell into one of two categories: privately financed societies with restricted membership, such as the prestigious state societies of Massachusetts, New York, and Pennsylvania, or state-supported societies, of which the Wisconsin state historical society undisputedly ranked number one. Geographically, privately funded societies more or less defined the East, state-supported public institutions the West.[47]

Within these two broad categories, however, Bourne found considerable diversity. Collecting priorities varied widely. The Kansas and Missouri state historical societies, for instance, emphasized collecting local newspapers; the Minnesota State Historical Society focused on town histories and works useful for the study of genealogy; the Draper manuscript collection of the Wisconsin society held the papers of families prominently associated with the vaguely defined "border" or "middle border" region. Organizational structure also varied. Some states supported a state historical society and a state library-archives as separate entities; others combined these functions in one agency. Some state historical societies—notably Wisconsin, Iowa, Missouri, Washington, Nebraska, Mississippi, Massachusetts, Rhode Island, and Pennsylvania—either were affiliated with state universities or had close ties with nearby universities. Moreover, upon closer scrutiny the line between private and public funding was not hard and fast. Only the state historical societies of Massachusetts, New York, and Pennsylvania were entirely privately financed. Maine, New Hampshire, Vermont, Rhode Island, Connecticut, New Jersey, and Maryland subsidized the publication of state records by private societies. States west of the Alleghenies, however, often provided operational support to their state societies. Even so, state-supported societies typically were allowed to generate additional revenue from membership dues, private donations, publications, and other incidental sources.[48]

Bourne perceived both advantage and disadvantage in this great, decentralized diversity. Principally, the advantage was that the westward spread of historical organizations was an integral part of the movement toward "a broader interpretation of American history," by which he meant history that incorporated the theme of westward expansion. The disadvantage was that a (presumed) sense of community among historians would devolve to "isolated effort." To combat the perils of decentralization, Bourne called for some type of formal affiliation to foster a common direction.[49] The dichotomy that Bourne articulated established the rationale for an annual conference of state and local historical societies under the auspices of the AHA: learned scholars *must* concern themselves with the collection and preservation of historical materials beyond the eastern states so that historians *could* write broader interpretations of American history. To accomplish this mission, the AHA turned to the person best able to grasp the magnitude of that challenge, Reuben Gold Thwaites, who was both a scholar and the administrator of the leading state-supported historical society in the country.

Thwaites convened the two-hour conference session at the Chicago meeting. Sixty-two delegates attended, representing state or local historical organizations in seventeen states plus the District of Columbia and Manitoba, Canada.[50] The format included two roundtable discussions, the first of which focused on the administration and organization of state historical bodies in relation to state governments. Thomas Owen, director of the Alabama Department of Archives and History, and Warren Upham, secretary of the Minnesota State Historical Society, opened the roundtable with prepared remarks. The second roundtable explored the possibilities of cooperation between state and local historical organizations, with prepared remarks by Shambaugh and C. M. Burton, president of the Michigan Pioneer and Historical Society. General discussion followed, from which there emerged consensus on the need to share information about holdings and the desirability of regional meetings to achieve greater cooperation. The assembly also voted unanimously to establish the conference as an annual event, and the AHA Executive Council approved a request for a subsequent conference the following year at the Baltimore meeting. Owen and Shambaugh were selected to organize the second conference, functioning respectively as chair and secretary.[51]

The Executive Council encouraged this new activity, as evidenced by subsequent actions. Thwaites not only was elected to the Executive Council at the 1904 meeting, but he also was asked to chair a subcommittee charged with preparing a special report addressing the "best methods of organization and work on the part of state and local historical societies." Shambaugh and Franklin L. Riley of the Mississippi Historical Society served as the other two members.[52]

Thwaites lost no time ordering the work of his subcommittee. The members devised a standard questionnaire that expanded the scope of Bourne's previous inquiry and divided up the task of information gathering. Subsequently, they met for two days in Iowa City to analyze the replies and draw some conclusions.[53] Shambaugh, who arranged the Iowa City meeting, took advantage of the occasion to promote local awareness of the centennial of the Lewis and Clark expedition. Thwaites delivered a public address on the significance of the expedition, which had passed through western Iowa, and Shambaugh arranged for newspaper coverage of his talk. Shambaugh also hoped to stimulate local interest in the upcoming Lewis and Clark Exposition in Portland, Oregon, that summer.[54]

Thwaites and Shambaugh then traveled to the exposition in Portland, where they promoted the work of the AHA on behalf of state and local historical societies. F. G. Young of the University of Oregon, also a member of the AHA Executive Council, took advantage of regional interest in the Lewis and Clark Exposition by organizing a conference of western historical societies. Young's intent, as Thwaites understood it, was "to stir up things on the Northwest coast and take advantage of our experience in the East—the East meaning everything east of the Rocky Mountains." In this endeavor, Young enlisted the aid of Thwaites and Shambaugh, arranging for them to conduct sessions where they explained the subcommittee's work and provided advance information about its findings.[55]

The second Conference of State and Local Historical Societies, held at the 1905 AHA meeting in Baltimore, was an important event. It solidified a body of members interested in discussing the work of state and local historical societies and, in so doing, justified the expenditure of time and effort that several people had devoted to launching the initiative. The second conference also brought forth a wealth of new information about what was happening across the country. In this respect, it proved to be a stimulus for further professional development and innovation. It is thus worth taking a close look at what transpired at the Baltimore conference.

Benjamin Shambaugh was asked to chair the second conference, owing to Thomas Owen's unanticipated absence. However, the two of them had worked together to arrange the program, which focused on the broad topics of "cooperation" and "publication," with two additional papers incorporated into the published proceedings but not actually presented at the conference: one on recent developments in the historical profession in Canada and another addressing the need for greater cooperation among historians and archaeologists.[56]

On the topic of cooperation, William O. Scroggs of the Harvard History Club called for more cooperation between academicians and historical societies, while S. P. Heilman described the organization and purposes of the recently formed Pennsylvania Federation of Historical Societies. Scroggs, who may well have been the most engaging speaker of the day if printed wit is any guide, expressed a certain sympathy for college professors. Individually, they often constituted a "department of one" in their respective institutions and were thus tied to a regimen of teaching the broad divisions of history as then defined: classical, medieval, and modern. What concerned him equally was that down the street or across town, local or state historical societies often were preoccupied with "the researches of local investigators or narrators whose chief delight is to stroll at random along the by-paths of history without regard to the guide posts that point to the greater historic highway." With such a gulf, how was cooperation possible? Scroggs argued that the gulf could be bridged by employing the methods of historical research, that is, the "source method," to new ends. To explain what he meant, he cited the example of a college instructor (unidentified) who had his advanced students research local topics "in connection with their study of some period of American history." The professor then directed his students to the library of the state historical society. Students whose research papers showed "special merit" were encouraged to present their work at the society's annual meeting, and some papers subsequently were published for wider distribution.[57]

Today, many history professors set their students to research in primary documents in local repositories, but it was an arresting concept in 1905. Scroggs perceived, however, that this teaching strategy would actually produce greater benefits for historical societies. "The problem to be solved," he judged, "is how to arouse the interest of these students in local history so as to secure their participation after leaving college in the work of historical societies. For what the societies need above everything else is active members who know enough history to give a local event its national setting and whose knowledge of the historical development of mankind is sufficient to prevent them from arriving at absurd conclusions."[58] Scroggs did not take the next cognitive step by reasoning that such teaching strategies might also encourage students to consider careers in the professional administration and management of state or local historical societies, but he nonetheless injected a remarkably fresh idea into the discussion.

S. P. Heilman reported on the cooperative mission of the Pennsylvania Federation of Historical Societies, organized in January 1905. This body may well qualify as the first statewide organization of local historical societies, although a regional gathering representing societies in the Mississippi River valley states held in St. Louis in 1903 and the regional conference held in Portland in August 1905 suggest wider activity. In any case,

Heilman reported that, in one year, two-thirds of Pennsylvania's local historical societies (twenty-four out of thirty-six) had joined the federation. The federation's goals were to aid and direct historical research, to encourage the formation of new local historical societies, and to act as a bibliographer for its member societies by publishing bulletins and document calendars.[59]

The South received special attention at the Baltimore conference. U. B. Phillips noted that although an "immense amount of documentary material" existed in and for the South, historians had used "extremely little" of it. In part this was because a "very great number" of documentary collections were in private hands and in part because "plantation records and other such 'unconscious' documents for the economic and social history of the South ha[d] been almost entirely ignored," both in their collection and in research. Phillips cautioned that only after historians had access to a critical mass of historical materials pertaining to "industrial subjects" would it be possible "to truly understand the life and policy of the people of the old South."[60]

Mississippi state archivist Dunbar Rowland amplified Phillips's remarks by advocating more trained archivists and official repositories, both state and local, for the care of primary historical materials. As a case in point, he noted that his agency had recently conducted a survey of county archives in Mississippi. In the process, surveyors had uncovered a cache of forty-one volumes of original documents covering the period 1781–1798. These constituted the Spanish archives of the Natchez District, a region along the southern reaches of the Mississippi River that was part of the territory Spain seized from England in 1779. Rowland further noted that the state law authorizing the Mississippi Department of Archives and History also enabled the department to take custody of valuable historical records residing in local repositories if such records were not in daily use.[61]

Thwaites summarized the report of the subcommittee charged with gathering data on the work of state and local historical societies, with the complete report incorporated into the published proceedings. The subcommittee's findings were based on information gathered from 123 local societies, seventy state societies or departments, twelve regional bodies, and eighteen national organizations, excluding the AHA. The responses represented approximately half of the known historical societies in the United States, then estimated to number about 420. It was a remarkable snapshot capturing the profile of state and local history in the United States for a brief, but key, moment in time.[62]

Of the seventy state societies or departments reporting, thirty-two had been organized after 1890; that is, almost half were less than fifteen years old. Of the remainder, the oldest societies were, of course, mostly located in the East and South. Wisconsin, Iowa, Minnesota, and Louisiana were the westernmost states to have organized state societies prior to the Civil War.[63] An early interest in history in these states can be attributed, at least in part, to their location along the Mississippi River, which allowed French, Spanish, and then American explorers, trappers, and traders to penetrate the interior regions, producing a mixed culture and documentary records that date from the seventeenth century.

Among thirty state societies or departments receiving some level of state funding, those receiving the largest appropriations were the State Historical Society of Wisconsin ($32,000) and the Minnesota State Historical Society ($20,000). Wisconsin ranked third among those possessing sizable endowments; Massachusetts came in first with $221,000, Pennsylvania second with $170,000, followed by Wisconsin with $53,000. Among twelve state societies reporting building assets, Wisconsin again ranked at the top; its new building on the University of Wisconsin campus was valued at $610,000. Iowa followed with building assets of $400,000, Pennsylvania with $300,000, and Massachusetts with $225,000. The report also listed several local historical societies, most located in the East, possessing substantial endowments in addition to building assets. In this connection, the report called attention to the many Massachusetts town societies that either were housed in historic buildings or had converted historic buildings to public museums, an "example well worth following" the committee believed.[64]

In library holdings, the largest state libraries were in Pennsylvania (reporting 315,000 titles), Wisconsin (280,000), and Massachusetts (155,000). Among local historical societies, only the Essex Institute in Salem, Massachusetts, reported a large library collection (400,000 titles). In contrast, nineteen state societies and forty-seven local societies reported library holdings of fewer than 10,000 books and pamphlets; thirty state societies and seventy-eight local societies reported no library holdings at all.

Membership varied just as widely, as one might expect. Among state societies, Pennsylvania (1,600) and the Society of Colonial Wars in New

York (1,034) were the largest, with most organizations reporting somewhere between 150 and 300 members. Only two local historical societies reported more than 1,000 members: the Bostonian Society (1,100) and the New York Historical Society (1,057). Thirteen local societies reported between 300 and 800 members. However, many state and local societies reported no membership figures, making it difficult to judge just how many people, nationwide, were supporting state and local history through membership dues.

In terms of organization and operations, the report noted that a great deal of "self-sacrificing enthusiasm" often substituted for professional administration and management—"everybody's business was nobody's concern." Likewise, "some of the more general societies, especially in the newer States, appear[ed] to be confused" about their purpose and the scope of their collecting. The report outlined several different methods of organization but recommended none. It did, however, present many suggestions for collecting, organizing, and presenting historical material to the public. Indeed, the authors asserted that the "matter of arousing and maintaining public interest is of itself an important function of an historical society." And the report strongly urged cooperation between and among historical societies, public libraries, and educational institutions at all levels. To its report, the committee appended the full text of information received from respondents.[65] As a corollary to the AHA's state and local history initiative, the association updated Griffin's "Bibliography of American Historical Societies." The revised and updated edition, published as volume 2 of the *AHA Annual Report for 1905*, also was compiled under Griffin's direction.

Shambaugh also chaired the third Conference of State and Local Historical Societies, held at the 1906 meeting in Providence, Rhode Island. By now, the roundtable format was set, and the two major topics of discussion were "public archives" and "historic sites."[66] These topics reflected, first, the fact that the work of the conference overlapped the work of the AHA's Public Archives Commission. While there was no overt competition between these two entities (so much to be done at this stage), they nonetheless were in the process of establishing distinct functions within the larger association. Second, the topic of "historic sites" reflected Henry Bourne's continuing role as a behind-the-scenes initiator; since 1903 he had been working on a preliminary survey of historic site markers in the United States.

Herman Ames of the University of Pennsylvania and chair of the Public Archives Commission summarized the work thus far accomplished. During the commission's six years of operation, it had solicited and compiled information on thirty-eight separate archives located in twenty-seven states.[67] This body of information provided enough comparative data for the commission to judge that the majority of states still had "no adequate system for the care of the archives." At the local level, "less ha[d] been accomplished," and the general condition of local records consequently was "much worse." On a more positive note, Ames reported that, between 1901 and 1906, eleven states had enacted legislation to establish official state archives.[68] The degree to which the commission's work moved these eleven states to legislative action was a matter of conjecture, but Ames was confident that the commission had been influential.[69]

Henry Bourne summarized what he had learned thus far in his investigation, still in progress, of historic site markers. From his remarks, it is clear that Bourne undertook this investigation for much the same reason that he undertook his earlier survey of state and local historical societies: he wanted the AHA to become more involved in this realm of public activity. Seeking to understand why local authorities, local historical societies, patriotic organizations, and state and federal government agencies marked historic sites, Bourne identified two related motives: "it originates both from patriotic sentiment and from desire to supply historical evidence for the future." He also noted that the practice of marking historic sites, while hardly new, was on the rise and was being "done more effectively." Much as Bourne had found advantage for scholars to concern themselves with the work of state and local historical societies, he also saw benefit in some kind of historic sites initiative. The benefit was in "its educational results, both in the general influence upon the older members of a community and in educational value to the pupils of the schools."[70]

The 1905 Baltimore meeting justified and solidified support for the Conference of State and Local Historical Societies. The 1906 Providence meeting revealed that, by then, the AHA fully considered the conference to be essential for carrying out the association's mission. In his report of the proceedings of the 1906 meeting, Corresponding Secretary Charles H. Haskins noted that the annual meeting now functioned, in part, as a "clearing-house" for the AHA's "varied forms of activity" but that "the greater part of the Association's work lies . . . in the organized labors of its officers and committees carried on throughout the year." These varied activities included, in 1906, publication of the *American Historical Review*, the awarding of various prizes for outstanding historical monographs, the Historical Manuscripts Commission, the Public Archives Commission, and the Conference of State and Local Historical Societies, which, beginning in 1909, was more commonly known as the Conference of Historical Societies.[71] The dancing parties of a decade earlier were a thing of the past, now just part of the AHA's institutional memory.

Bourne, Thwaites, Shambaugh, and Owen remained active in the Conference of Historical Societies for many years, but after playing key roles in its launch, they became actors amid a much larger cast. Jameson, too, also took an active interest in the work of the conference and frequently attended the meetings, which may seem surprising considering the low esteem in which he held state and local historical societies. However, Jameson shared the same desire as the other four men: to extend the professionalization of history to the state and local levels. Thus in 1907 Shambaugh, Thwaites, Jameson, and Owen were appointed to a Committee of Seven charged with investigating cooperation among historical societies and with locating and cataloging historical material in foreign archives. Chaired by Dunbar Rowland, the committee soon narrowed the scope of its work to locating and cataloging documents in French archives that related to the history of the Mississippi Valley.[72] Much of the bibliographic research was funded by contributions from about a dozen historical societies whose collections stood to benefit the most, but the project never would have been completed without substantial assistance and additional financial backing from the Carnegie Institution.

From the beginning, Jameson strongly advocated cooperation with the Department of Historical Research of the Carnegie Institution so as not to duplicate French-language materials already available in the United States, and this turned out to be a wise decision. Active work began in 1909 after several state historical societies collectively had donated about $2,000 to pay research assistants in Paris, who worked under the direction of Waldo G. Leland, Jameson's chief assistant at the Department of Historical Research. By 1911, approximately 10,000 documents had been abstracted, and the committee was nearly out of money. Additional contributions allowed the bibliographic research to continue, although by now the committee understood the magnitude of this undertaking and realized that much more money would be needed to edit and prepare the catalog for publication and to underwrite the cost of printing. Work continued until war broke out in Europe in 1914, by which time most of the estimated 25,000 documents in French archives had been abstracted. At that point, the committee was forced to suspend bibliographic research, although Leland continued with the editorial work as part of his staff assignment at the Carnegie Institution.[73]

As a side note, it is of some interest that the committee survived a 1915 attempt to unseat the AHA "establishment" in control of the AHA. Certain historians grew increasingly resentful of the *American Historical Review*'s bias for publishing articles on European history and the token leadership positions held by historians located outside the Northeast. Resentment boiled to a head in 1915, when Dunbar Rowland fomented an insurgent group whose primary goal was to democratize the AHA by ousting Jameson as editor of the *American Historical Review* and Frederick Jackson Turner from his longstanding seat on the Board of Editors. Ironically, the founding of the MVHA in 1907, which drew its support from Americanists in the Midwest, solidified the strength of the AHA "establishment" and thus indirectly contributed to rising discontent.[74]

In any case, the Committee of Seven continued to exist with no change of members, although by this time the only place of activity was Jameson's Department of Historical Research. Work resumed after the war, and by the end of 1919 Jameson could report that the abstracting was nearly finished and that Leland was in the process of editing the material for publication. The Committee of Seven submitted its final report in 1920. Altogether, contributions to the project totaled nearly $3,000, enough to cover the cost of research assistants in Paris but not enough to see the catalog to publication. After having absorbed the cost of editing, the Carnegie Institution offered to publish and distribute the catalog, a proposal that the Conference of Historical Societies readily accepted.[75]

Aside from the work of the Committee of Seven, the conference initiated no other large projects between its inception and World War I. Actually, by 1915 several people believed that the conference was in danger of becoming "merely another session of the AHA" and that there was need for a change that could make it a more useful annual assembly. The method of organizing each year's conference included sending a circular to all American and Canadian historical societies. The annual circulars asked each organization to supply updated information on its funding, legislation, organization, membership, publications, collections, and related activities and to appoint a delegate to the next annual meeting. Del-

egates to the Conference of Historical Societies were given the same priv-
ileges as members of the AHA in order to encourage attendance, but the
strategy did not work very well. Usually, about one hundred societies submitted updated information each year, but fewer appointed delegates to
the next conference and even fewer of the delegates actually showed up.
Even so, the annual gathering included between fifty and one hundred
participants, and conference attendance gradually increased.[76]

Shambaugh, Owen, and Heilman were appointed as a Committee of
Three in 1915, charged with developing recommendations about the future of the conference. Reporting in 1916, the Committee of Three presented a set of recommendations based on the premise that the conference still had an important reason for being. These recommendations,
adopted unanimously, called for the AHA to recognize the conference as a
semi-independent organization operating under the auspices of the AHA;
for the conference to be supported by annual assessments on each society
that became a member of the conference; and for the conference to have
control over its own funds but to furnish the AHA with an annual report
of income and expenditures. The AHA approved this plan at its business
meeting, with the details to be worked out at the 1917 annual meeting.[77]

The details never were worked out satisfactorily, but this reassessment,
plus the domestic importance of World War I, infused the conference
with new vitality. Unfortunately, the new sense of purpose did not last.
Shambaugh's last major contribution to the Conference of Historical Societies was to chair the 1925 meeting. He chose to focus attention that year
on a single question: "How can the work of collection and publication of
historical societies be made more effective for the purposes of general history?"[78] His choice of topic is revealing. By 1925, few academic historians
were taking part in the Conference of Historical Societies. Over the years,
conference chairs often had selected topics that bridged the gap between
scholarly concerns and administrative or operational issues, but that top-
ical bridge was not a consistent feature from year to year. Nuts-and-bolts
professional issues just did not interest very many academicians. Julian
Boyd, a contemporary observer, stated that, after 1914, "the conference
. . . made no appreciable progress in furthering the primary object for
which it was established." He also noted that the conference "succeeded
chiefly in enlisting the support of the societies of the Central West and of
those closely allied with universities. For, although the conference invari-
ably voiced the best standards of scholarship and cooperation, its voice

was that of the parent body and not the joint product of those actively in charge of the administration of the historical agencies of the country."[79]

AHA members may have thought that the organization had done its part and done it well. By the mid 1920s, the directors of many state historical societies held doctoral degrees; the Thwaites and Shambaughs of professional history were increasingly the norm. Boyd, speaking in 1934, believed that state historical societies generally were on solid ground under the leadership of a new generation of trained scholars, including, in his estimation, Joseph Schafer in Wisconsin, Theodore Blegen in Minnesota, Harlow Lindley in Indiana, Herbert Kellar at the McCormick Historical Association in Chicago, and Dixon Ryan Fox at the New York State Historical Association.[80] The situation at the local level was hardly comparable, but state historical societies by and large were operating on a professional basis.

Additionally, the degree to which patriotic societies and genealogists had become a familiar presence within the conference could only have troubled many scholars and academics. One of the founding purposes of the conference had been to check the influence of genealogists within state and local historical societies. Certainly, this purpose motivated Jameson, who had adamantly expressed his frustration with genealogists in 1897: "The addiction of historical societies to genealogies arises not from devotion to the primary and public purposes for which they were instituted, but from a weak desire to placate people who, it is thought, may in time, if sufficiently indulged, turn from their personal and private interest in their ancestry, and begin to take an interest in history. They may, but meantime is American history being rightly used?"[81]

Moreover, few academic historians shared Henry Bourne's accommodationist view. Over time, the AHA catered increasingly to the scholarly elite, so much so that by 1939, when Allan Nevins proposed that the AHA sponsor a popular historical magazine, the membership soundly rejected his idea. Nevins struck back by openly attacking the profession in the pages of the *Saturday Review of Literature*, denouncing the "entrenched pedantry" in universities and learned societies that "benumbs and paralyzes all interest in history."[82]

Whatever factors weakened the conference, after the Committee of Seven finished its work in the early 1920s, Jameson focused his attention elsewhere. The same is true of Shambaugh, who ceased to be active in the conference after 1925. And Thwaites, who had shared Jameson's exasperation with the parochialism of local historical societies, had died in 1913. In an environment of increasing polarity during the late 1920s and 1930s, the Conference of Historical Societies limped along; reports of activity became increasingly sketchy. In 1926 the conference published its *Handbook of American Historical Societies*, a long-awaited update of the 1905 compilation by Thwaites, Shambaugh, and Riley; the 1926 edition was revised in 1936 under the title *Historical Societies in the United States and Canada—A Handbook*.

In 1933 Herbert Kellar instigated a reassessment of the relationship between the conference and the AHA, and he then became the driving force for reorganization. The 1939 meeting, chaired by Christopher C. Crittenden, director of the North Carolina Department of Archives and History, was largely devoted to discussing the merits of separating from the AHA. This was formally accomplished at the 1940 meeting, when the conference adopted a charter and chose a new name: the American Association for State and Local History (AASLH). Crittenden, who also chaired the committee that established the new organization's goals and purposes, subsequently was elected the first president of the AASLH.[83]

Applied History

Drawing from the tenets of the New History and from his own involvement in professionalizing the disciplines of history and political science, Benjamin Shambaugh began to assemble the components of what he would call "Applied History." As editor of the MVHA's *Proceedings*, he took the liberty of introducing the concept to his professional colleagues in 1909. "I do not know that the phrase 'Applied History' is one that has thus far been employed by students of history and politics," he wrote. "But I believe that the time has come when it can be used with both propriety and profit." At this point in time, Shambaugh discerned at least one "concrete expression" of applied history: legislative reference work. He pointed to the state of Wisconsin, the seat of midwestern progressivism, where the state library, administered by the SHSW, had established a legislative reference department to collect and arrange research materials specifically for the use of state legislators. Shambaugh proposed to take this idea one step further. Observing that "thus far the legislative reference departments [there were others] have, in the collection of data, emphasized current information," he announced that the SHSI would begin to investigate the historical development of current state legislative issues.[84]

Between 1909 and 1913, when the first volume of the Iowa Applied History Series appeared, Shambaugh codified a definition. New History was at the heart of it. "Applied History," he wrote, "is indeed, the natural outcome of scientific history, itself the inevitable result of the development of the newer anthropological studies—especially archaeology, ethnology, sociology, politics and administration, economics, comparative religion, and social psychology. In fact, these social sciences, which have developed so marvelously under the inspiration of the doctrine of evolution, have involved historical study in a revolutionary process which is giving birth to a 'New History.'"[85]

Applied history, as Shambaugh initially implemented it, essentially involved the historical analysis of legislative developments to inform the body politic, meaning elected officials and their constituents. But it was policy analysis with a mission—to uplift the political, social, and economic institutions of democracy. "The foundation upon which Applied History rests is the scientific law of the continuity of history. . . . Indeed, it is the recognized validity of this law that affords substantial assurance that Applied History is not a dream but a sound and intelligent method of interrogating the past in the light of the conditions of the present and the obvious needs of the immediate future to the end that a rational program of progress may be outlined and followed in legislation and administration."[86]

In practice, however, applied history would be more than mission-oriented policy analysis. Competent historical analysis required the meticulous gathering of evidence, preserved and made accessible in professionally administered public archives. Moreover, to Shambaugh, applied history inherently was state and local history. "Here [in the American commonwealths] the records are marvelously rich in experiments in civil and criminal law, in the application of constitutional limitations, in labor legislation, in the regulation of common carriers and public utilities, in taxation, in the administration of roads, in domestic relations, in the protection of women and children, in the conservation of health, in the maintenance of order, in the exploitation of natural resources, in the promotion of industry, and in the democratization of education and politics. To wisely use the results of all these experiments in efforts to solve the problems which confront each generation is to carry out a program of Applied History."[87]

At times Shambaugh glossed applied history with a belief in midwestern exceptionalism. For him, the great Middle West stretched from the Alleghenies to the Rockies, encompassing the Ohio and Mississippi Valleys as well as the Great Plains. In this vast midcontinental region, state and local history was particularly important because, according to those who elevated Turner's frontier thesis to ideology, the history of development in the Middle West, more precisely the development of democratic institutions in the Middle West, would lead to a greater understanding of United States history.[88]

The scene now shifts to Iowa for a closer look at Shambaugh in his own element, following his career from his days at the University of Iowa and the University of Pennsylvania to his death in 1940. Without doubt, he was among those who pushed the major professional organizations toward outreach and greater involvement in public affairs. At the same time, others pushed for higher standards of scholarship in the profession. While Shambaugh certainly supported the rising standard of scholarship that was a hallmark of the professionalization project in history, it is also fair to say that he was far more interested in making history useful to society. Above all else, he was a practical scholar. But how did this play out at home, in his day-to-day professional life? What did applied history, as it expanded and evolved, mean in reality, not just in theory?

2

A Gift of Fate

FROM SCATTERED passages in Swisher's manuscript, one learns that Benjamin Shambaugh was thirteen when his father died. Benjamin was one of ten children born to John Shambaugh, a successful farmer in Clinton County, Iowa, and his wife, Eve Anna Ziegler. Five sons and two daughters survived to adulthood. With such a large family to provide for, the Shambaughs made a practice of reinvesting the profits from farming into ever more land and continually enlarging their farmhouse. They valued education and helped to erect the country school their children attended, but it was financially impossible to provide all of them with anything more.

Benjamin, born in 1871, and his brother George, one year older, had the good fortune of being the two youngest children. According to a family story that Swisher recounts, John Shambaugh told the president of Carleton College, once a guest in the family home, "These two little ones, I am going to send to the University." Benjamin, who was present and heard these words, later "recalled how he had looked up into his father's face and received a reassuring glance." John Shambaugh did not live to see his two sons achieve his aspirations for them, but he provided for their higher education in his will. It was thus their gift of fate to be last in birth order. Benjamin treasured the special advantage his father gave him, and he used this gift of fate to forge a dual career as an academic and as the leader of a state historical society. George went on to become a physician. One senses—Shambaugh himself never said as much—that he somehow felt obliged to return that gift over and over, to his students and to "the commonwealth," meaning Iowa.

In the fall of 1888, Benjamin Franklin Shambaugh registered as a freshman in the State University of Iowa. He was then but seventeen years of age. But tall, athletic and attractive, with something of his father's dynamic personality, he could be depended upon for industry and leadership. Well-groomed and well-poised, even in those early days, he looked the part of an affable and distinguished young gentleman.[1]

In June 1892, Mr. Shambaugh was graduated from the university with the degree of Bachelor of Philosophy. His name also appeared among the honor students on the commencement program. For Benjamin F. Shambaugh college days had been busy, but happy days—days of development and growth. He had participated in many curricular and extra-curricular activities. He had gained experience as a public speaker and attained recognition as an editor [of the *Vidette Reporter* and the *S.U.I. Quill*].

Graduate study in the early nineties was an innovation at the State University of Iowa. There was at that time no graduate college, no graduate school. Provision was made, however, whereby advanced students might pursue graduate study. Benjamin F. Shambaugh was one of the first to embrace this opportunity. In graduate study at the university, as in many activities in later life, he was a maker of traditions, a frontiersman, a pioneer.

Moreover, as a graduate student, he was known for his independent thinking—his ability to express opinions, and for his philosophy of life. Within a month after he had entered upon graduate study he wrote: "I believe that the life which nature has lifted to greatness ought to do much for the masses below it. The great man should give generous aid to those who aspire to his high rank. Greatness should be useful."[2]

Iowa's flagship university, the University of Iowa, was founded in 1847 as the State University of Iowa, and it developed haltingly during its first four decades. The university did not even begin offering classes until eight years later, in 1855, and for lack of students was forced to close between 1858 and 1860. When it reopened under the presidency of Rev. Silas Totten, the curriculum also was reorganized, reflecting the older, eastern liberal arts tradition that was familiar to Totten in his previous post as president of Trinity College in Hartford, Connecticut. Charles Schaeffer's tenure as university president, 1887–1898, marked the beginning of academic specialization in the faculty. Schaeffer, trained at the University of

Pennsylvania and at Harvard, had previously been vice president and dean at Cornell University, and he brought with him then-current theories of curriculum design and faculty development.[3] Thus Benjamin Shambaugh, entering the university in 1888, was in the first generation of University of Iowa students to be trained within a modern academic framework. He also seems to have been an eager student and was especially influenced by one professor, William R. Perkins.

The teaching staff of the State University in the decade of the eighties was small, but it compared favorably with that of older institutions of learning in that day. Among the teachers whom Mr. Shambaugh was to remember gratefully throughout his own long years of teaching were men of wide learning and culture.

William R. Perkins is credited with giving much of the inspiration and encouragement that resulted in Mr. Shambaugh's early historical researches. "Why doesn't someone write the story of Iowa towns," inquired Professor Perkins—"They are just as important as the New England towns—as important as the cities of Greece!" "Why not?" mused young Shambaugh. Out of this suggestion developed Mr. Shambaugh's first monograph in Iowa history—"Iowa City, A Contribution to the Early History of Iowa."

That [Perkins] had a significant influence upon his life and activities is revealed by the fact that, speaking before a university convocation in 1926, Dr. Shambaugh set forth something of his own educational philosophy and paid high tribute to those teachers who inspired and directed his early thinking.

"There was William Rufus Perkins," he said. "A man small of stature, highstrung, temperamental. Charming manners and refined tastes bespoke the gentleman and the scholar. . . . During five days of the week about forty students assembled in the northeast room on the second floor of Old South Hall. They constituted the class in Grecian History.

"As the bell in the Old Stone Capitol strikes the hour, Professor Perkins enters the room. He is carrying a manuscript in his left hand. His clothes are faultless. Cuffs and collar immaculate. With nervous step he goes to the desk. He unfolds a specially devised lecture stand. Upon this he places his papers. From the breast pocket of his coat he takes a freshly laundered handkerchief. Unfolds it. Returns it to the pocket. He then carefully adjusts his glasses, and places the ribbon meticulously over his right ear.

"From a carefully prepared manuscript he reads his lecture word for word. It is a summary interpretation of Greek life, dealing particularly with the Age of

Benjamin F. Shambaugh, 1892. *Courtesy University of Iowa—University Libraries, Special Collections.*

Pericles. . . . Presently the intellectual and spiritual atmosphere of the classroom became charged with something more than history; it became permeated with that indefinable art sense of value, proportion, rhythm, and beauty—without which there is no culture, no real life.

"From the classroom of Professor Perkins we carried away something more than notebooks filled with factual information: we felt that somehow we had become possessed of that most precious of all the gifts of education—the art sense of discrimination."[4]

Perhaps the careful preparation, the immaculate appearance, the poise, the dignity, and the urbanity which Dr. Shambaugh displayed in the classroom throughout the years may be traced in part to the impressive and abiding influence of Professor Perkins.

It is not clear precisely how Shambaugh made a vital connection between studying Greek history and researching the history of Iowa towns under Perkins's tutelage—Swisher's manuscript does not tell—but one would like to think that it was not due to Perkins's natty attire and fastidious habits. His air of midwestern chauvinism, however, may have been catching. Moreover, Shambaugh took most of his history courses under Perkins, so of course he would have been influenced by the man.[5] In any case, during Shambaugh's undergraduate years, he certainly received enough exposure to new currents of historical thought to spur an interest in local and institutional history. He may even have read Frederick Jackson Turner's 1891 essay, "The Significance of History," which encouraged the study of local history within the context of world history. Whatever the sources of his inspiration, by the early 1890s Shambaugh was part of the upcoming generation that AHA president Edward Eggleston would praise in 1900.

Early in his graduate days Mr. Shambaugh advocated the study of local history and local government. He expressed the view that the real life and activities of the nation are developed through the growth of the forty-eight commonwealth units. Every local community is a part of the great national unity. [Later,] he expressed the view that: "An appreciation of these facts has within recent times given to the study of American history a new perspective; and we are beginning to study our history from the bottom up instead of from the top down."[6] Thus, he contended that an understanding of the commonwealth is fundamental, and that such an understanding can best be obtained by a study of the smaller units of government. Hence, for his master's thesis at the State University of Iowa he chose to make a thorough and scientific study of a local area, and selected as his topic "Iowa City, The Historical Capitol of Iowa."[7]

No previous attempt had been made to write the history of Iowa City [which served as the territorial and then the state capital from December 1841 through 1855]. Accordingly, the task involved considerable research and original investigation. Fortunately, Iowa City had always been the seat of the State Historical Society of Iowa, and there had come into the library many local historical documents which might otherwise have been destroyed or lost. In the library, newspapers, letters, original manuscripts and miscellaneous papers were available. From these Mr. Shambaugh gleaned much that has now become the recorded history of the city and the commonwealth.

During his year of graduate study at the state university, Mr. Shambaugh was awarded a scholarship for advance study at Columbia University. A like honor was conferred upon him by the Wharton School of Finance and Economy of the University of Pennsylvania. He accepted the latter award and in the fall of 1893 became a resident of Philadelphia and a student at the university which more than a hundred years earlier had been founded by Benjamin Franklin.

At the University of Pennsylvania, Shambaugh's courses included French history under James Harvey Robinson and the history of economic theory under Simon N. Patten. Shambaugh kept lecture notes from these courses, and eventually they were preserved with his papers. Shambaugh also retained his notes from a special lecture series at Penn during July 1894, which included lectures on political economy by Patten, Arthur T. Hadley, Frank H. Giddings, and John B. Clark; taxation by E. R. A. Seligman; economics and politics by J. W. Jenks; and environment and race relations by R. Mayo-Smith.[8] Study at Penn thus exposed Shambaugh to some of the top scholars of the day. Even so, he seems to have been processing the scholarship in terms of its applicability to state and regional matters.

During his period of graduate study at the University of Pennsylvania Mr. Shambaugh continued his researches in Iowa history. Early in 1895 the State Historical Society published two monographs prepared by him. These contained original documents relating to the acquisition of Louisiana, the Territory of Louisiana and the Territory of Missouri. Other monographs dealing with materials relating to the Territory of Michigan, the Territory of Wisconsin, the Territory of Iowa, and the constitutions of Iowa were published later.

In March 1895 Mr. Shambaugh was graduated from the University of Pennsylvania with the degree of Doctor of Philosophy. The following month, accompanied by his brother George, he sailed for Germany where he studied in the universities of Halle, Leipzig, and Berlin. Here both Benjamin and George gathered many memories of an old world culture that was to enrich their lives always.

Shambaugh's own professional career would take him back to the University of Iowa, but he deliberately maintained a tie with James Harvey Robinson, something he did with many colleagues whose judgment he valued. For the most part, this was a professional correspondence—the two sent one another their respective publications on occasion—but in 1903 Benjamin and Bertha Shambaugh stopped for a personal visit with the Robinsons during a month's vacation in the East.[9] Thus it is certain that Shambaugh considered Robinson an important mentor, and he quite likely saw himself as carrying the torch of cutting-edge scholarship back to his alma mater when the University of Iowa offered him a professorship in 1896.

Among President Schaeffer's faculty recruits at the University of Iowa was Isaac A. Loos, a student of William Graham Sumner's at Yale. Loos is said to have had "ambitious designs for courses in economics, sociology, and anthropology, as well as political science. Schaeffer wished to form a School of History and Political Science, whereas Loos preferred to orient political science toward the other social sciences."[10] The two of them were responsible for bringing Shambaugh back to campus as a faculty member.

Dr. Loos was himself interested chiefly in economics and sociology, but he knew of the growing needs in the field of political science. President Charles A. Schaeffer, endeavoring to start the institution on its way to becoming a real university, was anxious to have a thoroughly prepared, aggressive, young political scientist to develop this new field. President Schaeffer and Dr. Loos had both known Benjamin F. Shambaugh intimately during his college days. They knew of his abilities, his hopes, and his aspirations. Accordingly, when Mr. Shambaugh entered the University of Pennsylvania to specialize in political science, his former president and head professor hoped that he might later return to Iowa to reorganize and develop courses in political science.

With this thought in mind, Dr. Loos, in the summer of 1894, attended a series of lectures given by leading economists at the University of Pennsylvania, where Mr. Shambaugh was still pursuing his graduate study. After making some inquiry, Dr. Loos wrote to President Schaeffer concerning Mr. Shambaugh and his recent activities. . . . [Loos] entertained the hope that Mr. Shambaugh might be invited to join the faculty at the university.[11]

Thus it was upon the recommendation of Dr. Loos and with the approval of President Schaeffer that Mr. Shambaugh was named as "fellow in Political Science and History" at the State University of Iowa in March 1895, just a few days before he received [his] degree. Soon thereafter he left for post-doctorate study in Germany, returning to the university for duty in January 1896.[12]

When Dr. Shambaugh began his teaching career, he was young in appearance and young in years. Yet withal, he was dignified, stately, impressive. The youth who had come to the university in 1888 had gained not alone knowledge and learning, but also dignity and poise. . . . Moreover, there had come into his life an influence that was to remain, to sustain, comfort, and inspire him through the years. On August 11, 1897, he married Miss Bertha M. Horack, the sweetheart of his college days.

The campus to which Dr. Shambaugh returned as a teacher in 1896 was not essentially different from the one to which he had come as a freshman eight years before. A beginning of the period of expansion [was] made under the leadership of President Schaeffer. In 1896, the General Assembly passed a one-tenth mill tax levy, yielding a maximum of $55,000 annually for five years—the money to be available for building purposes at the university.

With the turn of the century, the new administration [of George E. MacLean, who became president in 1899 following Schaeffer's untimely death at age fifty-five in 1898] made many changes and marked many advancements. In July 1900, a committee of the Board of Regents made a report on nomenclature. Thereafter, what had formerly been departments were called colleges and what had been designated as chairs became departments. Thus, the Collegiate Department became the College of Liberal Arts, and new departments were established within that college. One of these was a Department of Economics and Sociology, with Professor Loos in charge. Another was the Department of Political Science, with Dr. Shambaugh as Professor and Head of the Department. . . . In a period of twelve years—from 1888 to 1900—he had advanced from the status of a freshman in the university to the rank of professor and head of a department, which had been established in conformity with his wishes.

During a one-year interim period before MacLean was selected as the new president, Shambaugh and one other faculty member, botanist Thomas Huston Macbride, reportedly were considered as internal candidates to succeed Schaeffer.[13] Shambaugh must have been considered a rising star, for he had been a faculty member for only two years. To have made the transition from former student to presidential candidate in such a short time provides a clue to Shambaugh's commanding presence in the university community.

MacLean, however, was a wise choice. During his tenure, 1899–1911, he continued the building program begun by Schaeffer. He also reshaped the curriculum toward a separate graduate division, established in 1900, with supporting undergraduate departments, despite considerable internal conflict as well as outside intervention by regents and legislators.[14]

[The Department of Political Science] was established with small resources. At first, Dr. Shambaugh was the only member of its instructional staff. His salary was not large, the equipment was scant, and the students were not numerous. But Dr. Shambaugh was not one to despise the days of small things. . . . Although the department was at first small, fundamental courses were offered to students in the College of Liberal Arts, and more advanced courses were open to students entering the College of Law. With increased enrollment, additional staff members were secured and courses were offered in local government, American constitutional law, American political theory, and political parties. Thus, the Department of Political Science grew in numbers, in strength, and in popularity. Meanwhile, new courses were offered and new approaches were made in the study of government. Among the courses presented were: Introduction to Political Science, Modern Governments, Actual American Government, Comparative State Legislation, Political Parties, Municipal Government, Jurisprudence, Constitutional Law, American Political Theory, International Law, and Government of Colonies and Dependencies.

By 1916 the [Department of Political Science] had come to be one of the strong departments of the university—offering a total of almost thirty separate courses. Its faculty consisted of eight members, each a specialist in his own field. Aside from its teaching program, the department had developed an extensive research program and was widely known for its activities along this line. The Political Science Department was unique, too, in being the only department in the United States in which a course in Oriental Politics was presented by an Oriental. This policy was established by Dr. Shambaugh in 1913, when he invited Dr. Sudhindra Bose, a native of India, to become lecturer in Oriental Politics at the university.

Aside from his purely academic interests, and aside from his activities with the State Historical Society, [Shambaugh] was frequently called upon to participate in extra-curricular activities. There were frequent requests for public addresses— requests that became more numerous with the passing of the years, until he was at length impelled to decline many more invitations than he accepted. . . . Moreover, Mrs. Shambaugh came to have almost as much interest in university affairs as did Dr. Shambaugh himself. Their home at 219 North Clinton Street came to be regarded not alone as the Shambaugh home, but as an ever-ready guesthouse for students, alumni, faculty members, and university visitors.

[By 1930] the Political Science Department staff consisted of four professors, three associate professors, and a lecturer. Meanwhile, the number of courses had been increased to include virtually all subjects taught in any department of political science in any of the great universities of the country.

In the field of research and publication the department likewise had an established reputation. Collaborating with the State Historical Society it developed an extensive program of research in history and government. . . . A report of the Brookings Institution of Washington, D.C., in referring to these researches and others of like character in 1933, said, "It is probable that no political science department in any other state university has served its constituency in a more comprehensive, persevering, and practical manner."[15] Dr. Shambaugh was in a very large measure responsible for these researches. As an organizer and director of scientific research, he held, for many years, a place unique among the political scientists of America.

From 1857 to the early 1860s, the University of Iowa was entirely housed in the Old Stone Capitol, the seat of state government until the capital was moved to Des Moines; the SHSI occupied one room or another until it was moved off campus in 1862. When the university began to erect new buildings in 1863, Old Capitol's functions were reduced, but it continued to house the library (until the early 1880s), classrooms, and departmental as well as administrative offices. Shambaugh's political science classroom is believed to have been located on the first floor. In 1902 the Department of Political Science moved to the newly completed Schaeffer Hall, as did the other academic departments, which left only the Law Department and university administrative offices in Old Capitol.[16]

Closely affiliated with the program of expansion and growth during President [Walter A.] Jessup's administration [1916–1934], Dr. Shambaugh served always in a large capacity. One of the building projects in which he took a special interest in the decade of the 'twenties was the restoration and remodeling of the Old Stone Capitol. For more than thirty years, he had seen buildings on the university campus become obsolete and replaced with more modern structures. The Old Stone Capitol stood through the years the most revered, the most historic building in Iowa. It had stood the storms of eighty winters.[17] It was becoming weathered and worn. As early as 1905, Dr. Shambaugh had recommended fireproofing this building. But that had been long delayed. At long last, in 1921, plans were made for extensive repairs. Three years later the work was completed. No one was more interested in the preservation of this old landmark than was Dr. Shambaugh. . . . The writing of his book, *The Old Stone Capitol Remembers*, was prompted by his high admiration and respect for this historic old building. In 1939—Iowa City's centennial year—after publication of this book, former President John G. Bowman [1911–1914] wrote to say: "As I look at the picture of the Old Stone Capitol, I realize that you are more responsible than any other man for the preservation of that building."[18]

The Old Stone Capitol was rehabilitated between 1921 and 1924. Margaret Keyes, who has documented the building's history (with emphasis on its restoration in 1970–1976), does not credit Shambaugh as being an instigator. This does not mean that Shambaugh played only a ceremonial role in preserving the building during the 1920s, however, for he often worked behind the scenes. In any case, Keyes reports that calls for repairing and fireproofing the venerable edifice came from many quarters after the turn of the century, but it took a nearby fire and at least two lightning strikes to move the state legislature to action. In 1917 legislators appropriated $50,000 for "restoring, fireproofing, and remodeling" the building, but World War I delayed the start of work until 1921. The rehabilitation included adding the west portico, which John F. Rague, the original architect, had designed but which had never been built. The interior was substantially altered, and realtered in subsequent years, to adapt the building to university needs. Importantly, Old Capitol became the site for Shambaugh's Commonwealth Conference from 1923 to 1930 (see Chapter 5).[19]

Dr. Shambaugh's longtime service as a university professor and administrator is indicative of his faith in the Commonwealth of Iowa. It was his interest in local history and government that induced him as a young man to return to Iowa for his teaching career. Back of his desire to train his own men in political science was the deep-seated belief that those who best understand the commonwealth can best serve it. It was this hope and confidence in his homeland that impelled him again and again to decline invitations to go elsewhere. Asked on one occasion if anything could "pry him loose" from Iowa, he replied, "No, I'm afraid not. I have thought my way out. If I have any ability or talent, it belongs to Iowa."[20]

Stow Persons calls the period from 1908, when the Graduate College was established, to midcentury the university's "era of creative anarchy." These were decades where a combination of institutional stability and organizational flexibility allowed "a generation of aggressive, creative individuals" to "initiat[e] new programs and leav[e] a long-lasting stamp on the overall profile of the university." Persons does not list Shambaugh's name among faculty members who were considered "anarchists," but there is no doubt that Shambaugh contributed to the evolution of the university's "distinctive character" during the thirty-two remaining years of his career.[21] Shambaugh's two major contributions were to separate history and political science from the social science complex and to forge an extraordinary relationship between the university and the SHSI.[22] In order to do the latter, he first had to bring the society back to its legislatively mandated home in the university.

Dr. Shambaugh once said: "I dream of the day when Iowa history not only will be translated into folklore, but transmitted into the hearts of our people."[23] When Mr. Shambaugh was a student at the university, the State Historical Society of Iowa was an institution which had as yet gained but little prominence. Housed in a large room above a hardware store on Washington Street in Iowa City, the library and physical properties of the society were neither attractive nor readily accessible. The room was lighted by windows in the front and the rear, aided by a somewhat befogged skylight in the center. There were bookcases along the walls on either side, and in the center of the room were long, low, glass-top display cases containing a variety of unlabeled curios and "specimens."

Placed about the room between the cases and against the walls, where space was available, were larger objects of varied interests—a small musical instrument, some photographs and maps, an ox yoke, a spinning wheel, a looking glass labeled "one hundred years old," some Civil War flags, and John Brown's cannon. The room was heated by two stoves—one on either side. Near the bookshelves were two tables and a few miscellaneous chairs.

The library was open to visitors regularly on Wednesday and Saturday each week, "and at other times when desirable." Young Benjamin Shambaugh, because of his special interests, was permitted to enter the room at his own convenience to pursue historical studies. On such occasions it was his custom to build his own fire, wipe the dust from the table nearest the stove, and spend hours in the pursuit of historical data.[24]

Outwardly the historical society presented a dismal aspect. But deep underneath the surface there was that which inspired confidence and gave hope of a much brighter day. Well-founded by sturdy pioneers in the decade of the 'fifties, fostered through the years by interested statesmen and educators . . . the State Historical Society had a substantial rooting in the past—a good foundation on which to build. It had collected and preserved valuable pioneer documents, records, and relics. It had made a beginning in the publication of pioneer history—the early issues of *The Annals of Iowa* and *The Iowa Historical Record*. But its program of extensive research and publication, its carefully designed plans for presenting historical data in a more popular form, its vision of writing Iowa history as "folklore" lay still in the future.[25]

When Dr. Shambaugh returned to the university as a member of the faculty in 1896, he had in mind plans for a closer affiliation between the university and the historical society. Although he carried a full teaching schedule in the university and had numerous administrative duties, he found time to serve as a member of the Board of Curators of the historical society and to continue his interests in historical research and editorial work. One of the first major extra-curricular activities that he undertook was the compilation and editing of the *Fragments of Debates of the Iowa Constitutional Conventions of 1844 and 1846*. No complete contemporary journals of the proceedings of these conventions were written, and no extensive private journals were available. Hence, the fragments gleaned from contemporary newspapers, giving both the Whig and the Democratic viewpoints, became historically significant.[26]

As a member of the Board of Curators, Dr. Shambaugh's influence upon the development of the society was clearly apparent. Early in the year 1900 he recommended that the society bind for permanent preservation twenty-five sets of *The Iowa Historical Record*.[27] In June of the same year, upon motion by Dr. Shambaugh, a committee was appointed to confer with the university relative to obtaining rooms in the new Liberal Arts Building. The pursuance of this motion resulted in a removal of the State Historical Society from its antiquated room on Washington Street to the new and commodious university building later known as Schaeffer Hall, where the society [remained until 1959].[28]

The move to Schaeffer Hall meant that the SHSI was housed in the same university building as the political science department. This made it convenient for Shambaugh to function in both of his official capacities. Frank

W. Bicknell, a syndicated newspaper correspondent whose articles appeared nationwide, played a part in promoting this convenience for Shambaugh. Bicknell, by virtue of his profession, cultivated a network of political back-scratchers and informants and, like Shambaugh, was a member of the historical society's Board of Curators. Lengthy correspondence between the two men reveals that Bicknell was quick to see Shambaugh's potential as an administrator who could build the society. Accordingly, he supported Shambaugh's ideas and initiatives, solicited his personal friendship, and freely offered political advice. While the move to Schaeffer Hall was under consideration in 1900 and early 1901, Bicknell took advantage of whatever opportunities he had to speak personally with the university president and with university regents he knew, and he reported these conversations back to Shambaugh.[29]

Even though Bicknell supported Shambaugh in moving the historical society to Schaeffer Hall, he personally had reservations about the proposed new arrangement because the university had a long record of housing the society poorly and neglecting the care of its collections. Moreover, the state had just begun construction of a $300,000 historical building in Des Moines. Thus Bicknell's "private, confidential, personal opinion [was] that the interest of the cause would be served by concentrating nearly all the material in the state historical building in Des Moines. . . . We cannot hope to maintain two great historical collections in Iowa." Better, he thought, to devote the energies of the historical society "to the prosecution of such work as you [Shambaugh] are doing. In this way I think we can work in harmony with the state historical department, secure legislative help and retain our argument that we are really an auxiliary of the University."[30]

As the worm turned in the ensuing years, Bicknell's concept assumed more cogency. The period from 1901 to 1907 represents a difficult but immensely important transition period. During these years, Shambaugh became involved in the work of the AHA's Public Archives Commission and Conference of State and Local Historical Societies and cofounded the American Political Science Association as well as the Mississippi Valley Historical Association. At the same time, he essentially redefined the SHSI and then emerged in 1907 as its official leader. He began by revamping the society's publications. As a member of the Board of Curators, Shambaugh either offered to assume the duties of editor or was asked to do so. In either case, he became editor of the *Iowa Historical Record* in 1900. Then, in 1903, he replaced the old quarterly with a scholarly journal, the *Iowa Journal of History and Politics*.

In January 1903 the first issue of the *Iowa Journal of History and Politics* was edited by Dr. Shambaugh and published by the State Historical Society. This was something of an innovation in historical publications and attracted wide attention. Upon receipt of an advance copy of this journal, Judge Horace Deemer of Red Oak wrote: "I hasten to congratulate you on the splendid appearance and excellent quality of the publication. Am glad you dressed it so neatly, as the apparel not only proclaims the man but oftimes the magazine."[31]

Judge Deemer, a member of the Iowa Supreme Court, also supported Shambaugh's efforts to professionalize the SHSI. His letter to Shambaugh is an early example of the comments that Shambaugh routinely solicited to promote the work of the society, as well as his own. For example, to L. S. Rowe at Penn, who was then president of the American Academy of Political and Social Science, Shambaugh sent not only a copy of the first issue of the *Iowa Journal of History and Politics* but also a copy of his most recent book, *History of the Constitution of Iowa*.[32] Likewise, James Harvey Robinson received a complimentary copy of *History of the Constitution of Iowa*, which he pronounced "a most dignified volume."[33]

Dr. Shambaugh instituted another advance step in the preservation of state historical data through the editing and publication of important government documents. An early adventure in this field resulted in the publication of *The Messages and Proclamations of the Governors of Iowa*. This series of seven volumes embraced the state papers of all governors of the Territory and the State, beginning with Governor Henry Dodge of the Territory of Wisconsin, and continuing through the administration of Governor Leslie M. Shaw in 1901. When the first volume of this series was published by the State Historical Society, Professor Albert Bushnell Hart of Harvard University wrote to Dr. Shambaugh saying, "You have a regular knack for doing what ought to be done for every State in the Union. It is a great pleasure to see the intellectual development of that great and rich State, and you may congratulate yourself on your active part in this progress."[34]

When subsequent volumes in this series were issued, Professor Hart wrote again saying: "I am delighted to see that continued evidence of an interest in State history and State affairs in which Iowa is setting an example for all the other states. I hope you will not be weary of well doing."[35]

Thus, Dr. Shambaugh was early recognized as a leader in the preservation of documents of this type—a plan that has been followed with acknowledgments in other states.

There is no question that Shambaugh saw his efforts to preserve Iowa's official records and make them accessible to scholars as a necessary state-level counterpart to the work of the AHA Historical Manuscripts and Public Archives Commissions. As the SHSI's publications program evolved, the three volumes of *Documentary Materials Relative to the History of Iowa* (1897–1901), the seven volumes of *Messages and Proclamations of the Governors of Iowa* (1903–1905), and the *Executive Journal of Iowa* (1906) became known as the Public Archives Series.

Additionally, Shambaugh was following the example of Reuben Gold Thwaites in Wisconsin. Thwaites, like Draper before him, worked to increase the State Historical Society of Wisconsin's manuscript collections and to make them available to students at the University of Wisconsin. Between 1896 and 1901, Thwaites and his assistants translated and published seventy-three volumes of documents entitled *Jesuit Relations and Allied Documents*. This monumental undertaking established his reputation as a historical editor. This reputation was further enhanced with his edited volume of Louis Hennepin's *New Discovery* (1903), eight volumes of the *Original Journals of the Lewis and Clark Expedition* (1904–1905), thirty-two volumes of annotated reprints of *Early Western Travels* (1904–1907), and, in collaboration with historian Louise P. Kellogg, the Draper Series: *Documentary History of Dunmore's War* (1905), *The Revolution on the Upper Ohio* (1908), and *Frontier Defense on the Upper Ohio* (1912). In addition to editing documentary material, Thwaites also found time to author several books of his own.[36]

Shambaugh and Thwaites corresponded regularly, and especially during the early years Shambaugh often sought advice or support from the elder man. Particularly telling of their professional relationship, Shambaugh asked Thwaites to "express his views" of the SHSI in 1904, when Shambaugh was seeking an increase in the society's annual appropriation from the Iowa legislature. In reply, Thwaites wrote: "The publications of the State Historical Society of Iowa occupy a high place among similar publications in this country; and the *Iowa Journal of History and Politics* is particularly so interesting, valuable, and ably edited a periodical that [it] has commanded wide attention among historical students throughout this country. Your sister societies and the many students of history throughout the West have learned to regard the State Historical Society of Iowa as an institution of constantly increasing excellence and with a broad future before it."[37]

Continuing the policy of publishing unique and valuable public documents, the State Historical Society under the leadership of Dr. Shambaugh published the *Robert Lucas Executive Journal.* Concerning this publication, Dr. Thomas Owen of Alabama said: "I do not think I have yet seen any more excellent work, either from the editorial or typographical standpoint. The State of Iowa has constant cause for congratulation in having a man in her borders whose ideals are so high, and who insists on the very best class of work for her official publications."[38]

The year 1907 was a year of high adventure in the life of Dr. Shambaugh. For a little more than a decade he had been a member of the university faculty. For a similar period of years he had been officially connected with the State Historical Society and directed many of its activities. Early in 1907 it seemed advisable to re-organize the society and to place it upon a more practical basis. Pursuant to this plan the Office of Superintendent and Editor was established, and Dr. Sham-baugh was unanimously elected to that office. Moreover, 1907 was the year for observing the semi-centennial of the framing of the [Iowa] constitution of 1857 and also the semi-centennial of the establishment of the historical society itself.

Plans for making the semi-centennial observance an occasion of statewide in-terest were instituted by the Board of Curators in March 1906, when a commit-tee, of which Dr. Shambaugh was chairman, was appointed to formulate a pro-gram. An appropriation of funds provided by the Thirty-first General Assembly of Iowa, and supplemented by the historical society budget, made possible the fi-nancing of an appropriate observance, and Dr. Shambaugh both officially and personally exerted every effort to make this an occasion long to be remembered in the history of the state.

There was at that time only one surviving member of each of the three consti-tutional conventions—Samuel W. Durham, a member of the constitutional convention of 1844; J. Scott Richman, a member of the convention of 1846; and John Henry Peters, a member of the convention of 1857. These men were brought to Iowa City to participate in the semi-centennial program. In addition to this the governor of the state, the president of the university, and distinguished historians and guests from other states [including Thwaites] joined in the historic observance.

In order "to preserve something of the form and spirit as well as the facts of the anniversary," the speeches which were presented at the semi-centennial were preserved in their entirety and published by the State Historical Society under the title *Proceedings of the Fiftieth Anniversary of the Constitution of Iowa.*[39] This volume was designed to preserve the best thought concerning a half-century of constitutional growth. But it was also a fitting tribute to Dr. Shambaugh himself, who more than any other individual had guided the historical researches of a commonwealth and made possible this and many other volumes of its type.

In its reorganization, the program of the State Historical Society of Iowa was unique. Differing from those institutions which emphasize the collection and display of historical relics, the society placed emphasis upon a program of scientific historical research and publication. Instead of attempting to assemble the largest historical collection in one place, it endeavored "to compile, publish, and distribute the greatest amount of accurate, scientific historical literature. Instead of hoarding books and manuscripts for the use of the few," the society aimed "to make the history of the State accessible to the many."[40] All this was in conformity with Dr. Shambaugh's wishes. Indeed, much of it was the result of his conscious effort and deliberate planning for the society.

Building carefully for the future, the society placed an emphasis upon quality rather than quantity. Its publications—[in] printing and binding—were of a high standard. Since the society was engaged in critical historical research and publication, not alone for the immediate future, but for long periods of time, the Board of Curators had very wisely determined upon a policy of issuing publications of a substantial character. This policy, the superintendent and the board believed, would in the long run promote both economy and efficiency.

That the influence of the State Historical Society of Iowa was increasing and that its work was being widely recognized by historians there is abundant evidence. Frederick J. Turner, writing to Dr. Shambaugh in 1908, said, "The *Journal* [*of History and Politics*] always has interesting and valuable material, and the series of books which you are issuing are not only beautiful specimens of printer's work but are full of historical meat."[41] Upon receiving a copy of the Robert Lucas biography, Albert Bushnell Hart wrote [that] future generations "will thank you for preserving these materials of the epoch of great significance of which the memorials are perishing every day." Later he wrote, "It is astonishing what an abundance of good stuff you people in Iowa get out, and I hope that you will keep up the good work."[42]

Jacob Swisher may have considered Shambaugh's reorganization program of the SHSI "unique," but Shambaugh more likely thought that he was modernizing the society in accordance with the best professional practices of the day. Without question he was ambitious; he aimed to make Iowa one of the top historical societies in the country. But he was not a self-serving empire builder. As time would reveal, he had no higher career aspirations for himself. Rather, he sought to lay a foundation that would sustain scholarship in Iowa history for generations to come.

3

The Politics of Public Institutions

EARLY SURVEYS conducted by the AHA's Public Archives Commission and Henry Bourne's two-year investigation of state and local historical societies indicated that emerging organizational structures varied considerably from state to state. None of them, however, became more convoluted than Iowa's. The SHSI, established by an act of the state legislature in 1857, was placed under the State University of Iowa, an organizational structure designed to emulate that of the State Historical Society of Wisconsin, although practically speaking the SHSI operated very differently from the Wisconsin organization until Shambaugh became involved. The State Department of History and Archives (SDHA) evolved between 1892 and the early 1900s in Des Moines as an entirely separate entity from the SHSI, located in Iowa City. The state legislature appropriated funds to both, but the two remained distinct until 1986, when they were officially joined under the Iowa Department of Cultural Affairs.

Personalities, politics, and timing account for the establishment of two state institutions that duplicated one another in many respects. Shambaugh already was a very busy person—building the Department of Political Science, reforming the SHSI, helping to found two new national professional organizations, and assisting with the work of the Public Archives Commission and the Conference of State and Local Historical Societies— but he also found time to try to professionalize the SDHA. Shambaugh deserves much of the credit (or blame) for rationalizing the respective functions of the SHSI and SDHA in order to justify the existence of both. The story, which is an interesting case study in institutional history, is more important because it reveals the tension that Shambaugh experienced as he sought to establish the SHSI as an institution that served public interests without becoming a servant of politics, an institution that did not let standards of scholarship slip with the demands of political expediency.

Although the SHSI and the SDHA were separate entities, in practice the division never was clear-cut, since the institutional operations always overlapped to a degree. The reputation that Shambaugh built for the society, however, explains in large part why the current SHSI is physically split between two locations, Iowa City and Des Moines, a situation that baffles out-of-state researchers and confuses many Iowans. Parenthetically, one might add that, among those who understand the institutional genealogy of the SHSI, there is steadfast fealty to an Iowa City presence. Shambaugh cast a long shadow.

Near the turn of the century there was developing throughout the country an increased interest in public archives. As part of this widespread movement, Dr. Shambaugh made a study of Iowa archives. In a report published by the American Historical Association in 1900, he called attention to the fact that Iowa archives were not complete for any period of state history. In some cases, valuable documents were not carefully preserved. In other cases valuable original documents had been lost or destroyed by frequent removal. He therefore advocated the establishment of permanent archives in which important documents might be preserved without need of further removal.[1] The problem of the archives remained one of vital importance until a permanent archives building was obtained. Dr. Shambaugh was one of the first and one of the most consistent workers for this project until its final consummation.

The Historical Department, [later] known as the Iowa State Department of History and Archives, originated as a branch of the state library in 1892. Prior to that time, [Charles] Aldrich had collected valuable historical materials which he presented to the State of Iowa. In that year the General Assembly set apart three rooms in the basement of the capitol building for the "Aldrich Collection," and provided that the trustees of the Iowa State Library should appoint a person to be designated as "curator of historical collection." The trustees appointed Mr. Aldrich to this position. From this humble beginning the State Department of History and Archives developed.[2]

Aldrich himself explained the origins this way. "In the year 1884, Mrs. Aldrich and I presented to the State, through the trustees of the State Li-

Benjamin F. Shambaugh, circa 1915. *Courtesy State Historical Society of Iowa, Iowa City*

brary, a simple Autograph Collection, proposing, if it should be placed in cases in the Library, and properly cared for, to make further additions to its contents, as well as to illustrate it with portraits of the celebrities represented, adding also sufficient biographical data. This offer was accepted." The Aldriches added to the collection as the state legislature appropriated money to build cases to hold the historical artifacts, but, as he further explained, "no one else was willing to undertake to arrange the materials in the cases. I was therefore compelled to come to Des Moines and do this work myself, or let the enterprise fall to the ground." One thing led to another, and in 1890 the Pioneer Law Makers' Association petitioned the legislature to support the work of collecting and preserving historical documents relating to the territorial and early statehood periods.[3]

Aldrich, an enterprising early-comer to the state, thoroughly enmeshed himself in state affairs. By profession he was a newspaper publisher, but by inclination he was a political activist, as evidenced by the fact that at age nineteen he was chosen secretary of the first "free soil," or antislavery, convention in New York, his native state. In 1857 he headed west, settling in Iowa, where he edited and published the *Dubuque Times* and then the *Marshall County Times*. He served one term in the Iowa House of Representatives, 1882–1884, but prior to that he was appointed to serve as chief clerk of the House by four different assemblies of that body. Thus he was in the thick of state politics throughout the 1860s and 1870s, and he was continually drafting bills and lobbying for their passage regardless of whether he was in the legislature. These included a measure, passed in 1862, to require the permanent binding of public documents, which Aldrich sought because "in old times Iowa official publications were only bound in sleazy paper covers." He also promoted public interest in commemorating the pioneers, and some of the earliest brass plaques and historical monuments installed in Iowa were due to his efforts.[4]

In 1892 [the same year he was officially appointed curator of his own collection], Mr. Aldrich, an elderly man, began to cast about for a young and able assistant who might later succeed him as Curator of the Historical Department. Among the young men with whom he conferred in this connection was Benjamin F. Shambaugh. Mr. Shambaugh was then a graduate student at the State University of Iowa. He had recently made the acquaintance of Mr. Aldrich as he had now and again visited Des Moines in search of materials for his first published volume, the early history of Iowa City.

Perhaps before Mr. Shambaugh left Iowa City to pursue graduate study in the East, and certainly very soon after he arrived in Philadelphia, he received letters from Mr. Aldrich relative to serving the Historical Department. Pursuing this matter further, in December [1894] Mr. Aldrich, in passing from New York to Washington, D.C., stopped at Philadelphia to confer with Mr. Shambaugh concerning matters of mutual interest. Mr. Aldrich and Mr. Shambaugh must have appeared as unconventional companions, for there was a wide variance in their ages and in their training and experience. Mr. Aldrich was sixty-six years of age . . . while Mr. Shambaugh was but twenty-three and had the appearance of being younger than he was. Mr. Aldrich had been trained in the hard school of experience, while Mr. Shambaugh had enjoyed the educational advantages of two universities. Despite these differences they had mutual interests, for they were both absorbed in the task of preserving Iowa history. Moreover, their friendship ripened with the years.[5] In February 1895, a month before Mr. Shambaugh received his doctor's degree at the University of Pennsylvania, Mr. Aldrich wrote to him saying, "Some young man like yourself (one among a million) ought to be looking ahead to take my place."[6]

While Dr. Shambaugh was in Germany, he continued to receive letters from Mr. Aldrich, and upon his return to Iowa City . . . the volume of correspondence increased. . . . [O]ut of this early correspondence there developed plans for a conference at Iowa City. Accordingly, Mr. Aldrich came to Iowa City, where he and Dr. Shambaugh held a night session at the St. James Hotel. The details of what transpired at that meeting are not a matter of record. It is clear, however, that what was considered to be a liberal offer was tendered to Dr. Shambaugh as an inducement for him to accept a position in Des Moines. This was declined, however, and a little later another offer was tendered—Mr. Aldrich always contending that the greater opportunities lay at the state capital.[7]

In April 1896 Aldrich anticipated that the cornerstone for the new historical building would be laid that December, a tidbit of information he offered Shambaugh as inducement. "If I am able to bring it around," he continued, "how would you like a situation in this Department at say, $900 to $1000 per year? Should this come to pass, your work would be upon the same lines as mine at this time—with good prospects for the future."[8] Shambaugh apparently kept his options open, for in early May Aldrich made an even stronger appeal based on professional status. "We discussed Mr. Thwaites," he wrote. "Your position, so far as you are personally concerned, would be identical with his, and I do not think that he would exchange places with any man in the State University—not even the President." Once again, Aldrich mentioned the new building and all that it promised. "The erection of the new Building; the collection of materials for Iowa and Western History; the development of the Museum—to include an art gallery; the editing of *The Annals*, and the publishing of special monographs; furnish fields of the highest usefulness and opportunities for a clear-headed, educated man to distinguish himself. . . . Seriously, if you let this opportunity go by, I believe you will miss the most glorious one that will come to you in your lifetime."[9] But Shambaugh was not swayed.

Dr. Shambaugh, having in mind the good work that was being done in Wisconsin through the cooperation of the historical society and the university, was of the opinion that historical interests were best developed at an educational center rather than in a political atmosphere. "A Historical Society or Library cannot be built up by politicians," he said. "It must command the support of scholars, men of learning and sciences, men who devote the labor of their lives to purely intellectual pursuits. Nor can *one* man *alone* succeed in the work. He must have the counsel, advice and interest of others."[10] Thus, at the very beginning of his public career, Dr. Shambaugh chose to affiliate himself with educational rather than political interests.

Aldrich reluctantly accepted Shambaugh's decision but continued to hold open the offer of succession should he change his mind. Recalling the society's history of neglect and meager appropriations, Aldrich firmly believed that Des Moines held the advantage for advancing historical interests in Iowa. "The People are looking *here* for the development and establishment of a Museum & Historical Department. Here I believe it will be fairly supported—*generously*, with the advent of better times."[11]

Shambaugh, however, cast his lot with the old historical society, which still had an institutional tie to the university, tenuous at best, but nonetheless a base he could use to build the society into something more like the Wisconsin model on which it was purportedly founded in 1857. Access to a community of scholars and an aversion to political influence were his reasons for remaining in Iowa City. There is little evidence to suggest that personal or other unstated reasons also played a role. In August 1897 he would marry Bertha M. Horack; the two had been courting since 1890 when they met as undergraduate students. But in 1896 Shambaugh was only twenty-five years old, unmarried, his entire career before him. Benjamin and Bertha might just as easily have started married life in Des Moines. Moreover, he had been in his faculty position at the university for only a few months, having just taken up his teaching duties in January 1896. Shambaugh truly was at a point where he had two more-or-less clear career options before him. He was unfettered by personal ties, and he had no established professional identity to consider. It appears as though, even at a young age, his career choice was guided by a sense of purpose.

Despite their differences of opinion relative to matters of employment, Mr. Aldrich and Dr. Shambaugh continued to be the best of friends. For more than a decade after Dr. Shambaugh declined the liberal offers to become officially connected with the Historical Department, indeed, until the end of the career of Mr. Aldrich, in 1908, there continued to be a close friendship between the two men. Not infrequently, Dr. Shambaugh aided the work of the Historical Department. . . .[12] Further friendship between Dr. Shambaugh and Mr. Aldrich is shown by the fact that in 1902 the Historical Department published Dr. Shambaugh's *History of the Constitution of Iowa*, which was dedicated to Mr. Aldrich as "Founder and Curator of the Historical Department of Iowa."

[Likewise,] the new historical building . . . being erected in Des Moines was . . . of much interest to Dr. Shambaugh. An adequate building for the preservation of historical materials had long been talked of by Mr. Aldrich and Dr. Shambaugh. A measure for the erection of such a building had been approved by the 26th General Assembly [in 1896] and signed by the governor.[13] This act authorized the Executive Council to erect a memorial, historical, and art building, and made an appropriation of $25,000 to carry out the provisions of the law.[14] The original plans were altered somewhat, additional appropriations were provided, and in due course [a full decade] the new historical building was erected across the street north of the state capitol building.

During these years there was developing throughout Iowa an interest not only in the memorial and art features of the program, but also in its historical aspects.[15] For this phase of the program, Dr. Shambaugh was among the first to give expression to a concrete plan. He prepared a "Report on the Public Archives of Iowa" for the American Historical Association.[16]

At this point, Shambaugh began assisting the AHA Public Archives Commission and took a more active role in preserving public records in Iowa. During the commission's first year, the work concentrated on identifying AHA members in each state who were in a position to assess the status of public records. Shambaugh was asked to report on Iowa, which he did promptly. His "Report on the Public Archives of Iowa," which appeared in the AHA's annual report for 1900, was one of ten state reports submitted that year, the others reporting being Connecticut, Indiana, Massachusetts, Michigan, Nebraska, New York, North Carolina, Pennsylvania, and Wisconsin.[17]

[In a 1901 editorial, Aldrich wrote] that Dr. Shambaugh had recently visited Des Moines, that he had discovered many valuable papers packed in close quarters, so that they were not available for use, and that he had emphasized the fact that a "Hall of Archives" had become a public necessity. Moreover, Dr. Shambaugh had expressed the belief that such a building should be located at the state capital.[18]

When the Historical Department was organized in 1892, it was placed under a board of trustees of the state library, consisting of the governor, the judges of the [state] supreme court, the secretary of state, and the superintendent of public instruction, with the governor as chairman. From 1894 to 1917, Judge Horace E. Deemer served on the supreme court and for many years was, by common consent, the chief representative of the board of trustees in matters of historical interest. In 1903, Dr. Shambaugh wrote to Mr. Aldrich and to Judge Deemer relative to the specific fields of service of the historical society and the historical department as he envisioned them. He said that the historical society would emphasize publications and a library, and expressed the hope that the historical department would lay emphasis upon a building and a museum. Thus, he virtually conceded to the historical department its priority in the matter of archives and the equipment of a building for their adequate protection.[19]

[Two years later, in 1905, Shambaugh once again] advocated a "Hall of Archives" and suggested that he would be glad to go with Mr. Aldrich and Judge Deemer to confer with the governor relative to the matter if such seemed desirable. To Judge Deemer he expressed the belief that the preservation of archives was "one of the most important missions of the Historical Department."[20]

Well might there have been keen rivalry between the state historical society and the historical department—each pursuing its own course in the collection and preservation of historical data. But in a larger sense, and especially in connection with the establishment and development of the public archives, there was no rivalry, but rather a spirit of kindly cooperation. Dr. Shambaugh collaborated with Judge Deemer and Mr. Aldrich in sponsoring legislation for the archives. As a result, a measure passed by the Thirty-first General Assembly [1906] . . . authorized the Executive Council to provide and furnish a room in the [nearly completed] historical building to be known as the Hall of Public Archives and made an appropriation of $2,000 annually for three years to carry forward the work designated.[21]

Correspondence between Aldrich and Shambaugh reveals that the two men, probably working with Judge Deemer, began consulting with Governor Albert B. Cummins and various state legislators in 1901 to find a suitable space for a state archives. Shambaugh apparently wanted a sep-

arate building, but Aldrich wanted the archives housed in the new historical building, then under construction, even though he knew there would
be insufficient space to house public records for more than a decade or
two. When the legislature failed in 1902 to appropriate additional money
to add an extension to the historical building for the archives, Aldrich
complained that he had received a "black eye" while Shambaugh had received an increase in the appropriation for the historical society that
year.[22] As late as 1905 Shambaugh still held out some hope that the legislature might appropriate an adequate sum, $100,000–$175,000, to build
another wing on the historical building, which was still under construction.[23] It took until 1906 to secure just a small appropriation of $2,000 to
begin gathering public records from various state offices and placing
them in preliminary order for transfer to the historical building, finally
completed that year, but exactly where the archives would be located in
the building had not been determined. By this time, Aldrich was in poor
health, and Shambaugh therefore accepted the responsibility of planning
and supervising the work. Accordingly, he hired John Parish, one of his
graduate students, to take charge of arranging and classifying the records
and a clerk, Clara Neidig, to assist Parish.[24]

On the matter of rivalry between the SHSI and the SDHA, there was
more than Swisher wanted to admit. In late 1906, when he was very ill,
Aldrich dictated a letter to Shambaugh in which he confessed: "When I
commenced my work fourteen years ago, there was no good feeling between Des Moines and Iowa City. Amongst us that ill feeling has died
away. A large [factor] in the premises [?] has been the wise and judicious
action of our mutual friend, Judge Deemer."[25] Deemer, it would seem,
acted as a moderating force, and there apparently remained some linger-
ing distance between Aldrich and Shambaugh, even though it is not obvious from their correspondence.[26]

Aldrich could be temperamental, as the "black eye" letter suggests. In
1904 he received a gold medal at the Louisiana Purchase Exposition in St.
Louis for his outstanding contributions to historical work, awarded by a
committee of historians and anthropologists chaired by WJ McGee.
When Aldrich grilled Shambaugh on the details of his nomination, Shambaugh admitted that he had initiated the recognition and that he also had
served on the "jury of history." And when Aldrich finally received the actual item, not until mid 1906, he was disappointed to find that it was not
gold at all but an alloy, which, as he informed Shambaugh, "looks more

like bronze than the yellow metal. However, it is approved by St. Gaudens which I suppose is all the certificate it needs."[27] Whatever tension there may have been in the relationship between the two men, it was always tempered by mutual respect; when Aldrich knew his health was failing him, it was Shambaugh he wanted to stand in his place to make certain that the archives became a reality.[28]

Since Dr. Shambaugh had always been interested in this field, it is not strange that the trustees of the historical department should have looked to him for further leadership. About the middle of May, 1906, he was in Des Moines and was asked to confer with the trustees relative to the archives. At that time, he made some general suggestions, but preferred not to make any specific recommendations until he had made a study of what had been done in other states. Thereupon, the trustees authorized him to visit other states for the purpose of making such a study.

In the weeks that followed, he visited Madison, Wisconsin; Buffalo and Albany, New York; Ottawa, Canada; Washington, D.C.; Harrisburg, Pennsylvania; Montgomery, Alabama; Jackson, Mississippi; New Orleans, Louisiana; and St. Louis, Missouri, to study archives. On this tour he traveled at night in sleeping cars and conferred with archivists during the day.[29]

Shambaugh's itinerary indicates that he sought the advice of leaders in the movement to establish public archives. Alabama and Mississippi had been the first to establish a state archive as a separate department of state. The Public Archives Commission had promoted bills for state-supported public archives in New York and Pennsylvania, and by 1906 J. Franklin Jameson and Waldo Leland were directing a national effort from the Carnegie Institution in Washington, D.C. Moreover, Shambaugh and Thomas Owen, director of the Alabama Department of Archives and History, had worked together on the Public Archives Commission and the Conference of State and Local Historical Societies, so it was logical that Shambaugh would consult him.[30]

Although Dr. Shambaugh was at this time teaching a full schedule at the university and serving as [superintendent] of the State Historical Society, after making this survey, he consented to assume the duties of directing work in the archives. In pursuance of this work, he submitted his first extensive "Report on Public Archives," published in the January 1907 issue of *The Annals*. Meanwhile, actual work in the archives had begun with Dr. John C. Parish temporarily in charge.[31]

For his friend Frank Bicknell, Shambaugh wrote an energetic piece on the advent of Iowa's official public archives, which appeared in the *Mail and Times*, a Des Moines weekly that Bicknell published. "To-day the public records, the public archives of Iowa, are in a sense being rescued from the vaults in the Capitol where they have rested for decades. They are being arranged and classified preliminary to their removal to the Hall of Public Archives in the new Historical Memorial and Art Building. . . . Behold the workers have appeared in the field! . . . Surely Iowa has been aroused to the effort of preserving and publishing the unpublished books of the Commonwealth's history."[32]

The hearty quality of Shambaugh's rhetoric for this piece reflects, at least in part, the nature of his friendship with Bicknell. Shambaugh typically initiated correspondence with academic and professional peers whenever he was drawn into some direct association with them or when he was seeking a professional stamp of approval to promote the work of the historical society. As a result, many letters scattered through his correspondence bear the signatures of luminaries in the historical profession between the 1890s and 1940. However, he seems never to have sought informal camaraderie with male companions.

In this regard, his relationship with Frank Bicknell was something of an exception, probably because Bicknell's hunting and fishing buddies included Bertha Shambaugh's brothers, Frank and Claude Horack, so the intimacy of family was wrapped up in their friendship.[33] Even so, Shambaugh set limits; he politely deflected Bicknell's persistent invitations to join them, or him, for a few days of "gentlemanly shooting" during open seasons and probably never donned the pair of hunting boots that Bicknell once sent him. Shambaugh seems to have preferred the company of his wife when engaged in social activities and, in any case, was too engrossed in his own work to make time for "gentlemanly" relaxation. "Cordial," "diplomatic," "polite," "efficient," and sometimes "solicitous" are words that aptly describe the language in the vast majority of his letters, and the volume of them is astounding. Thus the candor that is evident in the Shambaugh-Bicknell correspondence is unusual, a factor that seems particularly significant in terms of reading Shambaugh's state of mind as the task of establishing a professionally administered state archives in Iowa became increasingly mired in politics.

That interest in the archives had become widespread is evidenced by the fact that, in January 1907, Governor Albert B. Cummins made reference to the work and recommended "such an appropriation as may be necessary to carry on the project with reasonable celerity."[34]

When the Thirty-second General Assembly met there were many applications for clerical positions at the state house. To increase the number of available positions, some of the legislators sought to find employment for them in the archives. Dr. Shambaugh always sought to avoid political appointments. Moreover, he sought to use only employees who were trained to do the work at hand. Accordingly, he wrote a clear, concise letter to members of the Senate in which he explained that only trained employees could be used. At the same time, in a letter to Judge Deemer, he expressed the hope that he might be able to keep the matter of appointments out of politics: "There is one thing that I certainly have no genius for doing and that is for taking care of clerkships created for the purpose of being filled by particular persons."[35]

Whether there was a resentment of Dr. Shambaugh's attitude relative to clerk hire, whether there was opposition to his policy of building up the archive, whether there was a general desire to curtail appropriations, or whether there was a belief that there should be a general reorganization of the Historical Department—all of these are matters of conjecture. Perhaps there were a variety of reasons involved. At all events, soon after the introduction of the measure for increased appropriations, there was agitation in the General Assembly to transfer control of the archives from the Board of Trustees of the State Library to the Executive Council. In this situation, Dr. Shambaugh wrote to Governor Cummins urging that the appropriation be increased and that management be left in the hands of the trustees.[36] Despite this request, a substitute bill was introduced in the Senate, the purpose of which was to transfer authority to the Executive Council. This substitute measure was passed and duly signed by the governor.[37] Thus, the General Assembly disregarded the advice and counsel of Dr. Shambaugh.

Before the bill was signed by the governor, Dr. Shambaugh had written to Judge Deemer explaining in detail why he thought the change was not for the best interest of the Historical Department.[38] He also asked to be released of further responsibility after the May meeting of the board, adding that he believed that the sooner the Executive Council was free to take over the work the better it would be. Thus, for a second time in his career, Dr. Shambaugh chose to pursue educational rather than political pursuits.

May 1908

James G. Berryhill exposed the scheme in the pages of the *Des Moines Register and Leader*. Unlike Swisher, who puzzled over political motives, Berryhill reduced the plot to political cronyism. In 1906 the legislature did authorize an appropriation of $2,000 annually for three years to fund the Hall of Public Archives. However, the next year a coalition of Republican senators and representatives conspired to pass a bill raising the annual appropriation to $6,000 and, in addition, transferring administrative control to the Executive Council. Immediately after the bill became law, the Executive Council discharged Shambaugh and Parish, then divvied up the $6,000 among cronies of Governor Cummins. J. H. Kelley, the representative from Polk County (Des Moines), was appointed "manager in chief" with a salary of $1,000 per year (despite a constitutional provision prohibiting the holding of dual offices); John Thompson, editor of the *Bystander* and chief whip for turning out the African American vote, was "employed" at a salary of $900; and four other close allies in the Cummins administration were similarly "employed" at like salaries. According to Berryhill, "The legislature was about to adjourn and the clerkships would end, and if these important members of the 'flying squadron' were not cared for they would be forced to go into private life and struggle for a living as ordinary citizens." Clara Neidig, who had been assisting archivist John Parish, was retained at wages of $9.37 per month for two hours of service per day.[39]

For history's sake, retaining Neidig was a fortunate mistake; two hours a day was enough time for her to observe what was going on, with ample time left for buttonholing well-placed people and writing letters to her former boss, Shambaugh. She seems to have been an articulate, efficient, indispensable office worker who knew how to keep the government bureaucracy working despite the constant turnover of political officeholders; in practically every letter she mentions that she either had an opportunity for another position in some state office or had spoken to some senator or commissioner about the possibility of other work. But she liked archival work and wanted to stay.

Neidig's letters suggest that she was not a timid person. She understood that she, too, might lose her job, but instead of fretting about it she approached the governor personally in an attempt to learn what her fate might be. When she sensed that the governor was politically embarrassed by what had transpired and apparently trying to distance himself from the perpetrators, she took advantage of the "unsettled" situation and spoke privately to someone identified only as "the power behind the throne" about the possibility of returning Parish to his position.[40] She also gave Shambaugh advance warning when the archival holdings were physically transferred in July to the "sky parlor," rooms situated directly under the roof of the new historical building where the materials were exposed to temperature extremes—"I am sure [this] was not your recommendation. The heat will be hard enough on the records, to say nothing of the people."[41] Neidig was also the first to notify Shambaugh when the Executive Council reassigned the directorship to a Mr. Davison in August 1907—"a thunder-clap, sure enough, as he had never entered my mind as a possibility. . . . He has been civil to me, but he is the last person I would have supposed would have been put in charge of the work. It truly looks as though the Council didn't know what to do with it [the archives], after all." When Davison set her salary indignantly low, relative to the salaries of the men with whom she was expected to share the work equally, Neidig determined to take the next better position that came her way.[42]

In a more urbanized state, say New York or Illinois, the archives debacle of 1907 might have been considered business as usual, but machine politics hardly existed in Iowa. Moreover, Cummins had a reputation as a reform governor. The incident thus reveals how thin a line separated political cronyism from political reform. The whole affair could only have been disheartening to Shambaugh, a classic model of the progressive professional: white, middle class, well educated, Republican in political persuasion, Protestant in religious inclination. At the very least, it gave him an enduring distaste for politics, and it may have patterned his response when he confronted another nasty legislative battle the following year.

As for John Parish, Shambaugh made a place for him in Iowa City. An increased appropriation for the SHSI enabled Shambaugh to hire an office staff. "I will have a clerk or secretary in my office and Mr. Parish has been appointed as Assistant Editor," he wrote to Bicknell. "This will relieve Mrs. Shambaugh from some of the burdens which have been imposed upon her heretofore."[43] The last line is one of the few bits of evidence verifying the important role that Bertha Shambaugh played during the early years of her husband's career. Quite simply, she made it possible for him to hold two full-time professional positions, to involve himself in the work of professional organizations, and to help manage the affairs of the historical department in Des Moines.

Precisely how much unpaid work Bertha Shambaugh contributed is not a matter of record, nor is it clear where she worked: perhaps she spent a few hours each day at the historical society offices in Schaeffer Hall, or perhaps the two of them worked on correspondence at home in the evenings. Wherever she worked, Bertha must have spent hours each day pounding away on a typewriter. What Shambaugh's massive correspondence files do reveal is that the operation of the historical society was intimately woven into the daily fabric of his personal life. Business and professional correspondence is interleaved chronologically with letters to and from family members and inquiries about household matters and travel arrangements. With the hiring of office staff in mid 1907, Bertha was free to devote more time to her own interests (she was an accomplished photographer; she painted; and she researched and wrote about the history of the Amana Colonies). She also found time to manage the many social events that took place in the Shambaughs' home.

By the end of 1907, Shambaugh had put the bruising public archives episode behind him and refocused his attention on the work of the historical society. "The fact is," he wrote to Bicknell, "that this year for the first time I feel that the State Historical Society has been able to raise its head above the clouds and see more clearly the work in all of its bearings relative to the preservation of Iowa history. For the first time ideals cherished for years are being realized in practical efforts."[44] Shambaugh referred to the publication of another biography and the seven volumes of the *Messages and Proclamations of the Governors of Iowa,* completed in 1907, "a plan of research work which I believe is unique and at the same time the most advanced step which has been taken by any historical society in the line of scientific research in state and local history."[45]

Early the next year, however, Charles Aldrich died, a sad event with serious implications for the future of the historical department, especially considering the state of disarray created by the previous legislative session. Shambaugh felt obliged to serve his now-departed friend by once again turning his attention to affairs in Des Moines.

After the passing of Mr. Aldrich [in March 1908], there were those who favored the appointment of Dr. Shambaugh as his successor. One of the leaders in this group was Judge Deemer. In September 1908, after Dr. Shambaugh had conferred with interested parties at the capitol, he wrote to Judge Deemer: "I came away from Des Moines fully confirmed in the belief that if ever there was a time to bring unity and cooperation in the Historical interests of the State without friction and without heartaches it is now."[46] Apparently, many things had transpired to make further unity possible. And to promote this interest, the Board of Trustees voted to name Dr. Shambaugh Curator of the Historical Department. A part of the plan for developing the Historical Department under the new administration was the establishment of a Legislative Reference Bureau in connection with the department. In furtherance of this plan, such a bureau was established on a temporary basis, and Dr. John Brindley was placed temporarily in charge—awaiting legislative action when the General Assembly should convene.

Meanwhile, there was much speculation about Dr. Shambaugh's appointment and the possibility of his severing connection with the university and the State Historical Society to become a resident of Des Moines. He was quick to explain, however, that his acceptance of the new office did not involve such radical changes: "I do not sever my connection with the State Historical Society of Iowa or with the University. If the work at Des Moines can be arranged as contemplated, there will be no difficulty in my carrying the additional responsibilities involved in the superintendency of the Historical Department at Des Moines."[47] It is evident . . . that Dr. Shambaugh's chief interests remained in his affiliation with educational interests at Iowa City. In writing to Dr. J. L. Pickard [former president of the university and former president of the State Historical Society], he stated that the work in Des Moines was assumed on condition that the desired legislation be passed and that it not interfere with the Iowa City work: "After spending ten years of the best part of my life in efforts to build up the research and publication work of the State Historical Society of Iowa, I shall not be tempted to leave the Society or do anything except that which will promote the interests of the Society."[48]

When the Thirty-third General Assembly convened in Des Moines in January 1909, Dr. Shambaugh was serving as curator of the Historical Department, but resided in Iowa City. Mr. E[dgar] R. Harlan was serving as assistant curator, and Mr. Brindley was developing a legislative reference bureau. But future developments rested largely with the General Assembly. In order to obtain the best results, Dr. Shambaugh drafted a bill for continued service of the department under the Trustees of the State Library for the organizing of a permanent legislative reference bureau, and for an additional appropriation for the Historical Department. When the bill was introduced, there was rumor than an attempt would be made to amend the bill on the floor of the House, giving control to the Executive Council. Dr. Shambaugh believed that this would not be wise; he also thought it would cast reflection upon members of the Supreme Court, who constituted the majority of the Board of Trustees.

Notwithstanding [Shambaugh's] viewpoint, a substitute measure was introduced and passed in the House. In the Senate, however, the measure was laid on the table. Thus, the Historical Department was left without any legislative change and without any additional appropriation.[49] With his legislative program rejected and plans for a legislative reference bureau defeated, Dr. Shambaugh tendered his resignation to Governor B. F. Carroll, who had recently succeeded Governor Cummins in office.[50] Thus, for the third time in his career, Dr. Shambaugh stepped aside from political influences to continue his educational pursuits.

Swisher relates this incident in muted tones and leaves much unsaid. Shambaugh's failure to win legislative approval for a permanent legislative reference bureau in Des Moines was a bitter pill to swallow at the time. Swisher, it must be remembered, wrote from the perspective of one who knew and worked closely with Shambaugh in the fullness of his career, and from that vantage point Shambaugh himself probably looked back upon the rejected proposal as only a minor setback in a long string of successes. However, the correspondence he maintained with John Brindley during the heat of battle suggests a deep investment of professional energy and identity. These letters also reveal much about Shambaugh's convictions concerning the value of history in public affairs and his uncompromising principles.

John Brindley had recently joined the faculty at Iowa State College (now University) in 1908, teaching in the department of economics. Unlike Shambaugh, however, Brindley was considerably more open to a professional situation closer to the center of state governmental affairs. He had just completed a history of railway taxation in Iowa and in the fall of 1908 began compiling information from states that had established legislative reference bureaus or departments. Shambaugh and Brindley quickly developed a comfortable professional relationship, and together they worked out the details of what both hoped would be a permanent bureau in Iowa.

From the beginning, Shambaugh maintained that legislative reference work and historical research "should be carried on together or in very close co-operation." He may have preferred to have charge of coordination in Iowa City, but he realized that a legislative reference bureau should logically be located near the statehouse. "I think I have grounds for saying that the research work which I have been trying to promote for several years in this State has something to do with a movement for a legislative reference department. I am desirous of bringing about co-operation between related interests and of preventing a dismemberment of work that should be kept together."[51]

Brindley respected Shambaugh's seniority, but he was Shambaugh's equal in this initiative. By mid October 1908, he had produced a manuscript analyzing the "legislative reference movement" throughout the United States. Since 1901, when Wisconsin established a legislative reference department under its state library, twelve states (not counting Iowa) had created similar departments or bureaus, and eight states were considering bills to provide for organized legislative reference work.[52] Like Shambaugh, Brindley considered "scientific" research, not merely library reference services, as "a *sine qua non* of well conceived legislation" and "therefore of social progress." In more direct language, he expressed his views this way: "There is nothing which prevents ultra-radical action and doctrinaire views from becoming the basis of legislation like a careful and thorough appeal to the facts of history." Based on his own investigation of other states and given the dual structure of state-supported historical institutions in Iowa, Brindley advocated a practical position: "that legislative reference work should not form a separate and distinct institution." Rather, "through correlation and concentration of effort" with the historical department, the historical society, and "allied institutions," Brindley projected that a legislative reference coordinator, presumably himself, could provide state legislators with "the maximum of expert service at the minimum of cost."[53]

Brindley's position paper was not merely an analytical exercise designed to clarify his own thinking. Johnson Brigham, the state librarian, favored making the legislative reference service a function of the state library and in fact drafted a legislative bill to accomplish this. Brindley adamantly opposed this organizational arrangement. In his considered opinion, the reference service should "be a *clearing house for what is imme-diately desired out of all the libraries in Des Moines and Iowa City or, for that matter, of any other place in the United States*. It will not itself be a library. In this way you will eliminate both of the fatal defects in McCarthy's Wisconsin system, viz., too much emphasis on current data, and the collection of a large mass of poorly arranged material."[54] Through timely and diplomatic intervention, Brindley and Shambaugh managed to persuade Brigham of the wisdom of a "clearinghouse" organizational structure.[55]

By this time, November 1908, Shambaugh had clarified his own thoughts, not only on the proper berth for legislative research work but on the entire administrative structure of the historical department. He therefore took the opportunity to draft a multipurpose legislative bill separating the historical department and the state library, although the two units supposedly would remain under the administrative control of one board (how this actually might have worked is unclear). The draft bill further authorized the Board of Trustees to establish a legislative reference bureau that would draw upon the resources of the state library, the historical department, and the historical society in order to carry out its work. Shambaugh's bill further requested a $5,000 increase in the annual appropriation to be earmarked for the proposed legislative reference bureau.[56]

Optimistic about a favorable outcome during the 1909 legislative session, Shambaugh helped Brindley arrange a leave of absence from his teaching post at Iowa State and established a temporary legislative research bureau in the historical building in Des Moines.[57] While he was acting as both curator of the historical department and superintendent of the State Historical Society, Shambaugh believed that he (briefly) held enough power to organize a permanent research bureau, "with branches at Iowa City and Washington, D.C.," that would handle the reference work more or less as "a present to the State," that is, without incurring an additional drain on the public treasury. Nonetheless, he had a backup plan, which he quietly presented to Brindley in confidence. "If I cannot organize and conduct legislative reference work in connection with the Historical Department, it will be my duty to organize the work as a feature of the research work of the State Historical Society."[58]

At this point, December 1908, Shambaugh did not foresee that his bill would run into serious political opposition in the legislature. He was mindful, however, that Brigham might change his mind again and seek political support for a legislative reference department directly under the state library. Thus Shambaugh and Brindley handled Brigham with kid gloves, seeking his counsel or approval every step of the way. In truth, there was reason to fear that Brigham might change his mind, for Aldrich's death had created something of a power vacuum in Des Moines, and rumors apparently were circulating that Shambaugh might take this opportunity to undermine the status of the historical department vis-à-vis that of the historical society.[59] But there is not a shred of evidence to suggest that Shambaugh ever harbored such ideas. On the contrary, it may by now have dawned on him that the historical department served as a buffer of sorts, drawing political meddling that might otherwise have been directed toward the historical society.

To the end, Brigham remained steadfast in his support, but by February 1909 Shambaugh's bill was in trouble from multiple political corners. There were threats to cut the $5,000 appropriation for legislative reference work, a proposal to consolidate the historical department and the historical society, an attempt to specify staff positions and fix salaries, and proposals to transfer control either to the Executive Council or to a new Board of Education. Shambaugh's first response was to draft a new bill that would establish a "legislative reference research bureau" under the State Historical Society (it is unclear whether this bill was ever introduced).[60] Then he urged Brindley, who for all practical purposes was "lobbying" the original bill, not to allow the sponsors to accept amendments: "Either the Historical Department will become thoroughly educational and scientific and divorced entirely from political influences, or it will become a political museum for the exhibition of fossilized politicians."[61]

A severe case of "grippe" kept Shambaugh from attending personally to his bill in Des Moines, although it is not certain that even robust health would have induced him into the fray directly. By late March, the bill had been so amended that he was ready to wash his hands of the whole affair. In effect, he did just that, by notifying the Board of Trustees that he was resigning as curator of the historical department. "I fully understand the necessity of compromise," he wrote Brindley. "Nevertheless, I believe that in the organization of the Historical Department it is not for me to propose and agree to compromises. My business has been to formulate fundamental principles and then to stand by them even though such firmness leads to my own elimination from the work of the Department."[62] Brindley, who had a fledgling career at stake, wanted to press on, accept a short-term compromise, and roll the legislative dice again in the next session.

Shambaugh, in response, cautioned him to "quietly repair the bridges between Ames and Des Moines. If the cast of the dice on Legislative Reference is against you, you must have a sure avenue of retreat. The situation
is too uncertain for you to stake everything on the final throw."[63]

It was wise counsel, for the bill died in a Senate committee, and Brindley subsequently resumed his teaching post at Iowa State the following
term. Shambaugh, who rarely betrayed his emotions, took the defeat
hard: "It would not be possible for me to give any adequate expression to
my feelings," he wrote Brindley; "and so I will not make the attempt. I am
trying to make myself believe that the situation in this State with regard
to higher education and all that goes to make up the sphere of higher education will soon change for the better." To Brigham, he was equally di-
vulging but less expressive: "It is unsafe for one to express his mind when
overwhelmed with disappointment. . . . Accordingly, I will not discuss the
recent history touching historical matters in this State."[64]

Frank Bicknell, a political realist, chalked up the defeat to a legislature
that was "one of rather less ability than the average" and encouraged
Shambaugh not to lose heart. "[L]egislatures are 'peculiar critters.' Not
many of them are appreciative of the best part of your work. They need to
be shown things, especially tangible things, such as buildings, museums,
books. Scholarly investigation is a thing that must come in along with
others." But Shambaugh confessed that the "past year [had] been a very
difficult and depressing one. . . . It seems almost criminal for the State to
have neglected the opportunity to vitalize the Department at Des
Moines."[65]

As far as Shambaugh was concerned, the Des Moines chapter of his career was irrevocably closed. In a letter to Lieutenant Governor G. W.
Clarke, he took the defeat in stride but noted: "It sometimes seems
strange and inexplicable that, while there is such generous appreciation of
the work of the State Historical Society from people and institutions outside of our State, so little in the way of commendation comes from our
own law-making body."[66] To Albert Cummins, who as governor had appointed him curator of the historical department but by then had succeeded to the U.S. Senate, he explained his reasons for resigning, regret-
ting that this left the historical department "just where it was when Mr.
Aldrich died."[67] To Bicknell, he made it clear that henceforth his time and
energy would be spent building up the historical society in Iowa City:
"The State Historical Society will push forward along the lines already es-

tablished with perhaps one or two additional projects." He would leave the department in Des Moines to cope as best it could with political interference. Shambaugh would make an effort "to coordinate or correlate the work of this Society with the great educational institutions of the State."[68]

In 1909, when the AHA Public Archives Commission sponsored the first annual Conference of Archivists, Herman Ames could justifiably take pride in recounting a decade of progress. West Virginia had joined the states of Alabama and Mississippi with separate state departments of archives and history. Several states had established commissions, divisions of records, or a state archivist: Pennsylvania, North Carolina, Delaware, South Carolina, Virginia, Arkansas, Texas, and Connecticut. Another group of states had designated their state historical societies to be the official state archive: Illinois, Kansas, Nebraska, Wisconsin, and Oklahoma. Two states and one territory (anticipating statehood) had established a state historian's office: New York, Maine, and the territory of Arizona.[69] Iowa alone had a state-subsidized historical society *and* a state-supported department of history and archives. If the politics of establishing public archives in other states even came close to the ups and downs Shambaugh experienced in Iowa, it was indeed a decade of remarkable progress.

4

A Deliberate Course: Applied History

ONE CAN only guess at the course Shambaugh might have set for the SHSI had the legislative outcome been different in 1909. Swisher and others have claimed that Shambaugh always had a "clear idea of his long-range plans," that he began "develop[ing] a plan for the type of institution he wanted the historical society to become" from the time he joined the Board of Curators in 1897, and that "his goal was to create a laboratory for scientific historical research and publication."[1] In a general sense, all of this is true; Shambaugh began with a progressive-era vision of the greater value of history to society. He embraced the notion of history as scientific expertise, and he was unshakably committed to utilizing the knowledge of history in public service. However, with respect to the policy studies that were to become the heart of applied history at the SHSI, Shambaugh was open to a more collaborative arrangement prior to the legislative fiasco, with the society in Iowa City providing a broad-based research and publications program and a legislative research bureau in Des Moines focusing more specifically on issue-driven policy research. The setback seems to have galvanized Shambaugh's resolve to prove the value of history in modern society.

In any event, the idea of a legislative research bureau certainly had been gestating for some time. When in 1902 the Carnegie Institution established a Bureau of Historical Research in Washington, D.C., for instance, Shambaugh solicited a brief descriptive article from the director, Andrew McLaughlin.[2] The Carnegie Institution and the Library of Congress were the institutions Shambaugh had in mind when he revealed to John Brindley his idea of a research bureau utilizing sources available in Des Moines, Iowa City, and Washington, D.C. He reiterated this intent in a pocket-sized booklet issued in 1908, called *Historical Research in the State Historical*

Society of Iowa and without doubt printed expressly to influence political leaders favorably toward the proposed bureau. "Neither partisan bias nor personal prejudice is allowed to enter into the work of those who are engaged in research for the Society," the booklet announced. "Manifestly the research work of The State Historical Society should be correlated with whatever is attempted along the lines of State legislative reference work."[3]

By mid 1909, Shambaugh had turned his attention to developing his "laboratory concept" of history in earnest as a function of the society alone; the historical department in Des Moines was not to be involved at all. From then on, he concentrated on building the SHSI's research capacity and strengthening its ties to the university. Having failed in his bid to establish a legislative research bureau in the state capital, Shambaugh transformed the concept into an institution that bore his personal stamp, an entity that filled a niche between the SHSI and the political science department at the University of Iowa.

To be sure, Shambaugh's "laboratory concept" was based on the society's research publications program, which at this point comprised the Public Archives Series and the *Iowa Journal of History and Politics*. But it was to become much more than that. As his concept has been summarized elsewhere, "the Society would serve as an institution to bring together a team of specialists (professional historians) in a common location, provide them with the best available resources (a reference library, research facilities, and travel funds), assign them to specific problems that were part of a larger whole (a carefully planned, long-term research program), and make the results of their research (monographic and journal publications) available to a larger public that could, in this way, benefit from their work."[4] By 1910, Shambaugh was referring to his research group as "The School of Iowa Research Historians," and its purpose was "to make practical application of investigations in State and local history in the solution of present-day political, social, and economic problems."[5]

Because Shambaugh held tandem professional positions, his scientific-laboratory approach to historical research was more easily workable. He groomed graduate students for applied historical research; routinely consulted with legislators and other prominent people in state affairs to cultivate an ongoing list of contemporary issues; then coordinated research assignments and supervised the research, writing, and editing.[6] Had the 1909 legislative battle gone the other way, the applied history research laboratory no doubt would have been structured differently, with John Brind-

ley playing a key role in Des Moines. But it was much simpler to implement the concept in Iowa City, particularly because the political science
department and the SHSI were housed in the same building on the University of Iowa campus. As it turned out, Brindley became an early
member of the team when he decided to pursue a doctorate under Shambaugh's tutelage.

The staff of paid employees of the society varied with the years and came, at
length, to include names of persons well known in their respective fields. Some
of these remained to become long-time employees of the society. Others left after a short time to become distinguished in other fields of service. Dr. Shambaugh always selected his assistants with discretion and care—choosing only
those persons who gave evidence of ability and a desire to succeed. Moreover,
having made a selection, he contributed of his own personality toward the success of his protégé. With these associates he shared his vision, his guidance, his
cooperative interests, and his enthusiasm. As a result, there was always that bond
of mutual interest and helpfulness that develops personality and gives strength
of character to the individual and to the institution. His employees commonly referred to him cordially as "The Chief."

By the second decade of the twentieth century, the research program was well
under way. The Economic History Series was begun in 1910, with the publication
of the *History of Labor Legislation in Iowa*. This was followed by an extensive series
on the history of education, the history of taxation, road legislation, work accident indemnity, economic legislation, banking, and [an] economic history of the
production of beef cattle. To these was added the *History of Social Legislation in
Iowa* in the Social History Series.

In 1912 the research staff of the historical society consisted of fifteen men
working either part- or full-time on research projects under Dr. Shambaugh's supervision and direction. Most of these men were graduate students at the university who devoted part-time to historical research—some of them being employed during the summer months by the historical society. The summer
program afforded opportunity for students and faculty members from other educational institutions to do research work at the university.[7]

The Iowa Applied History Series consisted of many monographs issued in six
substantial volumes between the years 1912 and 1930. These were for the most
part doctors' dissertations in the Department of Political Science. Since Dr.
Shambaugh was superintendent of the historical society and also head of the De-

partment of Political Science, he was able to correlate the interests of these two agencies in such a way as to make their combined contributions unique and outstanding in historical, social, economic, and political research.

The first two volumes of the Applied History Series dealt with a variety of governmental problems—road legislation, primary election, tax administration, home rule, direct legislation, child labor, the merit system, poor relief legislation, and similar topics. Volume III dealt with statute law making. Volume IV treated various phases of county government, and volumes V and VI dealt with municipal government.

The Applied History Series was never entirely distinct from the Economic History Series or the Social History Series. As the research and publications program evolved, there was considerable overlap. For instance, *Applied History*, volume 1, issued in 1912, included abridged versions of three longer works that appeared as volumes in the Economic History Series: John Brindley's *History of Taxation in Iowa* (1911), Brindley's *History of Road Legislation in Iowa* (1912), and E. H. Downey's *History of Work Accident Indemnity in Iowa* (1912). Likewise, the second volume included abridged monographs of John L. Gillin's *History of Poor Relief Legislation in Iowa* (1914) and John Ely Briggs's *History of Social Legislation in Iowa* (1915), both full-length works published as part of the Social History Series. As the Applied History Series lengthened, however, it tended to absorb the identity of the other two. In 1931, for instance, a reviewer observed that the Applied History Series "was the first study designed to present a comprehensive description and critique of the contemporary political devices of an American commonwealth."[8]

Some of the authors were graduate students trained by Shambaugh; others were academic scholars from various colleges and universities. Scholars in residence during the summer of 1912, as an example, included E. H. Downey of Kenyon College in Ohio; John L. Gillin of the University of Wisconsin; John Brindley and Louis B. Schmidt of Iowa State College; Louis T. Jones of Wm. Penn College in Oskaloosa, Iowa; Olynthis B. Clark of Drake University in Des Moines; John Parish of Colorado College; Henry J. Peterson of Iowa State Teachers College (now University of Northern Iowa); and Frederick E. Haynes of Morningside College in Sioux City, Iowa.[9] Some of them were former students of Shambaugh's, which meant that summer research at the SHSI also was a time of collegial reunion.

A newspaper reporter who observed the research program firsthand that summer, 1912, noted that the "lights gleam every evening from the third floor of the hall of liberal arts, where are located the offices, library and research rooms of the State Historical Society of Iowa. Here from 8 o'clock in the morning until 10 o'clock at night or later, a group of professors and scholars . . . are engaged in careful, scientific research in Iowa history and allied subjects."[10] Shambaugh did indeed take great pride and personal interest in his research group. "The summer in many ways is the most delightful part of the year to me," he wrote to John Parish, "since it now means the home-coming of the Iowa Research Historians."[11]

As the research program matured, more and more of the authors came from the SHSI's full-time research staff. Senior-level research associates typically held doctorates. Research assistants usually were University of Iowa graduate students working on a degree either in political science or in history. Research assistants also earned credit toward degree requirements for their work at the society, and master's theses as well as doctoral dissertations often were published as monographs in the Applied History Series or some other publication series.[12] Most of the researchers were, as Swisher notes, men, but not all. Among fifty-two people who held positions as research assistants and/or associates between 1912 and the mid 1920s, eight were women.[13]

All of these men and women, however, knew they were part of something special. Most of the men who spent summers or whole years on the research staff went on to academic careers elsewhere: Frank Garver as professor of history at the University of Southern California; John Gillin as professor of sociology at the University of Wisconsin; John Parish as professor of history at the University of California at Los Angeles (UCLA); Henry Peterson as professor of political science at the University of Wyoming; Howard Preston as professor of economics at the University of Washington; Louis Schmidt as professor of history at the University of Texas. Some—John Ely Briggs, Bruce Mahan, Odis Patton, Louis Pelzer, Jacob Van Der Zee—transitioned from graduate student to professor at the University of Iowa, inbreeding the political science department in particular. However, Cyril Upham went on to a career in banking and law and in 1938 was appointed deputy comptroller of the currency in the U.S. Treasury Department. Jacob Van Ek moved from teaching to become dean of the College of Arts and Sciences at the University of Colorado. Nathaniel Whitney left a position as professor of finance at the University of Cincin-

SHSI Research Room, Ruth Gallaher, foreground. *Courtesy State Historical Society of Iowa, Iowa City.*

nati to enter the corporate world as an economist for Proctor and Gamble and president of City Savings & Loan Company of Cincinnati.[14]

William J. Petersen, Ruth Gallaher, and Jacob Swisher had long careers at the SHSI. Petersen, hired as a research associate in 1930, assumed the superintendency in 1947. After Petersen became superintendent, Gallaher left the society in 1947 to teach political science at Asbury College in Wilmore, Kentucky. Swisher retired from his position as research associate in 1950. In a nutshell, a commensurate demand for applied historians in the professional realm of policy formation or in the professional marketplace as a whole did not evolve along with Shambaugh's research institute.[15]

The career paths of the SHSI research staff would make an interesting case study, as would the influence of the society's research program on the course and outcome of state legislation between 1910 and 1930.[16] What is more important here, however, is the concept behind the Applied History Series. Shambaugh clearly was responding to the high level of public interest in reform legislation that characterized the progressive era. "[A]s practical citizens, lawmakers, and public officials," he wrote in the introduction to the first volume in the series, "we demand reliable and complete information concerning the public questions which now confront us and which we are called upon to solve as best we can." He defined "applied history" succinctly as "the use of the scientific knowledge of history and experience in efforts to solve present problems of human betterment." As previously noted, he most definitely linked the Applied History Series with the New History, even going so far as to reference James Harvey Robinson's collection of essays, *The New History*, published the same year: "Henceforth the New History, leavened and enriched by the products of political and social science, promises to play a much more important role in the intellectual life and progress of mankind."[17]

Shambaugh also argued that applied history education was a legitimate function of state-supported universities: "Why should the State afford special facilities for training lawyers, doctors, engineers, agriculturists, and dairymen, and at the same time neglect the training of men and women for public service? It is utterly futile for us to talk about high-minded citizenship and ideals in public service without seriously endeavoring to provide that special training which will make men really capable and efficient public servants." To him, public service was the force behind applied history: "State institutions, like high-minded citizens, should be dominated by a zeal for public service."[18]

With lofty language, Shambaugh thus introduced the concept and embodiment of applied history: "[I]n bringing the history of our Commonwealth down to the present hour, in conducting scientific researches along lines of political, economic, and social developments, and in projecting a series of publications on Applied History, in which the language of the scientific investigator is translated into more popular form, the State Historical Society of Iowa aims to make a direct contribution to the public welfare by linking the public with the results of scientific research in political and social science."[19] One could say that *Applied History*, volume 1, was the genesis of public history's gray literature, although in this particular instance the pages were bound in sturdy blue buckram on which the title was embossed in gold leaf.

In planning and publishing the Applied History Series, Dr. Shambaugh won wide distinction for himself and for the State Historical Society. When the first volume of this series was published, Charles A. Beard . . . referred to it as a "splendid" volume. The essays, he said, "seem to me to be at the top notch." When the second volume appeared, Professor Beard [wrote], "The idea of the series is excellent and the execution is to be commended." Professor Roscoe Pound said, "The series is indeed a notable one, and I hope it may be continued."[20]

One of the most encouraging comments of those years of growth and development came from *The Nation*. Under the title of "Our States and Their History" the editor of that magazine said, "What is now wanted is inquiry into the constitutional, social, financial, and legislative record. An almost unique example of the response to this demand has just come from Iowa. It is embodied in a series of volumes issued by the State Historical Society, covering every department of state history. There have already been published the first two [volumes] devoted to the history of education, justly called by the editor [Shambaugh] 'the first adequate history of schools and educational institutions produced by any State'; a 'History of Social Legislation,' a 'History of Taxation,' a 'Political History,' and two volumes of 'Applied History,' the last representing systematic scientific research into the field of contemporary legislation." In conclusion, the editor of *The Nation* said, "The 'Applied History' series . . . shows admirably how experience may be a constant guide to the future."[21]

Shambaugh, of course, sent complimentary copies to professional colleagues, discreetly soliciting comments that might be useful for promoting the society's work. But it was not promotion simply for the sake of eliciting praise, for cultivating personal prestige, or to establish a distinctive reputation for the society. Rather, he seems to have routinely sent out complimentary copies with some hope that, by example, he could stimulate a movement among state historical societies and universities to engage scholars in the task of applying "the creative power of scientific knowledge in politics and administration" toward "a rational program of progress" in legislation and governance.[22]

While there was plenty of praise, not all reviews were favorable. "From the viewpoint of the *American Historical Review*," wrote Edward Fitzpatrick, "the first comment to make is that the essays of the volume [volume 2] are not in their primary intention historical. . . . [T]he promise of the definition of 'applied history' is not fulfilled in any of them. We expected a kind of natural history of the movements listed: of how in the light of their experience, or in spite of it, the people of Iowa progressed, or evolved their political, economic, social present status; and how, profiting vicariously from the experience of others, a new social programme was being evolved in the light of the history of local institutions. Such a promise is not fulfilled."[23]

"Institutional history" was not necessarily what Shambaugh meant by "applied history," but Fitzpatrick was neither the first nor the last to have difficulty understanding the term. Others would later substitute the term "applied politics" or "applied political science" or "applied social science." But Shambaugh chose to call the series "applied history." To him, the process of policymaking, intelligently approached, required a historical perspective on the issues and an analysis of proposed solutions. Fitzpatrick's critique, however, signaled that academic historians, or at least the AHA "establishment," would dismiss applied history because it did "not contribut[e] to knowledge from a scholarly viewpoint."[24]

Despite a perceived vagueness in the term, applied history became the centerpiece of Shambaugh's "laboratory concept," and the publications that fell into this category included not only the six-volume Applied History Series but the Economic History Series and the Social History Series as well and to a large extent the contents of the *Iowa Journal of History and Politics* (*IJHP*). Policy research articles frequently filled the pages of the *IJHP*; beginning in 1911, the journal regularly published a summary of legislation passed by each session of the state legislature, sometimes incorporating commentary on supporters and opponents of major bills or controversial measures that did not pass. In 1929 the legislative summaries became part of the Iowa Monograph Series, until budget cuts in the 1930s forced suspension of this series. From the mid 1930s until the 1970s, abbreviated legislative reports were incorporated into the *Palimpsest*, the society's popular history magazine.

Funding for the research and publications program came from the state legislature. In this respect, the Applied History Series proved to be a useful tool for increasing the society's annual appropriation. After plans for a separate legislative research bureau fell through, John Brindley turned his attention to finishing his research on state tax policy, which the society published in 1911 as *History of Taxation in Iowa* in the Economic History Series.[25] Through friends in the legislature, Shambaugh brought notice to the work, and the legislature, in turn, requested a copy for each senator and representative. Shambaugh complied and leveraged their interest to increase the society's annual appropriation by $4,000, bringing it up to $16,000. Likewise, volumes of the Applied History Series were sent to each legislator as they appeared, and the annual appropriations continued to rise. From 1917 to 1921, the annual budget stood at $24,000, at least half of which went to support research and publications. The research program not only attracted outside notice, but the expanding volume of publications attracted new members, and membership increased from 375 in 1910 to approximately 1,200 in 1922. A portion of this increase was attributable to the *Iowa and War* pamphlets, which stimulated greater interest in state and local history.

Despite increased membership, the $3.00 membership fee hardly covered the cost of the SHSI's member benefits and services, but state legislators regarded the publications program highly enough that, by 1921, Shambaugh was able to boost the annual appropriation to $44,500 so that the society could publish the Iowa Chronicles of World War Series in addition to its other publications, which now included the *Palimpsest.* The SHSI thus could maintain a heavy publications schedule without raising annual dues. Shambaugh managed to hold this funding plateau through 1925, when hard times forced the state into retrenchment. The society sustained budget decreases beginning in 1925, but, even so, funding remained comparatively high through the remainder of the decade.[26]

In terms of funding and programs, the period from 1910 to 1930 was the society's high tide. Success brought new members and widespread attention. It also brought more political meddling.

One of the most interesting phases of Dr. Shambaugh's work . . . was his contacts with the General Assembly. Dr. Shambaugh was skillful in presenting the needs of the society, and usually he was very successful in convincing members of the General Assembly of the merits of the work which the society was doing. Usually legislative appropriations were secured with little or no organized opposition, but this was not always possible. On rare occasions real controversies arose. . . . In 1915 a measure was introduced by the Committee on Retrenchment and Reform in the Iowa House of Representatives to transfer control of the historical society to the State Board of Education. But the Board of Education was not interested in such a transfer. Indeed, some of the members of that board were quite unaware that such a measure was being prepared. The bill itself did not reveal the author's name. Just who had conceived of such a measure was not a matter of public announcement. Dr. Shambaugh, however, was aware that someone, working through the committee, was attempting to direct public affairs. He resolved to meet the issue squarely. Going directly to members of the General Assembly, he explained the aims, purposes, and activities of the State Historical Society. Presently, the proposed bill was "peacefully sleeping in the morgue of the Sifting Committee."[27]

The most dramatic incident in Dr. Shambaugh's entire legislative experience occurred in connection with Senate File No. 356, commonly known as the Foskett Bill—a measure introduced in the Senate [by H. I. Foskett of Shenandoah] in March 1919 to dissolve the historical society and transfer its property to the state university. When this measure was introduced, Dr. Shambaugh was at home, ill of influenza. He knew, however, that the opposition could be met only by . . . gaining the confidence and support of the legislators. By correspondence through his office, by long distance telephone calls, and by the personal service of two representatives of the society who volunteered to go to Des Moines to contact members of the General Assembly, an aggressive educational campaign was inaugurated. Meanwhile, the bill was pending action in the Senate, and there was a period of anxious waiting. . . . Thus matters rested until April 7, 1919, when the bill came up in the Senate and was indefinitely postponed. Whereupon, one of the society's representatives in Des Moines wired to Dr. Shambaugh: "Three five six died without a murmur."[28]

But legislative contests were not always won. Sometimes measures designed to increase legislative appropriations for the historical society were indefinitely postponed, or lost in committee or on the floor of the House or Senate. On one occasion, when an important appropriation bill had been lost, Dr. Shambaugh's sense of humor came to the fore when he wrote to a friend saying, "The Historical Society Bill for an increased appropriation was laid to rest in the Senate Committee. Senator Maytag presided at the funeral services."[29]

Usually, however, legislators were kind to Dr. Shambaugh as he was kind to them. Usually they were generous and magnanimous in their support of the historical society, even as Dr. Shambaugh was generous and magnanimous in his service to the state. Usually liberal appropriations were granted, and no one appreciated this official approval of the work of the historical society more deeply than did Dr. Shambaugh himself.

In his 1934 retrospective of historical societies in the United States, Julian Boyd observed that state-supported historical societies in the Midwest had produced "two of the most significant features of historical society activity" during the twentieth century up to that point. One of these features was that the state historical body could be "an active member of state administration." The other was that the state historical body could carry out "a democratic program of education in state history." Boyd considered the SHSI, especially its Applied History Series, to be the prime example of the first type of activity and the Minnesota State Historical Society to be exemplary of the second. Speaking of the SHSI, he continued: "Here history is raised to the dignity of a coordinate agency of government, assisting through historical scholarship to throw light upon vexing present day questions. . . . It was such a public function as this that led John Quincy Adams in 1844 to declare that historical societies were among the most useful of human institutions. If legislative control acts as a brake on absolute freedom of research under these auspices, the scientific method is nevertheless employed."[30]

Although the Applied History Series and related publications formed the core of applied history as Shambaugh defined it, they were only part of the society's functions. The publications program as a whole was quite varied and included works that were more standard fare for state historical societies. Beginning with John Parish's 1907 biography of the territorial governor Robert Lucas, nineteen volumes in the Biographical Series appeared during Shambaugh's tenure as director. The Miscellaneous Publications Series included topics of cultural and social history, such as Bertha Shambaugh's *Amana: The Community of True Inspiration* (1908); Louis T. Jones's *The Quakers of Iowa* (1914); and Clarence Aurner's *History of Education in Iowa*, published in five volumes between 1914 and 1920.

The society's applied history line, however, dominated, and it also came to include the Iowa Chronicles of the World War, which Swisher mentions only briefly.

During the period of the First World War, a collection of twenty-four pamphlets was issued dealing with war topics. Following the war, the *Iowa Chronicles of the World War* were issued. This series dealt with welfare campaigns, welfare work, the Red Cross, food administration, and the sale of war bonds. The books on the sale of war bonds were used extensively again during the Second World War.

The Chronicles of the World War Series not only represents an episodic contribution to the SHSI's applied history initiatives, it highlights the type of scholarly engagement in public affairs that the AHA encouraged during World War I. Shortly after the United States officially entered the war, several state historical organizations began systematically collecting war-related materials. At the 1917 Conference of Historical Societies, the Department of History of the Indiana State Library reported that it was clipping newspaper articles from the "two leading daily papers of Indianapolis" in order to "add local color to the official reports." The Minnesota State Historical Society reported that it was collecting "posters and programs" of meetings as well as photographs, encouraging organizations engaged in war activities to save their records and encouraging families to save letters from those in military service.[31]

The SHSI had not yet started to document homefront activities, but "emphasis [wa]s being placed on military and war history" in the research and publications program.[32] Works in the Miscellaneous Publications Series during 1917 and 1918 included *Marches of the Dragoons in the Mississippi Valley* by Louis Pelzer and *Old Fort Snelling, 1819–1858* by Marcus Lee Hansen. Additionally, in July 1917 the society began publishing a monthly pamphlet series entitled *Iowa and War*, which featured "brief flag-waving sketches" of homefront activities throughout the state and which was published for the duration of the war, the last issue appearing in July 1919.[33]

Mixed motives drove historians to involve themselves in the war effort. First of all, the war was of such magnitude that historians, especially archivists and directors of state and local historical societies, realized the value of immediate collecting. But behind the acquisitions frenzy, which was predictable, ran a high spirit of patriotism that produced a zealous strain of enthusiasm among American historians for promoting and justifying U.S. participation. Historians generally believed that Germany had skewed the intellectual estate that had once been the hallmark of its universities. More to the point, American historians, many of them trained at German universities, felt betrayed. For some, the fact that President Woodrow Wilson held a doctorate in history probably reinforced whatever link they forged between history and patriotic service. Overall, however, there was a sense that participation in the war effort "would demonstrate the usefulness of history." But that sense of purpose was tempered with dis-ease at mixing scholarship and patriotic service, which inevitably obfuscated professional standards of objectivity.[34]

On the national level, the Carnegie Institution's Department of Historical Research took the initiative to organize a conference in Washington, D.C., in April 1917, out of which came the National Board for Historical Service. The propagandistic historical scholarship carried out under this board (which really was an arm of the AHA) in cooperation with the Committee on Public Information, *History Teacher's Magazine*, and other entities, constitutes a fairly well known chapter in the history of the profession.[35] Less well known is the effort to coordinate the work of state historical societies in preserving war-related materials. In 1918 the National Board for Historical Service appointed a committee to survey state-based activities and to draw up a model plan for the acquisition and publication of war materials that all states might adopt.[36]

Much of the 1917 meeting of the Conference of Historical Societies was given over to a roundtable discussion on the need for state and local historical societies to collect material related to the war effort. In 1919 and again in 1920 the conference met jointly with the newly formed National Association of State War History Organizations (NASWHO) to discuss the collection, preservation, and publication of war-related materials, including newspapers, articles, posters and other ephemera, photographs, letters from those in military service, and records of organized civilian activities.[37] Shambaugh served on the NASWHO executive committee.

These joint conferences not only revealed a great amount of work on the part of local and state historical societies nationwide, but they undoubtedly helped to focus and expand the scope of state and local efforts. By this time, at least thirty-five states had taken formal steps to collect and preserve materials documenting wartime service, either military or homefront. More than half of them had established special bodies: a war history committee, a state historian, a war records commission, or a board of historical service. In a smaller number of states, including Iowa, collection and preservation were carried out, or coordinated by, established historical agencies or some other institution with permanent archival facilities. Thus, in just two years' time, many state and local historical organizations, as well as universities, had amassed fairly sizable collections. Several institutions had assiduously collected posters, broadsides, and other ephemera that would otherwise disappear quickly; others had become the repositories for official war records, special state censuses or surveys, and records of civic organizations.[38]

The mixture of motives that underlay historians' participation in the war effort is evident in the responses that Shambaugh crafted for the society. The *Iowa and War* monthlies and the military histories published in 1917–1918 certainly nourished the growing mood of patriotism. The society also collected materials that time was likely to judge as valuable historical evidence, but Shambaugh adopted a judicious acquisitions policy that was geared toward documenting the state's collective war service history through the Red Cross, the United War Work Campaign, and similar organized efforts.[39] Through its *Bulletin of Information*, the SHSI encouraged local institutions, particularly public libraries, to take the lead at the community level.[40] The SHSI's greater contribution was a seven-volume chronicle of Iowa's homefront participation in the war effort. It is this effort that once again demonstrated Shambaugh's commitment to make history useful to contemporary society.

Early in 1919 Shambaugh announced that the SHSI planned to publish a comprehensive record of the state's role in World War I.[41] Several other state historical societies also drew up plans for publishing comprehensive histories.[42] By late 1920, however, Iowa reportedly was the only one that had managed to get a manuscript in print. The first volume of the Iowa Chronicles of the World War Series, *Welfare Campaigns in Iowa* by Marcus L. Hansen, appeared in 1920, and six additional volumes followed during the next few years. Iowa was considered to be "more favorably situated than any other State" to carry out its publishing plans precisely because Shambaugh had an established research and publishing program that enjoyed a stable source of funding.[43] The combination of an in-house research "laboratory" and a publications budget thus enabled Shambaugh to implement the Iowa Chronicles of the World War Series with relative ease.

"Relative" is the operative word, however. The World War I chronicles would have run more than seven volumes if Shambaugh had received all the state funding he sought, which was a special $50,000 state appropriation in 1919 to publish a roster of Iowans who had served in the war and to publish the planned comprehensive history of the homefront. But the state legislature appropriated only $20,000 for the roster. Disappointed but unswayed, Shambaugh simply used a portion of the large increase in the society's permanent appropriation voted by the legislature in 1921 to carry out a scaled-back publishing effort.[44] The flurry of patriotic zeal that precipitated a spurt of collecting dissipated quickly after the war, but Shambaugh managed to use this short peak to boost the society's budget.

Another legacy of World War I was the society's popular history magazine, the *Palimpsest*. The monthly pamphlet series, *Iowa and War*, was well

received among the society's members, in part because the pamphlets appeared regularly and in part because the articles were brief. Shambaugh had been considering adding a popular history magazine to the publications line before the war, so when *Iowa and War* demonstrated the viability of a monthly, the society continued to meet readership demand with the *Palimpsest*, the first issue of which appeared in July 1920. The *Pal*, as it came to be called, was the society's vehicle for "readable" history written in a more literary style, but Shambaugh insisted that authors adhere to the standards of research and writing on which the society's reputation was founded.[45] Swisher gives only brief mention to the *Pal*.

In publishing and distributing the *Palimpsest* to all parts of the state, Dr. Shambaugh realized one of his early dreams—the presentation of Iowa history in story form. On one occasion he said to Herbert Quick, "I have looked forward to the time when our history would be embodied in a literature that all men would read."[46] For the years 1920 to 1922, Dr. John Carl Parish served as its editor. Dr. John Ely Briggs became editor in 1922 and continued to serve in that capacity throughout the remainder of Dr. Shambaugh's superintendency. [After] 1940, these journals continued publication under the leadership of Miss Ethyl E. Martin, who for many years had been Dr. Shambaugh's executive secretary and assistant superintendent, and who succeeded Dr. Shambaugh in the office of superintendent, Dr. Gallaher and Dr. Briggs continuing to render editorial services as in former years.

Despite the brevity of Swisher's remarks, the *Palimpsest* actually represents an important dimension of Shambaugh's expanding concept of applied history. The intersection of historical scholarship, governance, and public service formed the core of applied history as Shambaugh originally conceived it. However, he always felt a responsibility to engage local interest in history or somehow to make historical scholarship interesting and available to ordinary citizens.

Like most pedigreed historians, Shambaugh considered antiquarianism and genealogy indignities to the profession, although he rarely made disparaging remarks. His approach to limiting the society's contact with genealogists was simply to concentrate the society's library and manuscript holdings on those materials that were most useful for scholarly research;

he left the collecting of newspapers and public records to the historical department in Des Moines. His approach to antiquarianism was to replace the *Iowa Historical Record*, a typical pioneer quarterly containing reminiscences of days gone by and paeans to old settlers, published from 1885 to 1902, with the *IJHP*.[47] Shambaugh advocated that history be used to serve the commonwealth, which to him did not mean catering to the narrow interests of local historical societies. Rather, he sought to edify the general public by raising the level of the reading material emanating from the SHSI.

In a literal sense, Shambaugh could afford to neglect genealogists and antiquarians because the society did not depend on member dues for its annual budget. Nonetheless, after the "research laboratory" was running smoothly, he turned his attention to figuring out how the society could better serve the general public. His thinking may have been influenced by general trends in periodical literature published by state and local historical societies. A 1916 survey and analysis of American historical periodicals by Augustus Shearer, which at the very least would have landed on Shambaugh's desk when it was published in 1919, indicated that there were fifty periodicals in the United States devoted exclusively to publishing history. This number did not include genealogy periodicals "which, though catering to a selfish, narrow-visioned, albeit industrious class, may some day be found of more use to the historical student than they have been as yet," nor did it include antiquarian publications, "the blind alley of history."[48]

Shearer's survey was quite a useful summing up of the state of historical journals and magazines circa 1915, and Shambaugh may have studied it, especially since the SHSI was then among the up-and-coming. Iowa had been one of the first states to "find a supporting constituency" for state and local history, and Shearer considered the *IJHP* as one among ten "more recent" state history quarterlies that showed "great promise" of achieving the same stature as the *Pennsylvania Magazine*, begun in 1877, and the *Virginia Magazine*, established in 1893. Newer trends in historical periodicals were running in two directions: one to "sectional" journals, such as the *Mississippi Valley Historical Review* (1914) and the *Southwestern Historical Quarterly* (1913); the other to specialized interests, such as the *Catholic Historical Review* (1915), the *Journal of Negro History* (1916), and *History Teacher's Magazine* (1909).[49]

Importantly, Shearer called attention to two "commercial exploiters" who had managed to tap into local interest in history and make money, for a time at least, by selling popular history monthlies and who also "deserve[d] credit, nevertheless, for keeping a high standard and for educating while popularizing." He referred specifically to *Dawson's Historical Magazine and Notes and Queries*, published between 1866 and 1875, and the *Magazine of American History with Notes and Queries*, published in New York by Mrs. M. J. Lamb between 1877 and 1893. There were plenty of history-related periodicals with "gaudy covers, profuse illustration, and unexpected headlines," which Shearer declined to name by specific title, but even so he admitted that these contained some worthwhile information and had a degree of educational value; the "trouble is that much well-written trash . . . passes for history along with the rest."[50]

How to make serious scholarship accessible to the general public was no less a dilemma to professional historians then than it is now, and Shambaugh must have been giving the dilemma the same consideration as Shearer. In any case, once the pamphlet series *Iowa and War* confirmed there was an audience for popular history that was not in the antiquarian vein, Shambaugh launched the *Palimpsest*. Just as he had aimed to prove the value of history in governance and public affairs with the Applied History Series, so he intended to demonstrate that popular history did not have to be trivialized in order to succeed. Moreover, he did not want the *Palimpsest* to become "a stepchild among the Society's publications."[51] Thus Shambaugh and the magazine's editors insisted that authors verify the accuracy of their material, even though articles appeared without footnotes, and sought brief works focused on a single subject. As it turned out, Shambaugh judged the demand accurately. With the *Palimpsest*, he succeeded in delivering state and local history to a wider public audience without sacrificing professional standards of scholarship.[52]

Wider dissemination, however, did not depend on increasing membership or marketing publications.[53] Because the society was state supported, Shambaugh was able to maintain low annual membership dues and, as appropriations increased, justify free distribution through libraries. Beginning in 1916, the society designated more than 150 college, university, and local libraries as official repositories for the society's publications.[54]

The society's reputation rested on its publications, and through the mid 1920s that reputation was very high. But as Shambaugh began to experiment with longer formats for general audiences, he seemed to lose touch. The Iowa press responded favorably to historical memoirs and impressionistic "literary" history, such as Thomas Macbride's *In Cabins and Sod-*

Houses (1928) and Irving Richman's *Ioway to Iowa: The Genesis of a Corn and Bible Commonwealth* (1931), both sans footnotes, but some scholarly reviewers began to judge the SHSI publications more harshly.[55]

When *In Cabins and Sod-Houses* appeared, reviewers were courteously interested in this new direction the SHSI was taking with its publications. Merle Curti noted that even though Macbride's book was "not a systematic treatment of the intellectual history of the founders of Iowa," it was still "valuable in that it represents the characteristic idealization of the frontier by one who was himself a pioneer."[56] Harlow Lindley was more favorably impressed, noting that the "narrative humanizes and vitalizes the historical period with which it deals." He believed that Macbride's work "should serve as a model of historical interpretation."[57]

Had Shambaugh limited the practice of sans footnotes to just the impressionistic, literary historical works, he would have made a wise decision. However, in the 1930s books published in the Biographical Series, even though purported to be based on scholarly research, appeared either without footnotes or were poorly documented. The response from scholars was predictably negative. Charles Payne's *Josiah Bushnell Grinnell* (1938) was judged "a pleasant, sometimes confused book that should have been a great book." Of Jacob Swisher's *Robert Gordon Cousins* (1938), one reviewer concluded: "Here is the career of another congressman, not critically but rather certainly presented." Shambaugh's own book, *The Old Stone Capitol Remembers: Marking the One Hundredth Anniversary of the Founding of Iowa City, Iowa,* even was lightly panned. Philip Jordan regretted that "no footnotes or citations to sources [were] available for those who might wish to trace many of the stimulating statements." H. C. Nixon noted that the text included "mention of documents" but that "sources [were] used primarily to adorn a tale rather than to prove an interpretation."[58]

Publications ruled the society's identity, for better or worse, but several other public programs for libraries, local historical societies, and schools rounded out its functions. These, too, Swisher chose to ignore as aspects of Shambaugh's career, and perhaps rightly so because Shambaugh had no personal interest in local historical organizations. He supported the *idea* of vigorous local historical societies—recall his leadership in the AHA's Conference of Historical Societies. However, even though he did not openly denigrate antiquarians and genealogists, as did many of his professional colleagues, he steered clear of becoming too closely involved with them.

Local historical societies were considered "auxiliary members" of the State Historical Society, an honorific designation that inferred a special relationship, but communication with them was primarily top-down and from a distance. Iowa's 1907 Conference of Local Historical Societies is a case in point. Shambaugh used the occasion of the fiftieth anniversary of the state constitution to stage a four-day celebration that was, in some respects, the SHSI's coming-out party. The proceedings, published in a volume exceeding 450 pages, included two conferences: one on the teaching of history and the second on the work of local historical societies. The opening remarks of the second conference indicate that the SHSI intended "to hold conferences from time to time" with representatives from local historical societies.[59] In fact, Shambaugh called them together only once more, in 1910, to meet in conjunction with the Mississippi Valley Historical Association, which held its third annual meeting in Iowa City.[60] Instead of conferencing with local historical societies on a regular basis, Shambaugh instituted a series of informational bulletins that were issued on an occasional basis between 1904 and 1942.

Under Shambaugh, the SHSI sometimes dictated to local historical societies through the intermediary of public libraries. In 1904, for instance, the SHSI collaborated with the Iowa Library Commission to produce "An Iowa Program for Study Clubs." This program, published in the society's *Bulletin of Information*, actually was a list of twenty-five topics in state and regional history—for example, Marquette's explorations in Iowa, the Louisiana Purchase, the Lewis and Clark expedition—deemed suitable for local study groups, together with appropriate bibliographic citations.[61] That same year the SHSI also published a prescriptive list of books on American and Iowa history for public libraries and suggested that "the public library in cooperation with the local historical society should make a business of collecting and preserving the data and materials pertaining to the life and history of the community." Packaged with this instructional article, which contained a precise list of the types of local history materials to be collected, were excerpts from a similar article taken from the *Proceedings of the State Historical Society of Wisconsin*, further evidence that, early in his career, Shambaugh consciously emulated the practices of Reuben Gold Thwaites in Wisconsin.[62] Moreover, the announced purpose of designating 150 public libraries as official repositories for SHSI publications, beginning in 1916, was to stimulate them to "become centers for the collection and preservation of local history."[63]

It was not until 1941, the year following Shambaugh's death, that local historical societies in Iowa were formally organized as a statewide association. Ironically, the impetus came through a door that Shambaugh had helped to open with the AHA Conference of Historical Societies. At the instigation of its successor organization, the American Association for State and Local History (AASLH), the Department of History and Archives in Des Moines, not the SHSI, took the initiative to organize what was billed as "the first" Iowa Conference on Local History in May 1941. A second organizational meeting was held in October to adopt articles of incorporation as the Iowa Association of Local Historical Societies and to elect officers. Ethyl Martin, who succeeded Shambaugh as superintendent of the SHSI, represented the society on the board, but the association was more of a grassroots organization, something Shambaugh never would have encouraged.[64]

If Shambaugh lacked a personal touch when it came to dealing with local historical societies, he nonetheless continued a path opened with the *Palimpsest*. To stimulate greater public interest in the magazine, each month the society prepared shorter pieces based on the articles, which were repackaged as the Iowa History Items Series. These monthly bulletins were distributed to newspapers throughout the state, and the items were written so that newspapers could reprint them without editing.[65]

During the 1920s, the society also collaborated with the Iowa Federation of Women's Clubs (IFWC) to experiment with outreach programs. The SHSI and the IFWC cosponsored an essay contest for high school students in 1923–1924. This initial venture led to Iowa History Week, which the SHSI and the IFWC continued to cosponsor every April between 1926 and 1938. Iowa History Week promoted historical activities in schools based on a different Iowa history topic each year, and the SHSI provided background information through the *Palimpsest*. The SHSI also promoted the event through press releases and radio announcements. The radio spots quickly became a series of radio programs broadcast daily just prior to and during Iowa History Week, then turned into a weekly radio discussion on topics in Iowa history broadcast over the University of Iowa's station, WSUI.[66]

The SHSI also produced a silent movie in 1923 depicting a reenactment of Father Jacques Marquette's discovery of the Mississippi River in 1673. Commercial theaters throughout the state screened the film, which came with a four-page pamphlet providing more complete information than the subtitles. Finally, the SHSI staff began taking to the road in the 1920s, traveling around the state to speak to community groups. For the cost of expenses, a local organization could schedule a speaker to deliver a slide-lecture on one of several standard topics.[67]

Historical research at the SHSI also embraced, to some degree, prehistory. After Shambaugh took an anthropological study trip with Duran J. H. Ward in 1903, he allocated a small portion of the society's budget to support Ward's study of American Indian mounds in 1904. The following year, the society supported Ward's photo-documentary study of the Meskwaki Settlement along the Iowa River near Tama. Ward's photograph collection, housed at the SHSI, became an important visual record of traditional Meskwaki culture for future researchers.[68]

During the early 1920s, Shambaugh served on the Iowa subcommittee of the National Research Council's Committee on State Archaeological Surveys. In this capacity, he and Carl E. Seashore of the University of Iowa organized a conference to initiate plans for a state survey, held in March 1922. Out of this came the survey work of Charles R. Keyes, a professor of German at Cornell College with an interest in archaeology. Keyes began the State Archaeological Survey in 1922 and continued work during successive summers, with support from the SHSI, until 1931; beginning in 1934, he conducted more extensive field investigations utilizing field crews employed under the auspices of New Deal work-relief programs. The SHSI-sponsored survey thus launched Keyes on a second, parallel career as an archaeologist, ably assisted in the field by Ellison Orr, a civil engineer with an interest in archaeology. By 1927, Keyes had sufficient field and archival data to propose the first outline of Iowa prehistory, which he revised in the early 1940s. Keyes and Orr, who both died in 1951, laid the scholarly foundation for archaeological research in Iowa.[69]

In emphasizing the society's research and publications program, Swisher rightly understood that this was Shambaugh's intellectual focus. And it was chiefly the policy research on which Shambaugh's professional reputation rested. Secure in this reputation, Shambaugh began to expand the society's identity through public outreach, particularly between the years 1923 and 1930, which also were the years of the Commonwealth Conference, the subject of chapter 5. The Great Depression years, however, forced changes. Because the research and publications program depended so heavily on state funding, declining appropriations during the depression years forced Shambaugh to curtail or abandon much of what he had spent so many years building. In the 1930s Shambaugh also began to turn inward, and this, too, probably played a part (see chapter 6). Even so, with the first signs of economic revival, he began planning for one more major series to commemorate Iowa's statehood centennial in 1946.

Iowa was admitted to the Union in 1846. As a fitting observance of the centennial of that event, Dr. Shambaugh conceived the idea of a Centennial Series of volumes of Iowa history to be published by the State Historical Society prior to 1946. Three volumes in this series—*Iowa Through the Years* and *Iowa Pioneer Foundations*, volumes I and II—were prepared and published under Dr. Shambaugh's direction. [Before his death in 1940] he also read and approved the manuscript for *Iowa: Land of Many Mills*, and suggested the publication of *Iowa: The Rivers of Her Valleys*. Although Dr. Shambaugh was not permitted to see this series completed, the work [was] carried forward by members of the society staff, and the Centennial Series [was] a substantial contribution to the observance of the centennial in 1946.

Shambaugh ambitiously planned to publish as many as fifty volumes in the Centennial Series, but wartime shortages brought the series to an end three years before the centennial.[70] Only a few works made it into print. Had Shambaugh lived longer, no doubt he would have found a way to extend the series, but this vision, along with many others, died in 1940 with him.

The State Historical Society of Iowa between the years 1907 and 1940 became an institution fashioned after the hopes and aspirations of its superintendent. Dr. Shambaugh was not without his critics. He was frequently referred to as an idealist, as a dreamer. But he was also an organizer and director of public affairs. Those who knew him best knew of his visions. But they knew, too, of his practical plans. He was a man of varied abilities of a high quality, one of the rarest of which was his ability to organize, direct, and supervise. If the State Historical Society became an institution after his own fashioning, it was because of his genius in this field.

Selecting his employees with care, training them with precision, sharing with them his enthusiasm and his visions, he was able to unify his staff and coordinate their labor into a single unit. Knowing legislators and legislative procedure and having powers of persuasion, he could obtain legislative appropriations to carry forward his work. Building up an institution and correlating it was another; he was able to strengthen both. The State Historical Society and the Political Science Department were thus effectively united and their strength was such as to merit comment. Reporting upon the activities of the historical society in 1933, the Brookings Institution of Washington, D.C., said: "In the number and scientific quality of its publications, as well as in their practical bearing on the political, economic, and social problems of the state, the superintendent and staff of the historical society have demonstrated their capacity to render notable public service, and, with respect to the type of historical research which they have conducted, have been surpassed by no other institution in the country."[71]

5

The Commonwealth Conference: 1923–1930

THE COMMONWEALTH Conference was perhaps Shambaugh's most innovative undertaking. Certainly it was the most complex, for it required teamwork among staff members and immense amounts of time to develop programs, secure speakers, invite participants, produce historical background reports, coordinate logistics, and promote events. In some respects, the Commonwealth Conference can also be seen as the apex of Shambaugh's career amid the full bloom of progressivism in Iowa. On the one hand, the conference implemented the highest ideals of progressive political thought inasmuch as Shambaugh designed the conference to involve a broad cross section of Iowa citizens in discussions of policy and governance. On the other, Shambaugh's motives for undertaking the conference signaled the beginning of his own retreat from progressivism, inasmuch as he viewed the conference as a counterweight to post–World War I education trends, which he thought flawed because courses in the history of law and government had been replaced by more general instruction in civics.

Above all, the Commonwealth Conference marked the conceptual transformation of "applied history" to "commonwealth history." Thus it also owed its origins to the New History. The Commonwealth Conference was the complete union of scholarship and public service that Turner had called for in 1891; it was Shambaugh directing his own version of what James Harvey Robinson called the "great contemporaneous task of human betterment."[1] The entire enterprise was directed outward to encompass an audience that mingled scholars, political experts, civic leaders, middle-class voters, and students. The whole purpose was to elevate policy above politics by raising the level of public awareness about important policy issues and fundamental matters of governance. Raising public awareness required historical perspective. In this respect, it is telling that the fourth conference (1926) became the basis for the last two volumes of the Applied History Series.

Born of the spirit of pioneer days and cradled in the Old Stone Capitol . . . the Commonwealth Conference was defined by Dr. Shambaugh as a "non-partisan forum" for the purpose of stimulating a creative interest in Commonwealth problems.[2] Thus he visualized it as something that had life and action, and so it was. . . . As a student at the university in the decade of the 'nineties and in the years that followed, Shambaugh had advocated the study of local problems. In support of this theory he stood almost alone. There was then but little support on the university campus for the study of local history and government. Despite this fact, Dr. Shambaugh had made a beginning in this field. He promoted and participated in the study of local problems, and arranged courses in the Department of Political Science in the field of state and local government. For a period of two decades, however, the growth was gradual.

In the decade of the 'twenties, the Commonwealth Conference came as something of a mutation—something new and different in the study of local governments. It was frankly an experiment in the study of government on a commonwealth basis—an experiment which might well have originated in Maryland, Maine, Ohio, or Pennsylvania. It might logically have developed and come to fruition at Harvard University, at Princeton, or at Yale. In reality, it was Iowan both in origin and development.

In the SHSI archives there is a handwritten program outline, in Shambaugh's hand and dated 1913, for the "First Annual Commonwealth Conference on the Public Welfare in Iowa." This conference seems to have existed in concept only, for the event itself never occurred. The holograph reveals, however, that Shambaugh began germinating the Commonwealth Conference in his mind a full decade before the initial assembly took place in 1923.[3] Swisher, however, credits Judge Martin J. Wade with precipitating the idea to fruition.

The conference, as such, originated in a suggestion made by Judge Martin J. Wade of the United States District Court. Judge Wade was an aggressive, forth-

Seventh Commonwealth Conference, 1930. Bruce Bliven speaking to crowd assembled on the steps of the Old Capitol. *Courtesy University of Iowa—University Libraries, Special Collections.*

right citizen and resident of Iowa City who preached the gospel of good government. He advocated the theory that emphasis should be placed upon an educational program for citizenship. He was instrumental in securing legislation that required the teaching of American citizenship in the grade schools and high schools of Iowa. He suggested also that the study of citizenship be given attention in colleges and universities. These were the very ideas that Dr. Shambaugh had fostered since his student days. More than a decade prior to this time, in his address "The West and the Pioneer," he had advocated a study of government "from the bottom up instead of from the top down."[4] The new emphasis that Judge Wade placed upon this subject afforded Dr. Shambaugh an opportunity to put into action the thoughts he had fostered and promoted for a period of two decades. When this opportunity came, he was quick to seize it; and with the hearty approval and cooperation of President Jessup, he organized and promoted the Commonwealth Conference.[5]

A 1922 exchange of letters between Shambaugh and Wade is intriguing because it sheds considerable light on Shambaugh's thinking at the time and on Wade's political philosophy. Shambaugh wrote a letter commending Wade for "stimulating the study of law and government in our schools by offering prizes for essays on constitutional freedom." He went on to expound at some length on his own notion of what "training for citizenship" should involve. "Citizenship is a very definite aspect of the life of the individual human being," he asserted. "A citizen is a member of the body politic. Training for citizenship, therefore, is nothing more nor less than the training of citizens for membership in the body politic. Concretely such training should deal specifically with the facts and fundamental principles of law and government and the relation of the citizen to the law and government of his country. It should not be confused with questions of good manners, morals, and religion." He squarely laid the cause of such confusion on progressive educational trends. "So-called 'community civics' and 'social problems' in the public schools is [*sic*] to no small extent responsible for the lack of knowledge of government."[6]

Wade snatched the bait and immediately responded with his own reproach of public education. "A lot of them [teachers] seem to have the notion that if a man will wash his face in the morning, and clean his fingernails, the highest notch of good citizenship has been attained." He included with his response a copy of the "Report of the Committee on American Citizenship," presented at the American Bar Association (ABA) meeting in August 1922, a reactionary document denouncing communists and anarchists who promoted anti-American propaganda and decrying the creeping influence of socialism through college professors and public school teachers. Wade's signature, which appears first, indicates that he either chaired the committee or was instrumental in its formation. Among the committee's recommendations was that the ABA follow the lead of the Citizenship League of American Schools and Colleges to promote patriotism through essay and oratory contests.[7]

Shambaugh may have been discouraged by a growing tendency to muddle what he saw as immutable principles of civic responsibility with the sociology of American political life, but there is no evidence that he shared Wade's reactionary conservatism. Thus it is unlikely that he proceeded to launch the Commonwealth Conference for the same motives that drove Wade to promote patriotism through the ABA. It is more likely that the emerging polarity of political voices and cultural values that produced so much social tension in the 1920s caused Shambaugh to see a need for a forum where political debate could be conducted in the spirit of civil discourse. Still, Shambaugh always invited Wade to a prominent place on the program each year.

As the format evolved, each conference typically ran for three days and consisted of lectures given by noted authorities followed by roundtable discussions. The participants, who included invited speakers and an audience drawn from political officeholders, judges and attorneys, mayors and county supervisors, public school administrators and teachers, college and university faculty, and representatives from statewide organizations such as the Iowa Federation of Women's Clubs, the Iowa Farm Bureau, the Women's Christian Temperance Union, the American Legion, and the Iowa Parent-Teacher Association. Everyone was expected to come prepared to debate and discuss specific issues of governance, which were announced in advance. The conferences were held during the University of Iowa's summer session so that students could attend conference sessions and faculty could participate in roundtable discussions.

Shambaugh worked with a university committee to arrange the conferences, which were free of charge and open to the public, even though a long list of Iowans active in public affairs received invitations and advance programs. Shambaugh, and perhaps others, viewed the conference as more than an opportunity to discuss current issues and problems of government and politics. It also was intended to function as "a school for leaders in citizen training and citizenship committee work." Toward this end, organizations were invited to schedule meetings of their "citizenship department, division, or committee" during the time of the conference.[8]

Subjects discussed at the annual conference sessions included "Problems of the American Electorate," "Costs of Government," "Local Self-Government," "Municipal Government," and "Political Issues" in various campaigns. The main subject at each session of the conference was divided into subtopics, and each phase of the subject was given careful consideration. Thus, a large share of the governmental problems confronting the people of the Commonwealth of Iowa was at one time or another discussed at the conference. Through the instrumentality of the Commonwealth Conference, the people of Iowa were afforded an opportunity to study and become interested in their governmental problems.

As chairman of the Commonwealth Conference Committee, Dr. Shambaugh prepared for the various conference sessions extensive program booklets. These contained not only the program . . . but also a well-selected compilation of queries, opinions, and topics for discussion. Thus, the program booklets came to be used as something of a textbook by persons participating in the conference, and they were distributed widely throughout the United States to persons interested in a scientific consideration of commonwealth problems. At one session of the conference this booklet was considered of such importance that the Director General of the Pan-American Union at Washington, D.C. directed that copies be sent to every Latin American ambassador and minister. At the same time, the Enoch Pratt Public Library of Baltimore requested that a copy be sent to each of its twenty-six branch libraries, and a western college ordered seventy-five copies to be placed in its library. The booklets consisted of from 32 to 48 pages and were issued in quantities of 20,000 copies.

The personnel of the conference varied with the annual sessions, but included always-outstanding lecturers and the leading political scientists throughout the United States. One of the speakers at the early sessions was Glenn Frank, editor-in-chief of *The Century Magazine* and later president of the University of Wisconsin. On one occasion he spoke upon the theme "American Problems." Again he addressed the conference on "State Universities in State Politics." Another of the early speakers was Senator Albert B. Cummins, who addressed the conference on "The Relation of the Federal Government to the State."

At the [1924] conference in which the "Problems of the Electorate" were discussed, Dr. Shambaugh, in presiding, gave expression to his own opinions and revealed his own attitude of mind relative to the common man and his responsibility in a democracy:

> No longer do students of political science regard the electorate as an unorganized mass of voters outside the government. For the electorate is in fact a department of the government, an arm of the Commonwealth, with an organization, personnel and functions as clearly defined as those of the legislature, the executive, or the judiciary. Indeed, the electorate is the fundamental department of the government from which in a very real sense all other magistracies receive their mandates. In other words, the American voter is the king of America. Whatever happens in government affairs that does not please him, the voter should take the proper blame upon his own shoulders if he has not voted or if he has not voted right. It is as reprehensible for the voter to stay away from the polls on election day as it is for a senator or representative to absent himself from Washington

when Congress is in session or for a judge to adjourn court to go to a horse race or a baseball game.[9]

At this session of the [1924] conference, James W. Garner, Professor of Political Science at the University of Illinois; A[ugustus] R. Hatton, Professor of Government at Western Reserve University and a member of the City Council of Cleveland, Ohio; and Judge Martin J. Wade presided at roundtable sessions.

When this conference closed there were only words of praise for its management and effectiveness. In reviewing its activities, Dr. Garner wrote to Dr. Shambaugh saying, "In conception, in arrangement, and in execution the conference was altogether admirable. . . . I sincerely trust that your president may be induced to give his approval to a continuation of the conference in future years. I feel sure that a number of other western state universities intend to follow your example in this respect."[10]

Garner also was president of the American Political Science Association (APSA) at the time, and Shambaugh may have invited him, in part, in order to build interest and support among his professional colleagues in the APSA. As was his habit, Shambaugh solicited feedback from those in attendance. Among those who responded, Perley Orman Ray of Northwestern University and W. J. Shepard of Washington University, both of whom served as roundtable discussion leaders in 1924, encouraged Shambaugh to make the conference an annual event.[11] Robert J. Kerner of the University of Missouri wrote a profusely congratulatory letter—"The absence of set papers gave a spontaneity and a vigor to the talks which in turn produced an atmosphere of complete freedom . . . where progressive thought and experience meet to suggest lines of possible solution for the often seemingly insoluble problems which lie ahead of our citizenry."[12] Feminist and political activist Laetitia Moon Conard penned a more candid assessment:

> The [roundtable] on World Politics was disappointing, in spite of the excellence of Mr. Garner and Mr. [Sudhindra] Bose. . . . Here the women were much interested but seemed unable without previous preparation to make worth while contributions. . . . Thanks to more progressive speakers—notably, Dean [Henry C.] Jones [University of Iowa College of Law], City Manager Carr and Miss Ruth Gallagher [*sic*], the [roundtable] on the Law was rescued from the stupidity in which it might have rested had the narrow vision of the Judge [Martin Wade] been maintained throughout.[13]

It was just this spirit of debate, if not yet the level, that Shambaugh hoped to encourage, and so the conference grew.

At the [1925] conference dealing with the subject "The Costs of Government," Dr. Shambaugh set forth clearly the aims and purposes of the conference as he visualized it. It is "the business of such a conference as this to carefully consider and frankly discuss public questions which confront the Commonwealth and the Nation. . . . It is no part of our task at this conference to press for dogmatic conclusions or political resolutions. This does not mean, however, that the expression of opinions is to be precluded from our roundtable discussions. On the contrary, discussion without opinion would be pointless and fruitless. But our opinions should be so voiced as to stimulate further thought rather than to close the mind to independent thinking. In other words, it should be possible for us in the course of our discussions to express opinions without becoming opinionated."[14]

[This] conference . . . received much publicity through the public press. The *New York Times* carried a long and favorable editorial on it. Daily comment appeared in the *Chicago Tribune* and leading Iowa papers. The *Chicago Tribune,* the *Des Moines Register*, and the *Christian Science Monitor* each had a special reporter at the conference, while the Associated Press and the local newspapers were well supplied with data concerning the conference.

Shambaugh actually orchestrated the publicity. The quote Swisher incorporated in the preceding paragraph comes from a press release prepared for distribution to newspapers following the opening plenary session, which took place on a Monday afternoon. Additional press releases containing quotes from notable speakers were prepared for evening and morning releases throughout the 1925 conference, culminating in the full-text release of Senator Albert Cummins's address, "The Relation of the Federal Government to the States," at precisely the hour he was scheduled to speak.[15]

The purpose of the conference, as restated by Dr. Shambaugh at this time, was "to consider, to weigh, and to discuss rather than to decide, conclude, and resolve—to stimulate creative interest in commonwealth problems rather than to formulate political conclusions." The conference was "not intended as a school for specialists," he said, "and the discussions [were to] be kept free from technical minutiae."[16] Participating in this conference, besides resident members of the faculty of the university, was a large group of well-known thinkers, teachers, and writers from all parts of the United States. A significant factor in the success of this session, as in all such sessions, was its social aspect. A luncheon at the Shambaugh home, a dinner at the Amana colonies, the president's luncheon at Currier Hall, a dinner and a breakfast for distinguished guests at the Shambaugh residence were a part of the program. The conference afforded representative university men from various institutions an opportunity to have a free exchange of ideas across the table on important public questions of the day.

Swisher missed another significant aspect of the 1925 assembly. The Third Commonwealth Conference included four women among the twenty-three roundtable discussion leaders. Previously, Ruth Gallaher, a research associate at SHSI, had been the only woman invited to participate in this manner. While it is true that men consistently dominated the program, accurately reflecting the status that men achieved in academic and professional life vis-à-vis college-degreed women, Shambaugh appears to have made good on his statement that the purpose of the conference was, in part, to train leaders among the citizenry, or the body politic, as he would have phrased it, which now included women voters. Two of the women were members of the State Board of Education, the third was president of the Iowa League of Women Voters, and the fourth was president of the Iowa Federation of Women's Clubs.[17] At the Fourth Commonwealth Conference in 1926, women were even more visible; sixteen of the forty-seven listed discussion leaders were women active in public affairs.[18]

The [1926] conference dealing with Local Self-Government was attended with peculiar and widespread interest. This was due in part to the management, in part to the distinguished personnel of the conference, and in part to a striking incident which occurred at the meeting. Public addresses were given by Dr. Arnold B. Hall of the University of Wisconsin and president-elect of the University of Oregon, and by Professor Charles A. Beard of Columbia University and president of the American Political Science Association. If the conference had not been nationally known before this date, it would have become so by virtue of Dr. Hall's address. "Some Problems Connected with Legislative Areas" was the subject of his address.

[In his speech, Hall] pointed out that whereas some problems of regulation could best be solved by legislating for large areas, there were other problems which could be solved more satisfactorily by legislating for more limited areas. . . . Illustrating the principle involved in areas of legislation, Dr. Hall made reference to the problems of child labor, education, and prohibition. In his opinion, these three problems could best be solved by state and local regulation, rather than by national regulation. He would, therefore, advise that their regulation be handled through state and local agencies rather than through amendments to the Constitution of the United States. . . . He declared that wherever attempts are made to accomplish results through national regulation of a problem that is local in character, the result is conspicuous failure in the enforcement of the law. He instanced the 18th amendment and its enforcement to date as illustrative of this point.

While Dr. Hall concerned himself with methods of regulation rather than with the moral or ethical questions underlying such regulation, he did go out of his way to say, when speaking of the 18th amendment, that he was "dry" and always had been "dry," that he was in favor of prohibition and its strict enforcement, but he thought that state and local regulation of the liquor traffic would have . . . accomplished more satisfactory results than our attempts at national legislation and enforcement.

Despite the care with which Dr. Hall presented his subject, his address was interpreted as being opposed to national prohibition. Accordingly, he was severely criticized. As a result, Dr. Hall and the conference received wide publicity.[19] Dr. Shambaugh later wrote to Dr. Hall to say that he hardly knew whether the conference had made Hall famous or whether Hall had made the conference famous.[20] At all events, there was much newspaper comment relative to the incident, and when Dr. Hall went to Oregon as president of the university, he found that his reputation had preceded him. . . .

Newspaper publicity began early when the *Chicago Tribune* and the *Des Moines Register* arranged for special correspondents to cover the conference. The Associated Press wanted texts of the principal addresses, and correspondents representing various newspapers throughout Iowa came to look over the ground. The *Chicago Tribune* commended the conference in an editorial entitled "America in Iowa." The *New York Times* carried an article on "Experts Discuss Self-Government." Throughout the conference newspaper interest was sustained; and when it was over, results of the conference were favorably reported.[21]

Harper Leech of the *Chicago Daily Tribune* covered more than one conference and commented extensively on the 1926 proceedings. Arnold Hall's provocative speech citing the Eighteenth Amendment as faulty governance prompted special coverage. Leech's article opened with the predictable grabber: "Prohibition was the headliner, almost the whole show, at the Commonwealth conference today." The closing, however, revealed that even a cynical newspaper reporter with by-line status in a major daily newspaper was impressed by the exchange: "The absence of the extreme utopian and moralistic notes, which have so long marked the public discussion of such questions . . . is perhaps the biggest news of the conference, because it may portend the passing of sensationalism and fanaticism in the political affairs of the midwest."[22]

For Hall, however, the publicity created a situation that briefly threatened his ability to lead the University of Oregon. "You will be interested to know," he wrote Shambaugh, "that the American Dry League, the Anti-Saloon League and the Portland Ministerial Association have demanded that I be ousted from the University of Oregon. Their position has been supported by a few of the local papers. All the papers of state-wide circulation, however, are coming to my rescue, but the matter still draws front page publicity in all the papers throughout the state, local and general." Hall was concerned enough that he asked Shambaugh to write a statement on his behalf to help "clear up in the minds of these people the suspicion that I am a wolf in sheep's clothing, using the mantle of respectability as a smoke screen behind which I am fighting the battle of the liquor interests."[23] Shambaugh complied and wrote a lengthy statement, which Hall deeply appreciated, but the matter blew over in a short while. Two weeks later, Hall could write that the regents had "refused to consider the matter" so he was "letting the animals roar."[24]

When the conference ended, the House Book—Mrs. Shambaugh's day-by-day diary—summarized the current impression under the title "Echoes of the Conference." The general feeling, the House Book recorded, seemed to be that this was the best of the conference sessions that had yet been held. For Dr. Shambaugh, the annual Commonwealth Conference had come to be almost an epoch in his career. He had devoted much thought and energy and time to it. He had come to live from year to year in anticipation of the next annual conference.

The 1926 conference did indeed raise the bar. The notoriety attracted by Hall's address may have assumed legendary status on campus, but the legacy of this conference and the next, as a whole, filled two volumes in the Applied History Series. The two-volume *Municipal Government and Administration in Iowa*, published in 1930, comprises one of the more comprehensive treatments of local government ever produced: more than 1,200 pages of text and footnotes. Shambaugh made it a point not to publish conference proceedings, believing that the true strength of the Commonwealth Conference lay in the spontaneous flow of ideas during open discussion. However, for the 1926 conference he had prepared a sixteen-page report, "Tentative Working Outlines for Researches in Municipal Government and Administration in Iowa," apparently distributed to the participants for discussion purposes.[25] Following the conference, the SHSI research staff, principally Gallaher and Swisher, spent the next four years analyzing the subject from every conceivable angle.

The first volume of *Municipal Government and Administration in Iowa* addressed the legal status of municipalities and the entities involved in municipal governance, for example, city council, mayor, city manager, and city clerk. The second addressed the functions of municipal administration, for instance, finance, justice, public safety, and city planning and zoning. "[An] example of applied politics at its best," wrote a reviewer. "One of the marks of the whole work is its touch of reality; experience, field work, inquiry, and questionnaire have entered heavily into the preparation of the chapters."[26]

The Fifth Commonwealth Conference continued the discussion begun in 1926, and the format remained unchanged. Banner speakers in 1927 were Charles E. Merriam of the University of Chicago and William Munro of Harvard, the latter also serving as president of the APSA at the time. Except for Gallaher, women's names disappeared from the printed program, suggesting that they did not participate in leadership capacities as they had before, a reversal that remains unexplained. Gallaher, however, gave one of six radio talks (scripted) that were broadcast during the week immediately preceding the conference.[27] Reporters from several Iowa newspapers plus the *Omaha World-Herald*, *Tulsa Tribune*, *Chicago Tribune* (Harper Leech), *Christian Science Monitor*, and the Associated Press covered the event. Clearly, Shambaugh's efforts to attract widespread media attention were beginning to pay off.

More important from Shambaugh's perspective, the idea of convening citizens in focused discussion of public affairs at the state and local levels had begun to take root elsewhere. Following the 1926 conference, William Anderson, director of the Bureau for Research in Government at the University of Minnesota, informed Shambaugh that he and others "were seriously considering the possibility of doing something of a similar nature at Minnesota."[28] Shortly before the 1927 conference, Charles Maphis of the University of Virginia sent Shambaugh a preliminary plan and statement of purpose for an "institute of public affairs" to be convened annually for two weeks each summer beginning that year.[29]

Maphis wrote particularly to inquire about costs. Shambaugh's reply reveals that expenses for participants ran between $1,200 and $1,800. Top-billed speakers received honoraria of $100 to $300 each, with discussion leaders and other speakers receiving less. Printing and distribution of the program would have added considerably more to the total expense, inasmuch as 20,000 copies of the program booklet, now running forty-eight pages, were distributed widely throughout the state, to members of the AHA, the APSA, and the Mississippi Valley Historical Association; to members of Congress; to city managers throughout the United States; to officers of the National Municipal League, the International City Managers' Association, and the National League of Women Voters; and to a selected list of newspaper editors across the nation.[30]

The Sixth Commonwealth Conference was even bigger. It also marked a departure from the exclusive focus on state and local government during the previous five assemblies. The impetus for switching to national issues in 1928 is not hard to fathom; by the time conference planning began in late 1927 native Iowan Herbert Hoover was the leading contender for the Republican presidential nomination.[31] "Political Issues of 1928," the exceedingly prosaic conference title, gave little clue to the lively mix of topics programmed for discussion or the preparation that went into this assembly.[32]

In preparation for the conference, Dr. Kirk H. Porter of the Political Science Department, made an extensive trip through the East, visiting Boston, New York, and Washington, conferring with political leaders, political scientists, and writers, and collecting data for the conference. The program booklet published for

this conference consisted of ninety-six pages—a booklet that was widely distributed and extensively used throughout the United States. As a result of widespread publicity, the conference was attended by representatives from some
forty educational institutions in twenty-one states.

Kirk Porter's gossipy notes of his research trip are more interesting to
read than the program handbook itself, although the *New Republic* did commend the compilation in a backhand sort of way: "we can hardly see why
anyone who has diligently read the handbook should need to go to the conference, or any conference."[33] Anyway, during his swing through Boston,
New York, and Washington, D.C., Porter personally interviewed more
than thirty people, including President Calvin Coolidge ("merely a mo-
mentary greeting"), Vice President Charles Dawes, members of the Iowa
congressional delegation, journalists, scholars, and political activists.[34]

Porter managed to find Vice President Dawes at an "unexpectedly op-
portune time . . . for a good fifteen minute talk," during which Dawes expressed the opinion that "economic issues overshadow everything else," a
prescient forecast in retrospect. In particular, Dawes believed that "a permanent agricultural policy and a sound giant power program [were] of
transcendent importance," a view shared by Nicholas M. Butler (president of Columbia University) and Albert Bushnell Hart of Harvard, as
well as journalists Bruce Bliven (a native of Emmetsburg, Iowa), Walter
Lippmann, and Norman Hapgood.[35]

Porter thought that Bruce Bliven, managing editor of the *New Republic,*
"was inclined to exaggerate," but Bliven nonetheless correctly predicted
that the Democrats would nominate Alfred Smith, the Catholic governor
of New York, and that, as a result, the "religious issue [would] obscure
everything else." Lippmann likewise was "[c]onfident of Al Smith's nomination. Hopes it will split Democratic party wide open—drive conservative democrats over to the eastern republicans, and leave progressive democrats to line up with western republicans." Hapgood, an "ardent disciple
of Al Smith," called the presidential hopeful "the exponent of modern democracy," just the "antidote for white collarites that affect young men."
Porter noted, however, that Hapgood's "own collar was very white."

Porter's brief notes concerning his interviews with Richard Buchanan,
publicity director for Democratic National Headquarters, and J. Bennett
Gordon, director of the research bureau at Republican National Head-

quarters, are humorous in view of the outcome of the 1928 election. The interview with Buchanan was "[a]lmost a total loss. Didn't seem to have an idea in his head except to wait and see what 'they,' the republicans, would propose, so that he could write a little news story making fun of it. Seemed to have nothing to do. Office meager and ill equipped. Material of little value. Spent two hours with him—largely wasted looking at publicity material." Gordon, on the other hand, was the model of professionalism: "Has a splendid fact-finding organization. . . . Keeps a line on all congressmen—can tell at a glance what bills they have supported and what opposed. Can tell in a moment who supported and who opposed important bills. Has catalogued and filed important speeches pro and con on important measures. All kinds of statistical data on elections so organized that it can be used intelligently."

Gordon's well-tuned organization might have impressed Porter for any number of reasons, not the least of which was the precision that Porter himself brought to the task of producing the 1928 conference. Porter directed a group of researchers who scanned the pages of more than twenty leading newspapers and magazines searching for statements of party policy, expressions of personal opinion, views of potential candidates, attitudes of organized groups, and editorials pertaining to election-year political issues.[36] He thus went to his interviews well prepared, and the program handbook reflected the immense amount of work that went into its preparation.

The topics selected for roundtable discussion were "Agricultural Relief," "The Government and Business," "The Federal Government and the States," "The Eighteenth Amendment," and "Foreign Policies." Following these general topics . . . twenty-two subjects were suggested in the program booklet for discussion. The first roundtable session was a popular one in which the McNary-Haugen farm relief bill was both highly praised and severely criticized. In this discussion, H. M. Havner, former attorney general of Iowa, and Harvey Ingham [editor of the *Des Moines Register*] played the major role, with other able speakers assisting on either side. The legislation halls in the Old Stone Capitol were well filled, with every chair occupied and standing room at a premium. Evidently somewhat perturbed at the crowded condition of the room, one of the visiting delegates sent an anonymous note to Dr. Shambaugh saying, "Professor, please put a little less lumber in your round table, and a little more in chairs for folks."[37]

"Capacity house" described the attendance at every meeting. Overflow meetings were held on the West Capitol Terrace. On one occasion there were three speakers, and as each finished his talk on the regular program, he went below to address the waiting audience from the steps of the Old Stone Capitol. The following evening it was planned to hold the main meeting on the Capitol Terrace. A thousand chairs were provided. Then suddenly, about 7:30, there was a light rain. Someone telephoned to Dr. Shambaugh, "The chairs are wet. What shall we do?" "Wipe them off," was the reply. A few moments later the chairs were dry, the weather was clear, and the setting proved to be a very good one.

Shambaugh had reason to bask in the adulation that came from all sides, for the 1928 conference was well attended and the roster of featured speakers included more notables than ever before. In addition to William Munro and Augustus Hatton, who were by now standards on the program, other speakers included Thomas H. Reed of the University of Michigan; Henry A. Wallace, then editor of *Wallaces' Farmer*; U.S. Representative L. J. Dickinson; and Victor Bohet of the University of Liege, Belgium. And women were once again listed in the conference program; the roster included four representatives of the National League of Women Voters and two women active in the national Republican Party.[38] As before, publicity was carefully orchestrated; favorable quotations were extracted from past correspondence, and eight feature stories were written for distribution to the press.[39]

Attendance throughout the sessions was good, and newspaper publicity was effective and widespread. Comments favorable to the conference appeared in the *Nation*, the *New Republic*, the *Chicago Tribune*, the *New York Times*, the *Tulsa Tribune*, and other out-of-state publications as well as in all of the leading newspapers and many of the smaller ones in Iowa. Between the sessions of the conference, there were numerous meetings of a political, educational, and social nature. One of these was a meeting of the officers of the American Political Science Association, for the transaction of such business as could be dealt with at a mid-year meeting. A meeting of Iowa political scientists from various parts of the state resulted in the organization of the Iowa Political Science Association of which Dr. Shambaugh was elected president for the ensuing year.[40]

For reasons that are unexplained, there was no conference in 1929, and the seventh conference, held in 1930, proved to be the last.[41] The University of Iowa had absorbed conference costs since 1923 as a public service, but it was an expense that could not be maintained in the face of budget cutbacks in the 1930s. It is unclear whether Shambaugh knew or sensed that the seventh conference would be the final assembly, but he nonetheless gave it the same degree of thought and planning that had gone into the others.

Prior to the convening of the Commonwealth Conference in 1930, Dr. Shambaugh had been elected president of the American Political Science Association. Thus, as head of the Department of Political Science at the state university, superintendent of the State Historical Society of Iowa, president of the American Political Science Association, and chairman of the conference, he was able to bring to the meeting an influence and prestige not previously enjoyed by the conference. . . . [A]t the opening session of the conference, [he] read a message from President Herbert Hoover, in which the aims and ideals of the conference were commended. Thus, this session of the conference opened with a new all-time high point of interest and enthusiasm.[42]

The theme for the conference was "Issues of 1930." The program booklet consisted of sixty-four pages. As in former years, this booklet contained preliminary announcements, the personnel of the conference, [and] comments and queries on the subjects selected for discussion. The program as outlined in this booklet provided for five roundtables. The subjects to be discussed were "Law Enforcement," "The Philippines," "The Control of Public Utilities," "Unemployment," and "Tax Reform."[43]

Prior to the convening of the conference, Dr. [Kirk] Porter gave a series of radio talks setting forth the aims and purposes of the various roundtable discussions. Newspaper publicity was, likewise, sent out in advance of the meeting. . . . Copies of the program booklet were also widely distributed to interested persons. The opening address was given by President Walter A. Jessup. Two other addresses were "Crime and Politics" by Frank J. Loesch of the National Commission on Law Observance and Enforcement, and "Administration of Justice" by Judge Harry Olson, Chief Justice of the Municipal Court of Chicago.[44] Another lecturer of national renown, Ruth Bryan Owen, daughter of William Jennings Bryan and member of Congress from the Fourth District of Florida, addressed the conference on the "Issues of 1930."[45] Brief addresses on "The Press and Politics" were given by Bruce Bliven, editor of the *New Republic*, and Ernest Gruening, editor of the *Portland Evening News*.[46]

The social activities of this . . . conference were comparable to those of other years, with the president's luncheon and numerous meetings at the Shambaugh home. A new and interesting feature this year was a breakfast for persons who had graduated from the university with the degree of Doctor of Philosophy in Political Science. Of the thirty-seven persons who had received such degrees, thirty-two were living in the United States and of this thirty-two, twenty-four were able to attend the Shambaugh breakfast.

If one can measure the success of a project by the personnel that is attracted to it, by the publicity which it is given in the daily press, and by the appraisal of one's colleagues, then this conference was highly successful. The Commonwealth Conference, with the passing of the years, had come to be an institution into which Dr. Shambaugh had put the best of his time and effort and ability. It had come, too, to a time and place of full fruition. From its small and inconspicuous beginnings, it had come to be one of the great educational conferences of its day. For this successful development, the university and the Commonwealth of Iowa were indebted in a large measure to the foresight, the skill, the enthusiasm, and perseverance of Dr. Shambaugh.

Despite its success, the Commonwealth Conference became one more casualty of the Great Depression. During its brief run, however, the conference considerably enhanced the University of Iowa's reputation for public service. Moreover, the Commonwealth Conference and other early public policy forums, such as the Williamstown Institute, served as prototypes and inspiration for later university-based policy research institutes such as the Bureau of Government Research at the University of Kansas, the Humphrey Institute of Public Affairs at the University of Minnesota, the Institute of Government at the University of North Carolina, the Institute for Social Research at the University of Michigan, and the Institute of Legal History at West Virginia University. The University of Iowa likewise revived the spirit and function of the conference in 1949 by establishing its own Institute of Public Affairs.[47]

In the broader picture, Shambaugh anticipated the role that "scientific experts" would play in national planning and policy formation during the 1930s, even if his own protégés were not among them. The roster of conference participants over the years is punctuated with the names of prominent scholars such as Charles Beard, Charles Merriam, and William Munro, who were outspoken and influential analysts of political structures, governmental institutions, and civic responsibility.[48] Merriam, who served as a member of Franklin Roosevelt's National Resources Board from 1933 to 1943, was among the scholars who found advisory positions in the planning bureaucracy of the New Deal. Other conference participants who found an official voice in governance during the 1930s were Raymond Moley of Columbia University, who became a member of Roosevelt's "Brain Trust," and economist Isador Lubin, who served as commissioner of labor statistics under Roosevelt.[49] And, of course, Henry A. Wallace served as Roosevelt's secretary of agriculture (1933–1940) and vice president (1941–1945).

Shambaugh himself never sought the wider sphere of influence that attracted men like Merriam, Moley, and Lubin; policy and public interest, not politics, were his intellectual passions. Moreover, he was philosophically inclined toward the individualism and volunteerism espoused by Herbert Hoover rather than the centralizing, regulatory control approach of Roosevelt. Shambaugh also seems never to have mourned the passing of the Commonwealth Conference, or if he did, he expressed himself privately. In accepting its fate, perhaps he rationalized that the conference had served its purpose and it was time to move on. Perhaps he sensed that the province of state governance was being reshaped by national events and that the purpose of the conference, were he to attempt revival, would require rethinking. Perhaps he was discouraged because his high-minded goals for the conference lay scattered on the shoals of economic disaster. Perhaps he was simply relieved to be free of the organizational burden he had created for himself, since the conference required increasing amounts of effort to plan and produce. Whatever remorse Shambaugh may or may not have felt, he began to steer his career in a very different direction in the early 1930s.

6

A New Deal in the Game of Life

CONSIDERING that Shambaugh once "dream[ed] of the day when Iowa history not only will be translated into folklore, but transmitted into the hearts of our people," it is difficult to fathom some of the actions he took during the 1930s. Humanists generally rejoiced at New Deal funding for culture and the arts, and the Federal Writers' Project (FWP), in particular, undertook initiatives similar to those Shambaugh had championed earlier. So it is curious that he did not take a keen interest in New Deal work-relief programs designed to document and promote regional history and culture. It is also extremely interesting that Swisher completely omitted this chapter of Shambaugh's career from his aborted biography, suggesting that either Shambaugh disassociated himself from the New Deal or that Swisher, writing in the mid 1940s, did not consider that SHSI's involvement in New Deal projects ever would be considered an important part of Shambaugh's legacy, or both.

In actuality, the State Historical Society was involved in white-collar work projects funded through the Works Progress Administration (WPA), but only reluctantly. The reason for this appears to have been double-sided. On the one hand, Shambaugh doubted the efficacy of funding historical initiatives through federal aid to relieve unemployment. On the other, the temporary nature of work-relief programs, their initially disorganized operations, and a bureaucratic inclination to disregard established professional expertise tended to confirm his generally low opinion of government-sponsored history. Thus Shambaugh belatedly cooperated with the Historical Records Survey and took an assertive stance with the FWP in assisting with the Iowa volume of the American Guide Series. Shambaugh was a more willing partner in an initiative that came from the Iowa State Planning Board: a small project to preserve and mark historic sites.

Early in 1934 the Joint Committee on Materials for Research of the American Council of Learned Societies and the Social Science Research Council drew up a plan for surveying local and state records under the auspices of the Civil Works Administration. The plan was ambitious in its scope: during an eight-week period, 2,700 workers would inventory public records held in counties, or comparable subdivisions, nationwide. Useful, if temporary, employment for white-collar workers was, of course, the reason for the plan, but it also was inspired by "the surveys and studies carried forward for some thirty years by the Public Archives Commission of the American Historical Association" as well as more recent statewide surveys conducted in California, Illinois, and Pennsylvania. A national database of local public records was the obvious goal, but the joint committee also believed that such a survey would "help to draw more scholarship into local history."[1]

Both of these were goals that Shambaugh supported strongly during the early part of his career, but when he was asked to serve as the state administrator for Iowa in this effort, he declined. Public records were the province of the State Department of History and Archives—he had helped to make it so. He therefore had good reason to refer the joint committee to the state archivist in Des Moines. However, even before the plan was announced, Shambaugh expressed reservations about the project's feasibility, stating that while a survey of county archives was "commendable," his "own experience with planning and executing the set-up, in respect to the State archives of Iowa, leads me to the conclusion that there are very few people who are competent to do satisfactory work." In essence, his sense of professionalism was so great that he did not care to be in charge of a program that would be staffed by nonarchivists, even if they were unemployed white-collar workers.[2] That he would simply decline to be involved reveals not only that Shambaugh had distanced himself from the historical department, but, more generally, that he had also distanced himself from archival issues that once had concerned him greatly. More important, he seems to have believed that applied history would be cheapened by associating it with government-funded relief work.

In any case, the Historical Records Survey did not begin until 1936, and then as a subdivision of the FWP under the WPA.[3] At that time, Shambaugh agreed to lend assistance to the survey, but he never really expressed much enthusiasm for it. From his vantage point, the project did not begin on a professional footing. Shambaugh was notified early in 1936 that he was on a short list of people to be "consulted in drafting the program for Iowa." However, it was a full eighteen months later that he was formally asked to be a project adviser.[4]

In the interim, the staff hired to work on the survey, which operated out of Des Moines, began requesting specific information from Shambaugh, not consulting him about a plan of work. For example, the assistant state survey director, Ray Stiles, requested a list of contacts among county historical societies. Shambaugh had the desired information extracted from the society's mailing list but, in a curt response, cautioned Stiles not to expect much help from the local organizations because "they are primarily interested in collecting material and reminiscences concerning old settlers and probably will have very little interest in the archives or county offices."[5] Stiles, somewhat taken aback by Shambaugh's cool tone, assured him that he had "no desire to impose upon your good nature," then proceeded to ask him to supply the Des Moines office with indexes to the collections at the SHSI and at the University of Iowa, adding that "if it should require the services of someone to do this work, I would be more than glad to supply someone qualified to make the proper copies."

Shambaugh sent Stiles a frosty three-page report on the society's holdings. In response to Stiles's request for copies of catalogs and indexes to the SHSI's manuscript collections as well as those at the University of Iowa, Shambaugh's report, possibly prepared by a staff member, contained the briefest description of the SHSI's collections imaginable, stated that the SHSI's manuscript collections were uncataloged and unindexed, informed Stiles that access by non-SHSI staff was limited, and further informed him that no SHSI staff were available to assemble the information he desired. As a historical document, Shambaugh's response reveals that he assigned low priority to good archival practices, but the message to Stiles would have been clear: if he wanted the information, he would have to negotiate with Shambaugh, and he would have to provide either personnel or funds, or both, to obtain it.[6]

After Don Farran took over as state survey director in 1937 and made the long-awaited professional courtesies, Shambaugh was much more cooperative.[7] Politeness returned to his letters, but he had little patience for naive assumptions, misstatements, and lack of professional deference. When, for instance, Farran informed him that only one set of the nationwide inventory of historical records would be provided to each state and that the historical department would be the likely recipient, Shambaugh politely but firmly insisted that it be sent to Iowa City rather than Des Moines. As a result, Farran recommended to the national office in Washington, D.C., that Iowa receive two sets but, in the event that only one set could be provided, "it be placed with the State Historical Society in Iowa City during the duration of Doctor Shambaugh's life," then transferred to Des Moines.[8]

Likewise, Shambaugh remained skeptical that WPA workers were competent. When Farran assigned some of his staff to compile state statutes and regulations covering county administration, with the intent of proposing legislation to prohibit the destruction of county records and authorize their mandatory transfer to the state archives, Shambaugh first reminded him that the SHSI had already compiled much of the legislative history and closed his letter with uncustomary but deliberate sarcasm: "I wonder how many WPA workers are qualified to do this work. It would seem to require some training in law, in history, and in the methods of research, in addition to a keen mind."[9]

No matter how he felt about WPA workers, Shambaugh responded to Farran's every request for advice or assistance, and their relationship was cordial while Farran was with the project. However, in the summer of 1938 Farran moved on to take charge of the Federal Theatre Project's Midwest Play Bureau in Chicago, then on to D.C. to work in the national headquarters of the Historical Records Survey. Thereafter, correspondence between the Des Moines survey office and the SHSI shifted to a more perfunctory level. Survey personnel changed, and after Shambaugh's death in 1940, Ruth Gallaher assumed the role of liaison.

When Congress terminated the Historical Records Survey in 1942, the work was far from finished and never to be resumed. Despite the publication of more than 2,000 inventories of municipal, county, and state archives, Farran later observed that the Historical Records Survey left a legacy of "chaos" in the states. Because few states had the facilities or capacity to store the quantity of research data generated during the six years the survey operated, "materials so carefully researched . . . were on their way to oblivion."[10] A tally of the work completed in Iowa indicates that twelve inventories of county archives (out of ninety-nine counties) were either published or approved for publication, with "a great many others in various stages of completion." Despite extensive research of church archives in Iowa, no inventory was published. The Historical Records Survey took credit for publishing *A Check-List of Iowa Imprints 1838–1860*, but in reality this checklist was largely compiled by Gallaher and published in the January 1938 issue of the *Iowa Journal of History and Politics*. "A Guide to Public Statistics" was prepared but never published. Likewise, several inventories of federal records in Iowa were prepared but never published.[11]

Throughout the life of the project, it was widely assumed that funding would resume at the end of World War II, an assumption that proved to be wildly unrealistic. One wonders what might have been accomplished, in Iowa at least, had federal administrators chosen at the very beginning to consult with professional historians in the state, had federal guidelines been permissive enough to allow either the historical department or the SHSI to operate the Historical Records Survey of Iowa, or had Shambaugh taken measures to assume more leadership.

Iowa: A Guide to the Hawkeye State, published in 1938, is now treated as a reference work, as are all the volumes in the American Guide Series, chock full with tidbits of information. Collectively, they represent a monumental compilation of state and local history—a fascinating slice of 1930s' Americana. They still appeal to readers and attract collectors, even if many of the listed points of historical interest are no longer extant and some of the facts are incorrect.

Shambaugh's very brief foreword to the Iowa volume explains that the SHSI "sponsored" the guide "in accordance" with a 1937 act of the Iowa legislature. He was careful to disclaim any responsibility for the contents, however. "While the Historical Society is pleased to carry out the will of the General Assembly," the foreword continues, "it can not claim any of the credit that belongs to the project which has found fulfillment in the publication of this book. Indeed, whatever merit there is in these pages belongs to the many Iowans who took part in their compilation. Likewise, the credit for the selection of subject matter and the responsibility for the arrangement and editing of materials go to those persons who have faithfully directed the activities of the Federal Writers' Project for Iowa."[12] It was a skillful dispatch with the mighty pen, for the words were full of double meaning. Stuffed correspondence folders pertaining to the Iowa guide tell the story behind its publication. Their contents reveal a similar pattern of skepticism and begrudging cooperation. In this instance, however, Shambaugh managed to wrest a degree of control over the final product.

In March 1936 the FWP staff in Iowa got down to work. Shambaugh and Gallaher both served on the state advisory board, as they did for the Historical Records Survey. In Gallaher's case, she considered this duty to be outside her regular responsibilities, for in agreeing to serve on the board she cautioned that there was "a limit to the amount of work one can do on the side."[13] Shambaugh himself seems to have had only a fuzzy idea about the role he and his staff might play in the Iowa guide project. In mid March he received a letter from the editor of the Iowa guide, Raymond Kresensky. Actually, it was a cover letter asking Shambaugh to read an enclosed essay written by one of his former students, Iola Thomas, who had found temporary work with the FWP. Kresensky half-apologized for sending the manuscript, explaining that "the essays for the guidebook, which are, by the way, stories prefacing the actual material of tours and trips, have to be simple. They are not written for technicians, though they should be correct, I know."[14]

The title of Thomas's essay was "Early Settlement of Iowa," which probably corresponds to the chapter in the published guide entitled "History: The First White Men; Territory of Iowa; Statehood; Government." If this is so (individual authors are not credited, and neither is the editor), then her manuscript either went through successive revisions or was totally rewritten because, except for subject matter, the two versions bear no similarity. In any case, Shambaugh's response was cheerful—"we will take pleasure in giving careful attention to Miss Thomas' story"—but packaged with thinly disguised irritation: "It would be very helpful to us if we had an outline setting forth the plan for essays . . ." and "Perhaps you might find it possible to visit Iowa City with a view to conferring with us."[15] This exchange set the tone for what became an increasingly strained working relationship between the SHSI and the Iowa FWP during the next two years.

After three essays arrived in quick succession for review, Shambaugh placed Kresensky on notice that he would not allow his staff to be overburdened with requests for assistance. "[I]t is, of course, not possible," he warned, "to look up every date, name, and figure given, nor to make note of all possible omissions. This would entail an endless amount of work, equivalent to doing the research over again." In the same letter, Shambaugh took another opportunity to question the competence of relief workers, notwithstanding that at least one of them was a former student: "The bibliographies which follow these essays are often not up-to-date; nor is the selection always good." So he sent Kresensky a bibliography recently published by the SHSI and instructed him to have his workers take a look at it.[16]

As it turned out, only Gallaher was overburdened with requests. She was much more pliable than her boss, although certainly with his knowledge and permission. Her letters to and from Kresensky are much softer in tone, sometimes even informal; she also accommodated his every request, supplying him with endless pages of factual corrections, rectified omissions, more precise wordings, and lists of published works that should have been consulted. If one were to reconcile the corrections included in Gallaher's letters with the published guide, the exercise would no doubt reveal that whatever accuracy the book holds is due in large part to her efforts, which must have consumed countless hours of time. Kresensky as much as admitted this in one of his letters: "My reason for sending you so much is that I feel one real authority should offer us help. You see we deal with so many consultants that I am of the opinion that one authority like you would help to unify the book."[17]

Like the editor and the anonymous authors who were employed as relief workers, however, Gallaher received no line of credit for her contribution. Actually, she may have preferred it that way. In response to a comment she once made concerning the number of errors she was finding, not to mention those undetected, Kresensky assured her that he was "not trying to anticipate a blame" that could be laid on her desk and that her name would "not be listed as final authority or any such thing."[18]

Kresensky himself found work on the guide equally frustrating at times and came to rely on Gallaher's store of knowledge as well as her good nature. After a year of working day in, day out on the content, he confided to her that the "three or four of us who have had some editorial, literary or journalistic experience and have always 'loved' the state of Iowa want to portray it honestly but we have the 'dead weights' of a relief proposition, much red tape, temperamental (artistic, they call it) differences, and not a little politics."[19] He must have been gratified when Shambaugh found the published guide "a very creditable book" and even moreso when Bruce Catton pronounced it "a first-rate job" in a favorable review.[20]

It seems clear that, whatever value social and cultural historians have attached to New Deal work-relief projects, Shambaugh did not view the history-related initiatives of the FWP as serious scholarship. How could he? The individuals placed in charge were not trained in history. Raymond Kresensky, a published poet, is a case in point.[21] After Gallaher had made lengthy and substantive comments on a number of draft essays, Kresensky confessed that although he was "a poet and one who goes into literature 'art for art's sake' I am beginning to appreciate the real literature in your society's publications. I think your books and articles—so directly associated with Iowa life—are more vital than the romantic stories . . . and the personal longings of poets disassociated from real life."[22]

Nevertheless, Kresensky did have a good feel for the elements of social and cultural history, and his letters reveal that he personally spent considerable time digesting the many books and articles sent to him for reference. He and Gallaher also exchanged ideas about what the subjects of "folkways" and "social welfare" should comprise, and when he initiated a sophomoric inquiry on the philosophy of history, she took the time to compose a thoughtful reply.[23] In other words, unlike Shambaugh, Gallaher did not shut out Kresensky intellectually, and, through her, the door to Shambaugh remained open. It seems fair to speculate that because of the time and intellect Gallaher invested in the Iowa guide, Shambaugh was obliged to take its publication more seriously than he otherwise might have.

Getting the manuscript published, however, was a struggle. First, the volume needed a sponsor to underwrite production costs. Shambaugh's three decades of publishing experience enabled him not only to get the manuscript into print quickly, it also allowed him to assume a measure of control over the final product. The federal government had not chosen to operate its programs through established state historical and cultural institutions, but FWP program administrators realized that institutions such as the SHSI were indispensable to get the work done. Shambaugh also realized this and deftly "made use of the proposed volume to gain support in the Iowa General Assembly for raising the Society's appropriation."[24]

Iowa's economy began to flag in the latter 1920s, then sank, with the rest of the nation, into the Great Depression of the 1930s. After the SHSI reached a peak appropriation level of $44,500 annually in the early 1920s, its funding fluctuated during the period 1925–1933, then declined substantially to $25,000 annually in the 1933–1935 biennium and rose slightly to $28,000 in the 1935–1937 biennium. The University of Iowa experienced a similar pattern of budget cuts, although the dollar amounts, of course, were much greater.[25] Because Shambaugh's applied history programs—especially the Commonwealth Conference, the biennial legislative analyses, and the policy histories—relied on state funding, either through the society or the university, these programs were suspended.

As things turned out, they were never to be revived. In effect, Shambaugh watched his own state-supported initiatives go by the wayside during the 1930s while the State Historical Society was more or less coerced into assisting new federally funded programs that were not organized by, supervised by, or staffed by professionals trained in history or political science or any other discipline Shambaugh associated with applied history. The wonder is that he confined himself to making so few dyspeptic remarks to be preserved in the archival record. During the 1930s, Shambaugh literally presided over the demise of his own career in applied history. That Swisher completely omitted this portion of the story from his biography of Shambaugh is revealing in the extreme.

Whatever sense of professional loss Shambaugh might have experienced, he nonetheless coped with changing times as best he could. In this respect, timely publication of the Iowa guide was Shambaugh's doing. In January 1937 Shambaugh and Gallaher received nearly identical letters (suggesting that all members of the advisory board received one) informing them that a bill would shortly be presented to the Iowa legislature seeking a state appropriation to publish the guide and further asking them to lobby appropriate elected officials in support of the bill, a copy of which was not enclosed with the letters.[26]

Neither Shambaugh nor Gallaher seems to have responded to this form letter, and there is a curious three-month lapse before the subject of funding the guide next appears in the correspondence. At that time, late April, near the end of the legislative session, Shambaugh informed George Keller, WPA state administrator for Iowa, that both houses of the state legislature had passed bills to increase the SHSI's annual appropriation, with the increase designated for publishing the Iowa guide, but that differences in the two bills remained to be worked out in committee. Specifically, Shambaugh informed Keller that the SHSI could only sponsor publication if the society's annual appropriation was set at $33,000, without the rider (in the Senate version) earmarking fully $7,500 for publication of the guide and without a provision specifying publication of a minimum 10,000 copies. Shambaugh insisted that the SHSI have the power to decide how many copies would be published and on what terms. Thus he more or less directed Keller to "inform Senator Breen and the Conference Committee that they (the W.P.A. Writers' Project) can not accept a provision for the publication of the Guide Book that would injure or embarrass the State Historical Society."[27]

An undated memorandum, apparently for in-house reference and discussion purposes, reveals that Shambaugh, possibly with his staff, spent time clarifying the SHSI's responsibilities vis-à-vis those of the FWP office in Des Moines and calculating how SHSI sponsorship would affect the budget.[28] Undoubtedly, private conversations preceded Shambaugh's letter to Keller. Nonetheless, it is clear from the letter's language and tone that by this time Shambaugh had taken control of the publishing process. The guide would either be published in accordance with standards set by the SHSI or Shambaugh would not allow the society to be involved.

Two weeks later, Shambaugh had the $33,000 appropriation on the terms that he wanted, and he immediately informed the project office in Des Moines that, even though the appropriations act would not take effect until July, "we should be pleased to have the manuscript of the 'Iowa Guide' placed in our hands at the earliest possible date."[29] But seven months later the SHSI was still "anxiously awaiting" a complete manuscript; in mid December Shambaugh sent a terse, one-sentence letter to Kresensky stating: "I do hope that you can get the final manuscript of the *Iowa Guide Book* to us next week."[30] On the eve of December 23, Kresensky notified Shambaugh that his office had finally "assembled the manuscript material" and that a packet was in the Christmas-season mail; five days later the packet arrived in Iowa City.[31]

Assembled manuscript material, however, was not quite the complete manuscript that Shambaugh wanted. The reason for delay was that, even though the SHSI was underwriting the cost of publication, the FWP national office in Washington, D.C., had to approve all copy. Raymond Kresensky was thus caught in the middle trying to appease both sides. Shambaugh insisted on a complete manuscript so that his staff could copyedit the work as a whole for accuracy and consistency, while the national office insisted on reviewing successive drafts of individual sections, written by a stable of anonymous writers, to ensure a uniformly lively narrative and to cut text so that the assembled pieces did not exceed set quotas for total length.

The published guide embodied a compromise more or less acceptable to all parties. During the early months of 1938, Kresensky and Gallaher negotiated a final manuscript as quickly as possible. The tenor of one lengthy letter suggests the differences they had to overcome or ignore in the process. In response to another long list of changes that Gallaher recommended, Kresensky replied that they would be "considered," but it is fairly clear that this would be the case only because the guide would bear "the Society's endorsement and is to be their book as well as ours." He added: "I know you can appreciate the fact that in many cases the actual facts might be lost, apparently, in the attempt at making interesting reading. The perspective in all cases has been that of a writer seeing all sides and attempting to interpret the scene, something that has never been done before."[32]

Meanwhile, Shambaugh negotiated publication details with Viking Press and the FWP national office. Shambaugh would have much preferred to use an Iowa press, but once he was assured that Viking was negotiating to publish the guides for several other midwestern states, he pressed the point no further.[33] No doubt it seemed odd to him, as it does in retrospect, that a federal program established to provide jobs and pump money into local and state economies would end up doing just the opposite: sending state money through a state agency to a large publishing house located in New York. He also anticipated having to justify the exporting of state dollars to Iowa legislators who had approved the increased appropriation. But to have stood on principle surely would have delayed publication indefinitely.

Shambaugh, moreover, wanted the published work delivered to bookstores in 1938 to commemorate the territorial centennial, so he kept cracking the whip.[34] At the same time, he withheld his signature from the publishing contract until he forced as many concessions as he could on the book's content. Tension reached a low boil in March 1938, when Henry Alsberg, FWP national director, sent a presumptuous cover letter with the still-not-quite complete manuscript and requested that Shambaugh sign the contract and wire Viking Press within two days to begin setting type.[35] Shambaugh responded with a telegram, as instructed, but the recipient was Alsberg, not the publisher. It reads, in part:

> Manuscript copy of Iowa guide received . . . . Do you want us to eliminate such obviously objectionable statements as Iowa "even has indications of culture," that Iowa farmers "distrust outsiders," that the Iowan is commonly "thought of as a great boaster" and that his "boasting is largely in self-defense impelled by a sense of cultural inferiority," that many of "the people were not proud of being in the center of the hog belt," that "the farmer, conscious of his own deficiencies is willing to pay high taxes for the maintenance of educational institutions"? . . . We should appreciate your reply before signing contract with Viking Press.[36]

Shambaugh's telegram provoked an immediate conference between the FWP staff in Des Moines and the SHSI staff in Iowa City. Two days later, Kresensky had agreed to another list of changes and corrections, and Shambaugh wired his approval of the publishing contract.[37] Differences over the length and content of the bibliography never were resolved to Shambaugh's satisfaction, but he nonetheless allowed publication to proceed in order to obtain a 1938 copyright date.[38]

The published guide appeared in late August 1938, a few months later than Shambaugh wanted, but considering the content and the number of people involved, a rather remarkable schedule. No sooner was the volume on bookstore shelves, however, than the FWP once again ignored the society's sponsorship. Three months after the guide went into distribution, the society was still waiting for the fifty free copies it was supposed to receive under the terms of the publishing contract.[39] Then there was the matter of copyright. In the contract with Viking Press, Shambaugh arranged for the SHSI to hold the copyright. The FWP staff understood this, but Kresensky nonetheless began granting permission to organizations requesting to reprint excerpts. He did so on the premise that public dollars had funded the content and therefore the material was "public property." When Shambaugh learned of this, he quickly instructed Kresensky to forward all such requests to Iowa City since "this Society is the only authority which can grant permission to reprint extracts from the *Guide Book*."[40]

The experience of simply sponsoring a publication was a new direction for the SHSI. Whatever the merits of *Iowa: A Guide to the Hawkeye State* as judged by reviewers, sales, and later scholars, the historical content did not really satisfy either Shambaugh or Gallaher. Despite the time that Gallaher spent reading and checking draft manuscripts, many of her suggested corrections went unheeded. Nevertheless, as the official sponsor and holder of the copyright, the society was placed in the position of responding to individuals with localized or specialized knowledge who began detecting the small errors that Gallaher had worked so hard to avoid.[41]

Perhaps it was a small price to pay. In the end, Shambaugh succeeded in rebooting the society's annual appropriation, and the society's name was linked, officially if not in spirit, with a new direction that historical scholarship began to take in the 1930s. As Robert Cantwell observed in 1939, when continued federal funding of the FWP seemed doubtful:

American history has never before been written in terms of communities—it has been written in terms of its leading actors, and of its dominant economic movements, but never in terms of the ups and downs of the towns from which the actors emerged and in which the economic movements had their play. It is one kind of experience to read, in Beard or in Turner, of the opening of the West, but it is another kind of experience to read of the rise and fall of Chillicothe in relation to the railroads, or of Galena in relation to the world market for lead. Everybody knows in a general way what happened when the railroads supplanted the canals, but nobody knew until the Guides dramatized it how many careers were deflected in the process or how many towns disappeared.[42]

Cantwell also could poke fun at the endless number of "secret rooms, invisible closets, hidden stairways and false halls" that, according to local lore, were built into homes; the amazing quantity of "spite fences, spite churches, spite towns . . . [and] spite railroads" dotting the American landscape; and the "majestic roll call" of "financiers and prostitutes who went broke . . . prophets whose positive predictions were so badly mistaken . . . engineers and technicians whose machines never worked . . . miners who never found any gold . . . [and] birthplaces of people who never accomplished anything." At the same time, he recognized that this great unfinished project would "revolutionize the writing of American history and enormously influence the direction and character of our imaginative literature."[43]

One other New Deal initiative contributed marginally to the advancement of historical interests in Iowa, the Historic and Scenic Features Project of the Iowa State Planning Board. Unlike the Iowa guide and the Historical Records Survey, which were initiated at the federal level, the Historic and Scenic Features Project was hatched at home. This difference may explain why Shambaugh was a more willing player.

The Iowa State Planning Board received its initial funding of $10,500 in 1934 from the Iowa Board of Conservation, which (with the Fish and Game Commission) had completed the *Iowa Twenty-five Year Conservation Plan* a year earlier.[44] The comprehensive 1933 plan sought to integrate the protection and enhancement of both natural and cultural resources—water, wildlife, soil, forests, parks and preserves, and historic and scientific sites were considered interrelated aspects of conservation—and it enabled Iowa to generate project-specific plans very quickly in order to receive federal relief aid through various New Deal programs. Iowa, for instance, had sixteen Civilian Conservation Corps (CCC) camps established and thirty-two projects under way within three months after the CCC was authorized in March 1933.[45]

Key personnel on the Iowa State Planning Board included many of the same people who had worked together on the twenty-five-year conservation plan. While the planning scope of the board was much broader, including a wide range of economic and social concerns, the Board of Conservation saw the planning board as another agency for accomplishing many of its conservation goals, hence the initial funding for operating expenses. As a result, the planning board's projects (there were fourteen in all, each with a separate technical advisory committee) reflected the resource conservation priorities identified in the twenty-five-year plan, priorities that included identifying, acquiring, preserving, and enhancing historic sites.[46]

Planning board member A. E. Rapp of Council Bluffs was assigned to chair the Historic and Scenic Features Project. Rapp was then serving on the Iowa Fish and Game Commission; in 1935, when this agency was combined with the Board of Conservation to become the State Conservation Commission, Rapp was appointed to serve on the new commission. Governor Clyde L. Herring appointed both Shambaugh and Edgar R. Harlan, curator of the historical department in Des Moines, to serve as two of the project's seven technical advisers.[47] Shambaugh, of course, would never have turned down a governor's request for service. In this instance, the *Twenty-five Year Conservation Plan* had been widely publicized and disseminated, as were the reports of the State Planning Board, and Shambaugh either knew personally or knew of the principal players involved. Thus he also would have understood the commission's goals and its organizational structure.

The term "project" really designated an activity area of each committee, and Rapp lost no time in soliciting suggestions from his technical advisers, as well as from a long list of local contacts statewide, about exactly what projects the committee should undertake.[48] As it so happened, Shambaugh was able to advance the discussion considerably because Jacob Swisher had just compiled information on more than a hundred historic sites in the state associated with some notable event or person.[49] For reasons that never were clearly stated, Shambaugh also began advocating restoration of a stone house located on a privately owned farm near Springdale, a Quaker settlement northeast of Iowa City.[50] The stone house, which was dilapidated and being used as a toolshed, derived its significance from a brief association with John Brown, who between 1856 and 1858 delivered escaped slaves to this location on the Underground Railroad and planned his advance to Harper's Ferry there.[51] By the 1930s, the house had become known as the John Brown House, a misleading designation but one that, as Shambaugh probably reasoned it, reflected historical status of appropriate national importance to justify any request for federal funding through New Deal relief programs.

In any case, by September 1934 planning for three specific projects was under way.[52] Restoring the John Brown House was one of them, and it was anticipated that workers paid through the Federal Emergency Relief Administration would carry out restoration. Charles R. Keyes, who had conducted archaeological investigations in conjunction with the SHSI for years, also was preparing to survey American Indian mounds in northeast Iowa, and Swisher had been working closely with landscape architect John Fitzsimmons of Iowa State College to tabulate and map historic and scenic sites across the state.[53]

The John Brown House restoration project produced high hopes, conceptual drawings, and an estimate of material and labor expenses ($4,000), but it never went any further.[54] In January 1935 Fitzsimmons notified Shambaugh that restoration plans had been "temporarily dropped due to the great amount of skilled labor necessary to carry out the project."[55]

In the meantime, the Historic and Scenic Features Committee of the Iowa State Planning Board began planning to reconstruct a log schoolhouse that had been erected in 1830 on the banks of the Mississippi River in the southeastern tip of Iowa.[56] The Galland Schoolhouse, as it was known, had been gone for about seventy years—the land was excavated for a canal in the 1860s, then submerged when the Keokuk Dam was constructed in 1913—but in 1924 the Keokuk Chapter of the Daughters of the American Revolution placed a bronze historic marker on a nearby spot to commemorate Iowa's "first schoolhouse." Then, landowners Timothy and Ella Harrington gave this tiny plot, twenty feet square, to the SHSI.[57] The society thus owned a "historic site" that lacked any authentic historic remains. This was, in essence, a project awaiting discovery; as it so happened, a local group took up the challenge and organized as the First Schoolhouse Committee.[58] But these plans, too, ran into a roadblock when "outside funds" were requested to pay for a labor supervisor. Shambaugh, still coping with severely reduced appropriations, could not squeeze the money out of his budget; consequently, this project also languished.[59]

By present-day historic preservation standards, the Galland Schoolhouse project would not merit consideration, and, in truth, even Rapp
questioned the logic of reconstructing a long-gone schoolhouse on a site it
never occupied.[60] A letter of response to Rapp's query reveals that, in just
a few months time, Shambaugh had begun to prioritize prehistoric and
historic sites within the state and to formulate long-term goals for their
acquisition and preservation "under some plan of State supervision."[61] He
even went so far as to request that the state legislature establish an annual
appropriation of $5,000 "for the purchase of historic sites and buildings
and for materials for directional markers to historic sites and buildings."
Cognizant that the Iowa Board of Conservation already had jurisdiction
over historic places that had been incorporated into the state park system,
Shambaugh suggested that this item be included in the conservation
board's appropriation, with the SHSI providing "advice and counsel."[62]

Considering that Rapp was appointed to serve on the State Conservation Commission, he would have been in a position to negotiate inter-
agency cooperation to establish a state-supported and -supervised historic preservation program, but there is no indication that he ever did.
Historic preservation thus slipped through cracks in the patchwork of
state and federal funding until 1938, when Louise Parker, another member
of the State Conservation Commission, took an active interest in restoring two historic sites in the state park system: Fort Atkinson, a military
fort associated with the period of American Indian removal from Iowa,
and Plum Grove, the home of Iowa's first territorial governor. Parker also
shepherded state land acquisitions for Effigy Mounds National Monument in northeast Iowa.[63]

In any event, after the John Brown House project fizzled, the work of
the Historic and Scenic Features Committee lapsed until 1936. In March
of that year Fitzsimmons met with Shambaugh and members of his staff
to outline a plan for marking selected historic sites, a project deemed suitable for WPA relief workers, who were to fabricate "temporary" wooden
markers.[64] By late 1937, this effort succeeded in placing wooden markers at
several historic sites throughout the state and signing 140 places associated with the 1846 Mormon migration across southern Iowa.[65] It was a
much less ambitious effort but the best that could be accomplished without someone in authority to champion historic preservation. And Shambaugh was not going to take up the cause. As he explained to one inquiry
about the lack of progress in restoring historic buildings, "The Iowa State

Planning Board may mark historic sites and may use W.P.A. labor in their restoration. But no funds were provided for these purposes, and since repairs usually require materials as well as labor, the Board has been unable to do much in such cases."[66]

The Galland Schoolhouse project did go forward, but the society had no direct involvement in the project. Rather, young men employed under auspices of the National Youth Administration reconstructed a replica, which was dedicated in October 1940, with Swisher representing the SHSI at the ceremony.[67]

Shambaugh's concept of applied history, with its heavy emphasis on policy research and democratic institutions, would seem to have been perfectly synchronized with the brain-trust approach to planning and governance during the Roosevelt administration. But New Deal–style planning was directed at national problems, and federal money flowed through states to the local level.

Moreover, during the interwar period, intellectuals shifted their attention from reform to regional culture and ethnicity, folkways, and "old things" in general. The search for answers to contemporary problems, guided by scientifically trained experts, began to give way to a widespread, if amorphous, search for national character in the "traditions" of its people. Artists and writers, in particular, embarked on what Michael Kammen calls "the emotional discovery of America," producing an overflow of artistic expression (and an outflow of disaffected artists).[68] Historians, by and large, were not among the intellectuals attracted to this egalitarian enterprise, but the generation of young, talented, sometimes aggressive idealists who staffed the upper echelons of WPA programs initiated under Federal Project No. 1 or who found employment because of them were either caught up in or influenced by its energy and spirit. These idealists developed the art of manipulating documentary material about "the people" into artistic and literary formats, often with a leftist message.[69]

Shambaugh simply was not interested in making the shift. He seems never to have considered investing whatever time and energy it might have taken to bootstrap new state initiatives from New Deal programs. Perhaps that would have been impossible, but he was not inclined to make the effort. Rather, he saw federal programs as mediocre efforts that the SHSI was obliged to rescue in order to avoid embarrassment or, as in the case of the Iowa guide, as a vehicle for regaining lost revenue.

Ironically, it was another progressive historian and Iowa native, Carl Becker, who absorbed the mood of the times and articulated a philosophy of history that would catch fire in the post–World War II era to inspire a new generation of historians. Although Shambaugh and Becker were born only two years apart, of similar backgrounds, and similarly influenced by Robinson and Turner (Becker directly as Turner's student) and progressivism in general, their paths apparently never crossed during their formative years. While Shambaugh was single-mindedly applying himself to graduate studies at the University of Iowa, Becker seems to have been undergoing an identity crisis that led him to abandon his studies at Cornell College in Mt. Vernon, Iowa, and head for the University of Wisconsin, a move that ultimately compelled him to shed certain elements of his Iowa upbringing, particularly Methodism and militarism.[70]

There is no correspondence to speak of between Shambaugh and Becker as they pursued their respective careers, suggesting that the two men probably had nothing more than a passing acquaintance in professional circles during their productive years. As professional historians, Shambaugh and Becker seem to have followed different instincts. Whereas Shambaugh embraced the history of the state and charted a high-minded course utilizing the methods of history to advance the progress of democratic institutions, Becker seems to have taken from his rural Iowa roots a sense of place and a fundamental, although intellectually detached, regard for ordinary people.

During the 1920s and 1930s, while Shambaugh experimented with disseminating history to popular audiences, Becker probed the relationship between history and memory and the intellectual processes that distinguished the historian from "Mr. Everyman." In much the same way that influential twentieth-century composers and artists, such as Aaron Copland and Grant Wood, abstracted the idea of the "common man" into modern creative expressions, so did Carl Becker draw on the "common man" to transform the way historians thought about historical knowledge and their role in crafting it. "History," he contemplated in his 1931 presidential address to the AHA, is "the artificial extension of the social memory"—not an exact science, not even an objective rendering of fact. Historians were bound by the same constraints as "Mr. Everyman," all "subject to the limitations of time and place" and drawing upon their memories of past events to make sense of the present and to anticipate the course of future events. But whereas "Mr. Everyman" reconstructed the past selectively "with something of the freedom of a creative artist," historians were the functional equivalent of tribal sages, trained and obligated to "harmonize, as well as ignorance and prejudice permit, the actual and the remembered series of events."[71]

Although Becker's 1931 address caused a stir in the historical profession, as did Charles Beard's "Written History as an Act of Faith," which followed two years later, Shambaugh did not participate in the debate over historical relativism that swirled around Becker and Beard during the interwar years.[72] If anything, he was moving in another direction. It is hard to characterize him as moving toward the political right to join what Novick has called "the defenders of 'the noble dream' of seeking objectivity."[73] Rather, in his own way he began retreating into his own philosophy of education. He turned his attention to developing a course titled "Approaches in Liberal and Cultural Education," commonly known as the "Campus Course," which is considered his chief legacy at the University of Iowa.[74]

In Swisher's manuscript, the chapter on the Campus Course is titled "An Adventure in Thinking." Bertha Shambaugh's editorial notes state: "This Chapter, Dr. Swisher acknowledged was the most difficult for him to write." She also reveals that three drafts of the chapter were written, the first by Swisher, the second by herself "at Dr. Swisher's suggestion," and the third by Ethan P. Allen, "Dr. Shambaugh's long time personal assistant in the Course," who "rearranged the material and cut both [previous] drafts." She considered Allen's draft "the shortest and perhaps the best for that," but even "he did not consider his treatment complete."[75] Indeed, it was not. This is the only chapter in the manuscript that has no footnotes, evidence that this is the point at which work stopped.

Oddly, since the Campus Course was Shambaugh's crowning achievement as an academic, his papers contain precious little pertaining directly to it: one folder only. It contains a few sheets of paper with random notes that probably were written for lectures: "Time Rolls On: History Is Fiction Agreed Upon," no date; "Science and Religion," 9 November 1932; and "Knowledge and Wisdom," no date.[76] Thus one is forced to rely on the collective memories of the three people who collaborated on this chapter, augmented by bits and pieces of related information. Yet, in retrospect, the Campus Course offers additional insight to the complexity of Shambaugh's professional persona, and this ultimately suggests another reason why he did not embrace New Deal cultural politics.

Shambaugh's idea for what became the Campus Course can be traced, first, to his presidential address before the American Political Science Association in 1930.

On that occasion he departed from the conventional time-honored custom of discussing a technical aspect of political science. Rather, he selected as his theme the broader subject: "The More Than in University Education." Vividly, he portrayed his dream of the university of the future: "I see the major emphasis everywhere placed upon freedom rather than upon restraint; upon wisdom rather than upon knowledge; upon states of mind and attitudes of soul rather than upon memorized details of information; upon the meaning of things rather than upon their factual content; upon the sanctity of the individual rather than upon the conventions of society; upon inner approval rather than upon external authority; upon likenesses rather than upon differences; upon unity rather than upon diversity; upon the creative faculty rather than upon the power of memory; upon the capacity for experience rather than upon the desire for possession; upon the use of leisure moments rather than upon the efficiency of working hours; upon human values rather than upon material accumulations; upon the art of living rather than upon the science of life; upon the teacher rather than upon the methods of teaching."[77]

Before "The More Than" became a formal address to his peers, however, Shambaugh delivered the prototype, his "Address to Freshman," in 1926.[78] Thus it appears that the idea for the Campus Course began germinating as he was developing the Commonwealth Conference in the mid 1920s. Another address to students, titled "Social Hygiene," undated but possibly also from the 1920s, provides another clue to his rationale for the Campus Course. In this lecture, he likened society to the human body, an organic entity in which the "structural unit . . . is the individual man or woman, just as the structural unit of the human organism is the cell." As sound health rested on good personal hygiene, so, too, the health of society rested on individuals who were "straight in thought, high-minded in aspiration, noble in ambition, and intelligent in action." But more than that, "Society" (capital S in his lecture notes) was "the accumulated wealth and riches of the ages—language, literature, art, science, religion," available to every individual "without price, freely without stint." In his organic concept of society, good social hygiene also required that individuals, the structural units of the body politic, contribute something "to the social progress of [their] own generation." Shambaugh's allegory was, in his words, "the practical philosophy of social life, the philosophy which begins and ends with social service—service to the community, service to Society, service to mankind."[79]

The Campus Course, in essence, was an opportunity for each student to synthesize his or her university education before stepping out into the wider world. In modern parlance, it probably would be called a "cap-stone" course in the humanities. One version of the Campus Course chapter, probably Allen's, notes that "Shambaugh believed that colleges and universities had forsaken their true mission in the trend to over concentration upon one field of study in the undergraduate curriculum." This version also explicitly links the Campus Course to Shambaugh's concept of applied history:

> Dr. Shambaugh had the ability to diagnose a system or program and the courage to attempt to correct the weakness of a prevailing system. And he had the peculiar power of bringing the classics up to date and associating them with today's world. It was a technique he used in "Applied History" in working out current problems on a historical foundation. He had an almost uncanny gift for looking into the future and of sensing trends. It was based not on *intuition*, but upon scientific analysis of the past. All this was brought into play in Dr. Shambaugh's last educational experiment, which he faced with a scholar's integrity and the full realization of the toil that goes into a great task.[80]

In terms of methodology, the course "combined three basic ways of presenting materials and ideas." Shambaugh lectured three times a week; under Allen's direction, students then engaged in small-group discussion in "an attractive conference room adjoining the beautiful library-lecture room"; and "personal interviews" with each student were held one or more times during the semester.[81]

Shambaugh himself traced his inspiration for the Campus Course back to James Harvey Robinson. As he began planning for the course in January 1932, he sent his old mentor a copy of the course proposal, "with which I have been playing for several years, and which may not be regarded as having passed the experimental stage. What do you think of it?" Robinson responded, "I think it admirable. I am especially pleased with the approach to Religion. I am confident that such discussions as are aroused will do much to relieve the tenseness of fundamentalist upbringing."

While Shambaugh was teaching the course for the first time that summer, he wrote again to Robinson, "This campus course is proving successful far beyond all expectations. . . . I never had such enthusiastic response to anything I have attempted in the classroom. The response almost frightens me. . . . Not a little of the vision of my campus course is the direct result of inspiration which came to me when I was a student under you at the University of Pennsylvania many years ago."[82]

To students, Shambaugh presented the Campus Course as a set of challenges, twenty-three to be precise. In large part, these "challenges" have the quality of little homilies, but three of them in particular seem to echo the strains of Roosevelt's speeches designed to raise morale and instill confidence in New Deal programs. Shambaugh challenged each student "to take a hand in a new deal in the game of life—with courage," "to be masters of our own destiny—without fear," and "to raise our lives to the plane of some kind of hopeful destiny—for ourselves, for our nation, and for all mankind."[83]

In presenting the Campus Course, Dr. Shambaugh gave much of himself. In writing and preparing the lectures he drew liberally upon other authors for the best thoughts of the ages. But in assimilating and presenting these views he reflected much of his own thinking, his own characteristics, his own personality. . . . As student groups completed their studies in Approaches in Liberal and Cultural Education, and as other groups came, Dr. Shambaugh never lost his spirit of adventure, nor his pioneer courage and fortitude. Like the true pioneer, he could feel the future beneath his feet. And in the end, he was prodigal of time, effort and energy in facing an objective that he deemed worthy.

Into Approaches in Liberal and Cultural Education Dr. Shambaugh put all of the frontiersman's risks and toil of creative work. Into it went all of his training as a scientific student of government, all of his experience in studying materials and methods of presentation, all of his broad knowledge of the inter-relationship of organized branches of learning. Into it went his ability to foresee trends. Into it went that indefinable something called personality. In it all there was the spirit of the pioneer, the spirit of adventure, the spirit of conquest.

Launched in a day of materialistic and semi-vocational trends in colleges of Liberal Arts, there was a stimulating challenge in Dr. Shambaugh's appeal "to think with the utmost freedom and with imagination, to think in every possible way—scientifically, humanly, socially, politically, spiritually, philosophically—

upon the everyday affairs of individuals and groups of individuals in their struggles of adjustment in these unhappy days."

That there was nothing new in the great fundamental of the Campus Course Dr. Shambaugh was wont to point out. It was old as what we call civilization— indeed it had made great civilizations.

Approaches in Liberal and Cultural Education was designed as a preparation for good citizenship by a scientifically trained student of government whose own facing of life's problems and thinking them through had brought the high conviction that,

> As education and the State are possessed of the same goal, which is civilization, so the school and government are under the same obligation to hold aloft the torch of culture along roads that lead to the fulfillment of the American Dream.

In brief, Dr. Shambaugh's "challenge to the modern University to provide inspiration and facilities for liberal and cultural education" was as old as civilization and as modern as today's earnest admonition amid our "crumbling certainties" for training in the art of living and thinking—to understand, appreciate and maintain the institution of democracy.

While recognized as a national figure in his own field, Dr. Shambaugh saw the relationship between various branches of organized knowledge too clearly to be an academic specialist. He was a liberal by nature and training. [Bertha's handwritten note indicates that she wanted this sentence reworked to read: "He never had been a liberal by nature and training."] And never was he more of the practical idealist than in this Adventure in Thinking. He planned, he studied, he experimented as the scientist in his laboratory.

Through an occasional summary of books recommended, or of topics under consideration, through conferences and discussions, and through a unique (and revealing) series of diaries, a fairly accurate estimate of the student's response to the challenge was made. . . . At the time of this educational experiment the closing two weeks of each University semester were devoted to "final examinations." In a pencil notation in Dr. Shambaugh's handwriting apparently addressed to his Campus Course class he refers to his departure from this time-honored routine:

> One of the reasons why I have not scheduled an examination for you is that the world is waiting to examine you in the fine art of living. The difference between a college examination and the world examination is that the world examination is continuous, without notice, without dates, without opportunity for special preparation. May I suggest that you examine your-

self. In the college examination you may fool others about yourself. But you cannot afford to fool yourself about yourself.

The Campus Course was offered "not as a criticism nor as a protest but as a practical way of bringing what may be called synthetic vision into liberal and cultural education and of focusing that vision upon life's essential problems." The experiment not only won the enthusiastic support of students but the respect of scholars at home and abroad. Will Durant called the Campus Course in actual operation the finest course he knew of in any American University. "It takes a brave University," he wrote, "to keep abreast with contemporary thought. The course on Approaches in Liberal and Cultural Education is an appetizing thing, just the sort of orientation which I believe every student should have who proposes to understand and enjoy life as well as make a living." There were many such letters of commendation and encouragement from educators, philosophers, historians, and students of government with the often-expressed hope "that through its influence the idea will be carried all over the land."

Preparations for the Campus Course lectures were made with all of Dr. Shambaugh's accustomed thoroughness, but as Dr. Ethan P. Allen, his long-time assistant points out, "Those typewritten pages form only the framework—the best of the lectures drawn from experience and the reading of a lifetime were given not from manuscript but on the spur of the moment with all of the sparkle that characterized his platform speaking. The setting—all that gave emphasis and meaning to a special occasion is as irreplaceable as the man himself with his ability to light the intellectual fires of his students with the spark of his own spirit."

In summarizing Approaches in Liberal and Cultural Education, Dr. Shambaugh would sometimes quite frankly present his own philosophy. In a larger measure than he may have thought, he was writing his own autobiography.

"Here," he would say, "are a few notes and memoranda which might be useful to me were I to write out a statement of my philosophy of life.

"I admit the Philosophy is important. It is more than important: it is everything. It is wisdom overflowing with the meaning of life.

"Philosophy is the high point in human thought, the peak of human achievement.

"The creation of Philosophy in one's life is the greatest triumph of the fine art of living.

"I would rather have men say of me that I am something of a philosopher than to have them say of me that I am good, or educated, or rich, or good-looking, or pious.

"Were I to reveal to you my philosophy of life adequately, I would give you nothing less than my own autobiography—the story of a farm boy destined for college by a legacy in his father's last will and testament. A man's philosophy is mirrored not in his words (in what he says he thinks and believes) but in how he lives, what he lives for.

"To me life has two great challenges: the challenge to make a living, and the challenge to achieve the fine art of living."

It was the habit of Dr. Shambaugh to close the semester with a brief inspirational message. Perhaps the one that most appropriately closes this chapter is his farewell:

We have met and talked and read and thought together for many weeks. And now we shall soon scatter to the ends of the earth. Shall we meet again? It is my hope that we shall. I want to believe that in sometimes tide we shall meet again, even though we scatter to the ends of the earth.

We shall meet again in the books we read in common. We shall meet on the plane of significant ideas—scientific, humanistic, philosophical, religious, and contemporary—which we think and cherish in common. We shall meet again in the dreams which we cast before us as we journey through life. Surely we shall meet again on the horizons.

It is my hope that wherever there is Truth, wherever there is Beauty, wherever there is Goodness, we shall meet again, not face to face, but mind to mind, and soul to soul, though we are scattered to the ends of the earth.

Practical idealist.[84] These two words sum up the complexity of Benjamin Shambaugh.

From one perspective, the last ten years of his career appear to have been a retreat from the challenges and opportunities the New Deal presented for applied history. From this perspective, he did not really take up the challenge to play his own "hand in a new deal in the game of life." Rather, he homed back to academia, his professional base, where he cocooned with students in the Campus Course, wrapping himself in silky cerements of adulation from which he would metamorphose out of this life to another realm.

From the Jacob Swisher–Bertha Shambaugh–Ethan Allen perspective, he devoted the last ten years of his life trying to provide inspiration to a generation of future leaders who were coming of age in a decade of uncertainty. The Great Depression did shake the foundations of American society. From this perspective, the Campus Course was his challenge to the new generation to join him in raising "our lives to the plane of some kind of hopeful destiny—for ourselves, for our nation, and for all mankind."

Although inspired by Robinson, on a more practical level Shambaugh seems to have conceived the course, in part, as an antidote to the perils of modernity. In a press statement, he asserted that "to many persons modern life seems to be mostly noise and confusion, speed and jazz, sound and fury signifying nothing. They see nothing in contemporary life but depression, moral bankruptcy, religious indifference, organized crime and legalized injustice."[85] Even if one allows for hyperbole, and Shambaugh was an experienced promoter, it seems likely that the Campus Course was his method of dealing with perceived social chaos, and there may have been a personal basis for his statement that "to many persons, life no longer seems to hold any special significance. They are not sure what they are doing is worth while."[86]

Bertha's notes echo her husband's own words. She wrote that the Campus Course, "like the Commonwealth Conference was a late flowering of a life-long working philosophy, and into it went all of his mature thinking on a great theme, all of his knowledge and technical skill gained through the years, all of his hopes for a better world obtained from a better understanding of it, all of his faith in an effective American democracy in the hands of an intellectual, moral, and spiritually trained citizenry."[87]

In turning his focus to the Campus Course, however, Shambaugh neglected to groom a successor. Obviously, he anticipated a much longer life, but that was not to be. Among his many protégés, there was not one who could provide the leadership and the vision that the SHSI needed to maintain its prominence in state and local history. Ethyl Martin, whom Shambaugh promoted from the position of a $40-per-month clerk in 1908 to assistant superintendent in 1930, succeeded Shambaugh as the top administrator, while John Ely Briggs took over his duties as the chief editor. Martin served ably in the administrative position and actively participated in the search for a more qualified permanent director (she held a bachelor's degree from the University of Iowa). She was inclined to seek someone from outside Iowa, but World War II made it difficult to attract professionals of the caliber desired. In early 1946 she nearly succeeded in securing a replacement when the Board of Curators offered the position to

Arthur Larsen, who had taken leave from his position as superintendent of the Minnesota State Historical Society to serve in the Army Air Forces's Historical Division during the war. Larsen, however, decided to return to Minnesota. As events transpired, Martin served as superintendent until 1947, when William J. Petersen, who had been a research associate at the SHSI since 1930, succeeded her.[88]

The difficulty in replacing Shambaugh suggests that wartime disruption was only part of the cause. In retrospect, Martin probably should be characterized as a transition figure. Shambaugh left no evidence that he was actively grooming a successor, but it is fair to say that had he been doing so he most likely would have chosen one of his doctoral students, and that person would have possessed a Ph.D. in political science, not history. This is the key. Shambaugh, who held advanced degrees in both history and political science, was intellectually grounded in both disciplines. Even so, he was a party to the very academic specialization that by the 1930s he had come to lament. Not only did he establish the Department of Political Science as one of the powerhouse academic units at the University of Iowa, he helped to found the American Political Science Association and once served as its president. By 1940, the academic disciplines of history and political science were no longer so closely entwined.

After Shambaugh died, the Board of Curators selected Martin as superintendent instead of Petersen, who also sought the position and was one of the few SHSI research associates to hold a Ph.D. in history. It took him seven years to reach his goal. During that time Martin carried out administrative functions in a manner that would have won Shambaugh's approval and, at the same time, scoured the professional ranks for someone she thought capable of filling his shoes. In Larsen, she thought she had found a worthy successor: someone from outside Iowa with the appropriate administrative experience and with a Ph.D. The fact that Larsen was a historian may not have been particularly relevant to her personally, but by this time it probably did matter to academicians at the University of Iowa, and the SHSI was then still located on the university campus. In any case, her quest ultimately failed.

Petersen, a strong personality in his own right, was nonetheless a far different leader than Shambaugh. "Steamboat Bill," a tag Shambaugh had hung on Petersen because of his consuming interest in Mississippi steamboating, brought a flare for publicity rather than scholarly publications, and he focused on building public interest in Iowana through public

Ethyl Martin and Benjamin F. Shambaugh, late 1930s. *State Historical Society of Iowa, Iowa City.*

speaking programs and historical tours. Petersen also revamped the society's publications program, discontinuing the *Iowa Journal of History and Politics* and placing more emphasis on the popular history magazine, the *Palimpsest*, and vastly increasing the number of illustrations in it in order to attract more readers and boost the society's membership.[89]

Swisher's unfinished biography of Shambaugh became a personal paean to a cherished mentor. He may have realized that he was simply too close to Shambaugh to treat his life with the same degree of scholarship that marks most of Swisher's published works. Nonetheless, a small portion of his text was edited into the pages of *Benjamin Franklin Shambaugh As Iowa Remembers Him: A Memoriam*, lovingly crafted by the staff Shambaugh left behind in April 1940. This volume gathered together "the flood of tributes" that poured into the society and to Bertha from across the state and the nation and the several eulogies delivered at his memorial service in the Old Stone Capitol. *As Iowa Remembers Him* is an amazing window to the essence of Shambaugh's legacy. To read through it is to understand that few could have matched his vision and administrative talent.

7

The Emergence of the Modern Public History Movement

No DIRECT link connects Benjamin Shambaugh to the emergence of the public history movement in the 1970s. Rather, the years between Shambaugh's deliberate attempts to promote applied history and commonwealth history and Robert Kelley's coining of the term "public history" in the mid 1970s are marked by a gradual progression of historians into the wider professional world, with World War I, the Great Depression, and World War II providing much of the impetus. And, as this progression took place, the profession began to fragment.

Thwaites, Shambaugh, Owen, Bourne, and others brought piecemeal professionalism to state historical societies, and a few of them advanced to prominent national positions. For instance, after directing the Minnesota State Historical Society from 1914 to 1931, Solon J. Buck taught at the University of Pennsylvania and directed the Western Pennsylvania Historical Society. Robert D. W. Connor, one of the original appointees to the North Carolina Historical Commission in 1903, became the first archivist of the United States in 1934. Solon Buck succeeded him in 1941.[1] More important, however, was the fact that historians engaged in local and state history or in the development of archives found less and less reason to settle for marginal status in the AHA. Thus, after the National Archives was established, the AHA's Conference of Archivists formed the independent Society of American Archivists. Likewise, the AHA's Conference of Historical Societies went its own way in 1940 and became the American Association for State and Local History.

Those who have studied the professionalization of history have focused considerable attention on the AHA's central role in the process. Clearly, as the association representing the majority of historians, the AHA exerted a powerful force in shaping a new, professional identity that was centered in the academy, with the doctoral degree in history as the basic credential for entering the fold. The counterpoint to professionalization was a gradual exclusion of avocational historians and of professional historians who practiced outside the academy. By tracing the credentials of those who held the AHA's highest office, it is possible to establish 1907 and 1927 as the beginning and endpoint of the professionalization project. Prior to 1907, AHA presidents were by and large avocational historians; after 1927, almost all of them were college or university professors.[2] Patricia Mooney-Melvin argues that in the process of excluding amateur historians, the "professional historical community" also turned its back on history education in elementary and secondary schools, on the general reading public, and on "the millions of Americans who received their education in history at the nation's historic sites."[3] Broadly speaking this is true, which accounts in part for the eventual emergence of new professional organizations to address the audiences of history that the AHA left behind. But the dynamics were complex: even as academically trained and employed historians moved to exclude avocational historians from their professional ranks, outside forces impelled professional historians to expand the purview of historical scholarship beyond the academy.

World War I

World War I not only stimulated homefront documentation at the state and local levels, it also advanced long-standing efforts to institutionalize historical consciousness within the military. During the 1860s, the United States Army initiated a historical publication series known as *Foreign Relations of the United States*. After the Civil War, Congress authorized both the War and Navy Departments to collect and publish war-related documents, which resulted in *The War of the Rebellion: A Compilation of the Official Records of the Union and Confederate Armies*, eventually comprising 128 volumes, and *Official Records of the Union and Confederate Navies in the War of the Rebellion*, comprising 30 volumes. Military professionals and historians quickly perceived the value of these documentary series. In 1903 the army established the General Staff, which led to the Command and General Staff School at Fort Leavenworth, Kansas, where military educators developed the "applicatory method" of analyzing past military actions. Shortly thereafter, the newly established Department of Historical Research of the Carnegie Institution and the AHA began pressing for greater scholarly access to military records; in 1912 the first conference of military history convened at the AHA annual meeting to discuss ways to foster cooperation between military professionals and civilian historians.[4]

World War I transformed these isolated military history initiatives into a more serious effort to document various aspects of the war as it was taking place. The navy established a historical section in the Office of the Chief of Naval Operations, independent of the Office of Naval Records and Library. Additionally, the U.S. naval commander in Europe, Admiral William S. Sims, established a historical section in his London headquarters. The War Department established the Army Historical Branch in the War Plans Division, and historical sections were attached to General George Pershing's command of the American Expeditionary Force (AEF) as well as the AEF Air Service. Likewise, the Marine Corps established a historical section in the Adjutant and Inspector General's Department Headquarters.[5]

The unprecedented nature of U.S. participation in World War I fostered an awareness of the war's implications not only for military history but political history as well. Efficient mobilization depended upon centralized coordination, and administrators of wartime federal agencies understood that they were making history. At war's end, the temporary agencies went away, and their records eventually might have, too, except that in 1934 the staff of the newly established National Archives began systematically combing federal offices hunting for important records. Among those retrieved "from the dark corners, the basements, and attics to which they had been relegated" were the records of the Shipping Board, the Fuel Administration, the Food Administration, the American Relief Administration, the War Industries Board, and the Council of National Defense.[6]

The Shipping Board established an Office of Historian, which existed from February 1918 until the end of August 1919. Fuel Administrator Harry A. Garfield gave his executive secretary, George E. Howes, the additional title of historian and editor and directed him to collect agency files from all the state and local offices. Using these records, Howes supervised preparation of the Fuel Administration's seven-volume final report. Herbert Hoover, head of the Food Administration, directed his staff to organize and preserve the agency's records as well as prepare administrative histories. As a result, four published histories documenting the wartime activities of the Food Administration appeared between 1920 and 1941. Hoover also made sure that the records of the American Relief Administration, based in Paris, were collected and retained. Bernard Baruch, head of the War Industries Board, directed his division chiefs to submit activity reports and brief administrative histories, which became the basis for the board's final report in 1921. Although the Council of National Defense briefly considered collecting and centralizing the records of all the temporary wartime agencies, this plan never was carried out.[7]

World War I elevated historical consciousness across the nation, but at war's end, just as interest quickly dropped at the state and local levels, so, too, did interest decline at the federal level. There were two notable exceptions. Immediately after the war, the United States Department of Agriculture (USDA) established an agricultural history and geography group for the purpose of studying long-term trends in agricultural conditions and production. Originally created in the USDA's Office of Farm Management, this group later became the Division of Statistical and Historical Research in the Bureau of Agricultural Economics. Division Chief Oscar C. Stine participated in the founding of the Agricultural History Society, which helped to forge a liaison with the academic community. The society published *Agricultural History*, but the first editor was a historian in Stine's division, Everett E. Edwards.[8] In addition to these developments at the USDA, the army continued to take history seriously during the 1920s. In 1921 a historical section was attached to the Army War College, providing a permanent berth for historians. Out of this grew an association of military historians, the American Military Institute, organized in 1933.

The Great Depression

The Great Depression spawned the second imperative for federal agencies to seek the services of historians and for historians to seek employment in the federal government, most notably in the newly established National Archives and in the National Park Service (NPS). In the National Archives, Robert D. W. Connor selected Solon J. Buck to serve as director of publications and as secretary of the National Historical Publications Commission. Connor, who owed his appointment largely to J. Franklin Jameson and other members of the AHA's inner circle, tended to hire professional staff members from among historians who had studied under these "AHA worthies," as Donald McCoy has called them. Connor began work at the National Archives with a staff of forty-two, and by the end of fiscal year 1938, the staff had grown to more than three hundred. Certainly not all were historians, but the professional staff included many who held graduate degrees in history from a relatively small number of universities and/or who were protégés of Jameson. Among those coming from outside the circle was Thomas Owen, who left the Alabama Department of Archives and History to direct accessions at the National Archives.[9]

In 1931 Verne E. Chatelain became the first chief historian of the NPS. Chatelain, who held degrees in history and law, had served a year as assistant superintendent of the Minnesota State Historical Society under Buck. This experience, in particular, helped prepare him for the challenges and opportunities that would come first as a result of Roosevelt's Executive Order 6166 (1933), which transferred the administration of all national parks and monuments, historic forts and battlefields, and the national capital parks to the NPS, and, second, with the subsequent avalanche of New Deal money for park development. Between 1931 and 1936 Chatelain established research and interpretation objectives for historic and prehistoric areas in the national park system, developed the Branch of Historic Sites and Buildings, and precipitated an influx of historians who were hired to research, restore, interpret, and administer historic sites.[10]

While the Great Depression created a job crisis for university graduates in many fields, including history, at the same time federal pump-priming enabled Chatelain to hire historians. "They were just flocking in to get jobs with us when there were no jobs in their field anywhere else," Chatelain recalled in a 1961 interview. "Conditions were unspeakably bad, and they were all glad to come." The NPS was permanently changed as a result. At the highest administrative levels a new perception took hold: "that here were many, many new historical areas, each of which demanded intelligent development and technical leadership of the highest order."[11] Federal dollars drove planning and development during the 1930s, and these activities demanded much of Chatelain's energy. Even so, he did not lose sight of the larger picture. Chatelain's tenure with the NPS was relatively short, but he is remembered precisely because he articulated a compelling rationale for developing the educational potential of historic areas in the national park system through research and interpretive programs. Moving in a direction that was little noticed among academic historians, Chatelain proclaimed that historic sites were both source material for the study of history and places where American history could be effectively taught to ordinary people.[12]

Chatelain left the NPS in 1936, exhausted from the frenetic pace demanded by New Deal projects.[13] However, the corps of historians he left at the NPS shouldered new responsibilities as a result of the 1935 Historic Sites Act, which authorized a nationwide survey to identify buildings, structures, and sites of cultural value for commemorating or illustrating the history of the United States. The 1933 consolidation of cultural properties under NPS administration; park development through New Deal work-relief programs, which also provided money to initiate the Historic American Buildings Survey (HABS) in 1933; and the mandate of the Historic Sites Act placed the NPS in the forefront of the emerging historic preservation movement in the United States. Park development projects, HABS documentation, and the historic sites survey all progressed steadily until the United States entered World War II, although interpretive programs flagged after Chatelain's departure.[14]

The history initiatives of the NPS also reflected growing popular interest in history. In 1929 Henry Ford opened a museum in Dearborn, Michigan, celebrating the triumphs of industrial capitalism and, nearby, Greenfield Village, an outdoor assemblage of restored historic buildings replete with Americana celebrating the folkways that industrial capitalism was erasing. Within five years the number of visitors climbed to nearly a quarter million and more than doubled in the next five years. Not to be outdone, John D. Rockefeller Jr. invested nearly $80 million in restoring, researching, and reconstructing buildings in Williamsburg, Virginia, to re-create a tidied-up version of the village as it appeared circa 1790.[15]

As Michael Wallace has observed, the history initiatives of the NPS, along with the Works Progress Administration (WPA) guidebooks and oral history collections, "reflected a populist shift away from the approach fostered by traditional and corporate elites, uncovering legacies of struggle and redefining American history as something that included common people as historical actors."[16] In this respect, the documentary impulse of the 1930s reflected Carl Becker's relativist approach to the study of history as "an imaginative creation, a personal possession which each one of us, Mr. Everyman, fashions out of his individual experience."[17] While the NPS initiatives certainly can be cast with the 1930s documentary impulse, it is worth noting that professional historians were not universally sought to direct the processes of documentation, preservation, and interpretation of historical material in federal agencies or programs. Shambaugh's experience with the Federal Writers' Project in Iowa demonstrates that Becker's relativist approach to the study of history, although based in sophisticated philosophical theory, quickly devolved to the notion that almost anyone could write history.

World War II

World War II interrupted the work of historians in the NPS and ended the work of the WPA, but it provided a new imperative for contemporaneous documentation of military operations and war mobilization. In March 1942 Franklin Roosevelt ordered all executive departments and agencies to preserve wartime records. To oversee this effort, the president established the Committee on Records of War Administration (reorganized as the Advisory Committee on War History in October 1943) with representatives from the AHA, the National Archives, the Library of Congress, the American Council of Learned Societies, the American Political Science Association, the American Society of Public Administration, and the Social Science Research Council. By war's end, approximately forty federal offices had established historical units or undertaken historical projects. These included special efforts to protect cultural treasures in war areas and public records in occupied territories.[18]

 Roosevelt's order to preserve wartime records had far-reaching effects in the military branches. World War II brought civilian scholars into service as military historians and, as a result, produced among military professionals a greater appreciation for the standards of scholarship observed by civilian historians. By and large, professional historians transformed "drum and trumpet" history into a respectable scholarly pursuit.

The navy responded to the order by calling up reservists with scholarly credentials in history. Secretary of the Navy James Forrestal also established a new history department, the Office of Naval History, which was merged in 1949 with the Office of Naval Records and Library to become the Naval Records and History Division.[19] Staff and command agencies throughout the War Department began collecting records to document the army's wartime activities. The Army General Staff created a new historical branch in the Intelligence Division, with a civilian scholar as chief historian. The Army Corps of Engineers also recruited civilian historians. Even though the corps' historical section went through an initial period of disorganization and produced little of value during the war years, the historical program survived and in 1946 became a separate historical office reporting directly to the chief of engineers.[20] Likewise, the Army Air

Forces established a historical division, which carried over when the air force became a separate military branch in 1949. The Joint Chiefs of Staff also established a history office during the war.[21]

In many respects, the careers of Maurice Matloff and Forrest Pogue exemplify the maturing of history scholarship in the military. Matloff had completed all but his dissertation at Harvard when he enlisted in the armed services, and he spent the last six months of his enlistment assigned to the Fourth Air Force Historical Headquarters in San Francisco. After the war, he joined the Historical Division of the War Department where he and other historians worked under the chief historian, Kent Roberts Greenfield (wartime head of the Army Ground Forces historical section and former chair of the history department at Johns Hopkins University), to write the history of the army in World War II. Matloff, who initially thought this might be a temporary position, ended up making his professional career as a civilian historian in the army, eventually succeeding Greenfield as chief historian.[22]

Matloff credited Franklin Roosevelt for issuing a blanket directive to all executive departments and agencies and Dwight D. Eisenhower for solidifying the army's history program at the end of the war. After Eisenhower became army chief of staff, he directed that "professional historians be given access to all the Army records of World War II, and be allowed to write the history; that they document it objectively, using the best standards in the historical profession; and that they be permitted to 'call the shots' as they saw them."[23]

World War II also shaped Forrest Pogue's career as a professional historian. After receiving his doctorate from Clark University in 1939, Pogue returned to his native state, Kentucky, to teach at Murray State Teachers College (now Murray State University). In 1942 he was drafted into the army where he, too, eventually ended up in the Historical Division of the War Department. After his tour of duty ended, Pogue continued to work as a civilian historian in the army until 1952. In 1956 he became director of the newly established George C. Marshall Research Foundation, where he remained for the next eighteen years. During that time he wrote the first three volumes of his biography of Marshall, completing the fourth volume after he went to the Smithsonian Institution to direct the Eisenhower Institute for Historical Research.[24]

"At the time," Pogue recalled years later, "government-sponsored history was not a professional thing to do. If you were assigned to do this in the army, well, it was a decent thing to do. But there was the great danger that you would become a propaganda agent for the army and that you would sell out to it." Pogue and other recent Ph.D.'s who spent their military time as historians, however, brought professional standards of scholarship with them. "I think it was a great thing that he [Kent Roberts Greenfield] was a professional historian. . . . And the field commanders stood by us when we took the point of view that we did not write history for the purpose of selling the army as an all-perfect organization."[25] Matloff concurs: "As for the significance and impact of the [seventy-eight-volume] Army series of World War II, I would suggest that it made official history respectable in the United States."[26]

The Postwar Era

When all the military branches were incorporated into the Department of Defense in 1947, the reorganization that followed extended to historical offices. In 1949 Louis Johnson established a historical office in the Office of the Secretary of Defense (OSD), which, since that time, has produced syntheses of national security policy as well as documentary collections detailing the department's institutional history. Civilian scholars under contract have written much of the history emanating from the OSD. The Joint Chiefs of Staff elevated history to a section in 1955 and three years later to the Historical Division in the Joint Secretariat's office. Since its inception, civilian historians have principally staffed the Historical Division.[27]

After World War II, certain functions of the Army War College Historical Section were merged into a new Historical Division of the War Department, which set to writing the official history of the army in World War II. Another reorganization took place in 1950, when the division became the Office, Chief of Military History (OCMH). Its functions included not only general reference, unit histories, and staff support but managing historic properties as well, and gradually expanded to include supervising the army's museums and art collections. In 1973, the OCMH was redesignated the Center of Military History (CMH), and publications increasingly focused on Cold War events and military-civilian concerns, specifically, civil defense and the integration of the armed forces. The Naval Records and History Division, renamed the Naval Historical Center in 1971, remained under the leadership of military professionals until the mid 1980s, when Secretary of the Navy John Lehman appointed the first civilian scholar as the director. This change was integral to Lehman's effort to shift naval history from reference works and a pre–twentieth-century focus to a broader program encompassing post–World War II narrative history, utilizing contract historians, and recognizing outside scholarship through grants and prizes. Historical programs in the air force likewise expanded after the Office of Air Force History was established in 1969. Command history programs predominate in the air force, providing historical information and analyses to support policy formation and planning. However, scholarly history directed at both military and public audiences has been a guiding principle, and for its vast output the air force relies heavily on civilian staff historians and on scholars who research and write under contract.[28]

In the post–World War II era, the number of historians in federal agencies other than the military branches also continued to grow. And, as the number of nonacademic professional historians increased, so did concern about the quality of their work. As Martin Reuss has observed, "There is some irony in this since academic historians and historical societies had been among the most outspoken advocates of government-sponsored history when federal historical programs were first being established."[29]

The importance of history was most evident in the NPS. The cadre of historians Chatelain helped to establish in the 1930s became, as Charles Hosmer has noted, "an elite guard of nationally minded preservationists. They were the first professional group to see the true scope of the federal program, and they quickly grasped the importance of bringing private historical organizations more strongly into the planning work being done by the federal government."[30] Movement in that direction took shape in 1947, when Ronald F. Lee, NPS chief historian, and Horace M. Albright, a former NPS director, came together with civic leaders outside the federal government—including George McAneny, president of the American Scenic and Historic Preservation Society; Christopher Crittenden, director of the North Carolina Department of Archives and History; historian-archivist Waldo G. Leland; and AHA executive secretary Guy Stanton Ford—to organize the National Council for Historic Sites and Buildings. The principal function of the council was to cultivate interest in and financial support for a proposed federally chartered body modeled after the British National Trust. This goal was met in October 1949 when Congress chartered the National Trust for Historic Preservation.[31]

Within the NPS itself, historians were busier than ever. Automobile

tourism swelled the number of park visitors, with a corresponding increase in the number of park historians, some of whom now were engaged
in site interpretation. NPS director Arthur E. Demaray also added park
administrative histories to the list of historians' responsibilities. Demaray's successor, Conrad Wirth, expanded the historical program even
more with MISSION 66, a ten-year development program that resulted in
new visitor centers; exhibits, leaflets, and other interpretive programs;
and a national historic landmarks program—all aimed at enhancing the
visitor experience.[32]

As MISSION 66 reached its sunset year, 1966, the NPS centralized its
history research program in Washington, D.C., under the administration

of chief historian Robert M. Utley. The same year, passage of the National
Historic Preservation Act (NHPA) vastly expanded the NPS's historic
preservation functions. Federal law established the principle that cultural
resources of state and local significance also were worthy of federal recognition and required federal agencies to consider the effects of their "un-
dertakings" (for example, highway construction, flood control, or urban
renewal projects) on historic and prehistoric resources. The NHPA triggered both expansion of and reorganization within the NPS. A new Office
of Archaeology and Historic Preservation oversaw the work of Utley's
History Division as well as the Archaeology Division, the Historic Architecture Division, and the National Register of Historic Places. Passage of
the 1969 National Environmental Policy Act and President Richard
Nixon's subsequent Executive Order 11593 firmly linked cultural resource
protection into the environmental review process. NPS archaeologists
and historians were increasingly called upon to implement and monitor
compliance with federal regulations requiring the identification and eval-
uation of cultural resources likely to be affected by federal, or federally
funded, development projects.[33]

Richard Hewlett and Wayne Rasmussen, like Forrest Pogue and Maurice Matloff, were veterans of World War II who went on to distinguished
careers as historians in federal agencies. Hewlett, after receiving his doctorate in history from the University of Chicago in 1952, went to work as
an intelligence specialist with the U.S. Air Force. A year later he accepted a
position with the U.S. Atomic Energy Commission (AEC). For the next
five years, as a program analyst in the Progress Reports and Statistics
Branch in the Division of Finance, he compiled and edited classified reports for the Joint Committee on Atomic Energy and the National Secu-

rity Council. Then, in 1957, Hewlett was appointed the AEC's first chief historian, and his initial assignment was to write a history of the commission. Acting on advice from Kent Roberts Greenfield, Hewlett fortified himself with a historical advisory committee and began writing scholarly history from his position within the agency. Hewlett continued to serve as chief historian of the Energy Research and Development Administration (ERDA), one of the two agencies (the Nuclear Regulatory Commission being the other) that succeeded the AEC in 1975, and of the Department of Energy (DOE), which superseded ERDA. During these years, he brought more historians into the agency and established a reputation for scholarly integrity, in part by publishing through university presses rather than the Government Printing Office.[34] When the Nuclear Regulatory Commission established its own history office in 1976, chief historian Roger Trask and his successors followed Hewlett's model.[35]

In 1939 Wayne Rasmussen began his career inauspiciously as a file clerk at the USDA, although he soon moved to the historical section of the Bureau of Agricultural Economics. At the same time, he pursued a doctorate at George Washington University as a part-time student. Drafted in 1942, he was assigned to the army's Psychological Warfare Division and then to the Information Control Office. After the war, he returned to graduate studies and his former position at the USDA. When Everett Edwards died in 1952, Rasmussen, in his words, "inherited" the position of chief historian. Unlike Richard Hewlett, Rasmussen also inherited a long-standing relationship between a professional organization, the Agricultural History Society, and the federal agency for which he worked. Therefore, he had relatively less difficulty building the UDSA's historical program into a policy-oriented research division. However, like Hewlett, he considered that the historian's primary responsibility was "to bring historical perspective to bear on current problems."[36]

David Trask also could be considered with this generation. Although born a bit too late to serve in World War II, Trask served two years in the army during the Korean War (1952–1954) between earning his M.A. and Ph.D. in history at Harvard. Through this army experience he developed an interest in foreign policy and military history that would later draw him into public service. Before he entered public service, however, he taught for eighteen years and wrote three major books on U.S. war aims and foreign relations during World War I. Then, in 1976, he left a full professorship at SUNY Stony Brook to direct the Office of the Historian at the U.S. Department of State. During the five years he served as director, his office researched and wrote several historical reports to provide needed background for managing the Iranian crisis that began in 1979. While this gave him an opportunity to demonstrate the efficacy of history, he also faced a major obstacle. On the decision-making side, he met "resistance to receiving advice that doesn't fit the desired policy." On the policy research side, he had difficulty finding historians "who are capable of doing this sort of thing, who are prepared to do it."[37] Frustrated by the experience, Trask moved on in 1981 to become chief historian of the CMH.

Hewlett, Rasmussen, and Trask stand out among historians in the federal government who sought to bring scholarly integrity to the civilian agencies they served and strove to demonstrate the value of history in policy formation at the highest levels. However, in the post–World War II decades, federal agencies, as they proliferated, also came to value history as a means to preserve and disseminate institutional memory: by collecting historical records, through oral history programs designed to capture transient information held by retiring employees, by researching and preparing commemorative exhibits and publications, and by developing public information materials. Consequently, more and more professional historians filtered into the federal bureaucracy, sometimes by ones and twos, sometimes in sizable numbers. The National Aeronautics and Space Administration established a history office in 1959, the Federal Aviation Administration in 1960, the Social Security Administration and the Department of Labor in 1962, the Food and Drug Administration in 1967, the Forest Service in 1971, and the National Science Foundation in 1972. Likewise, when the Smithsonian Institution added the Museum of History and Technology in 1964 (now the Museum of American History), it began employing professional historians to research, manage, and interpret its vast collections.[38]

Writing in the mid 1980s, Jack Holl noted that, after World War II, "a new, and impressive, national monument" developed around the Mall in Washington, D.C. Indeed, many of the buildings that line the mall are of post-1945 construction, but Holl referred not so much to the impressive architecture as he did to the increasing recognition given history and the value of historians in the federal government. "Almost unnoticed by the profession itself," he wrote, "the United States has created a monument to history perhaps without precedent in human history. The visible parts of the monument are familiar enough, the Smithsonian Institution, its museums and galleries, the National Archives, the Library of Congress, the United States Capitol, and the Supreme Court, along with Washington's public monuments and memorials. Less visible are the federal government's extensive historical programs."[39]

If historical conscientiousness is one mark of a maturing society, then World War II also is a convenient demarcation point for the advancement of professional history in the private sector. In the early 1940s the American Association of Museums identified eighty businesses with museum programs, usually small and typically staffed by retirees. At the same time, only one corporation had an archive. Scholars interested in studying the development of business and the U.S. economy were the first to call for corporations to preserve their records and make them available for research. Not surprisingly, however, business leaders did not find scholarly interest a compelling reason to do so. Wartime mobilization was the catalyst. During the late 1930s, Firestone Tire and Rubber Company engaged William D. Overman, then curator of history and archivist of the Ohio State Archaeological and Historical Society, to organize the papers of Harvey Firestone and his sons. The company's role in production for the war effort convinced Harvey Firestone Jr. that the company should be actively preserving all of its important records.[40] Consequently, in 1943 Firestone hired Overman as a permanent employee to establish the first professionally staffed corporate archive in the United States.[41]

The reason corporate museums preceded corporate archives is not hard to fathom. Internal museums provided a place to showcase the achievements of a company through the display of products and other business artifacts, a practice that could foster company pride and employee loyalty or that could demonstrate a tradition of progress and corporate stability to clients, customers, and investors. In other words, museums had public relations value. The need for archives, conversely, did not become apparent until the volume of accumulated records began to exceed the capacity of company records offices and libraries or until some critical event triggered an internal assessment of records management practices. Although preservation of records related to wartime production prompted Firestone Tire and Rubber to establish a formal corporate archive, Overman noted that Harvey Firestone Jr. had a broader goal of establishing a corporate memory bank that could be referenced for helping to solve day-to-day problems without reinventing the wheel and for long-range planning.[42] "At Coca-Cola," states Philip Mooney, "the need for documentation in a 1941 trademark case underscored the need for the formal maintenance of a historical collection."[43]

Although relatively few business firms immediately followed Firestone's lead by hiring a professional archivist, in the post–World War II era corporate executives slowly began to recognize the value of archives for preserving institutional memory, for commemorating anniversaries, for long-range planning and decision-making, and for legal purposes. INA Corporation, a predecessor of CIGNA; Time, Inc.; Armstrong Cork; Alcoa; Lever Brothers; Eastman Kodak; Texaco; Ford Motor Company; Sears Roebuck; New York Life Insurance; Eli Lilly; Procter and Gamble; Coca-Cola; and Bank of America established archives during the 1940s and 1950s.[44] Larger firms, of course, had the resources to fund archival departments from overhead. By 1960, when the Society of American Archivists conducted the first systematic survey of business organizations in the United States, fifty-one respondents reported the existence of "business archives" or "business historical collections," a number that increased to nearly two hundred by 1975. This growth, however, did not immediately translate into substantially increased employment opportunities for professional historians; only about a third of these business archives were staffed by full-time archivists.[45] Moreover, professional archivists who did go to work for corporations were by and large individuals who "were interested in using archival resources to assist companies in meeting their current business needs; they were far from the business historians who wanted access to records in order to write scholarly articles and books."[46]

The American Association for State and Local History (AASLH) also found a larger general audience in the postwar era. *American Heritage*, launched in 1946 as a quarterly journal aimed at improving the teaching of state and local history, initially failed. After the AASLH changed the format in 1949 to a popular history magazine featuring articles written by well-known scholars, *American Heritage* found its niche; within five years circulation reached 20,000. Indeed, the magazine was so successful that demand outstripped the association's ability to handle production. In 1954 the AASLH transferred publication to a New York publishing firm.[47]

Although the popularity of *American Heritage* signaled widespread lay interest in history, its success did not translate into a broad-based, or significantly larger, AASLH membership. As George Rollie Adams has noted, "the 'hard core' of AASLH members had always consisted of the professionals of the large organizations. The Association had attracted relatively few members from academe or the public schools."[48] In search of a broader membership base, the AASLH hired a staff and pursued a dozen initiatives to increase its visibility, raise professional standards, publicize the work of historical organizations, and improve the quality of state and local history being taught in the schools. Although the AASLH was criticized from without for trying to be "all things to all people," leadership remained committed to a broad-front approach, believing, as William T. Alderson stated it in 1970, that state and local historical organizations "not only must serve the needs of scholars and researchers in studying the records of past events, but . . . also must bear the primary burden of helping the average citizen understand his heritage."[49]

Thus, by the early 1970s, historians were liberally scattered throughout federal agencies, historians were continuing to professionalize state historical organizations, and archivists were working in both private corporations and public institutions. The Society of American Archivists, the AASLH, the National Trust for Historic Preservation, and the American Association of Museums addressed the professional needs and issues of historians who worked in archives, in state and local historical organizations, in museums, and in agencies or organizations that cared for historic places.

Moreover, since the late 1930s a small number of history departments and historical institutions had developed specialized training programs in response to the profession's gradual expansion. In 1939 the history department at American University in Washington, D.C., began offering courses in archival administration that were linked with internships at the National Archives. Out of this collaborative effort grew the National Archives Summer Institute, which, since 1945, has been providing basic instruction in the principles and techniques of archival practice. In the 1950s the University of Delaware established professional museum training through the Winterthur Museum and the Hagley Foundation; Radcliffe College established a program in historical administration; and the Cooperstown Graduate Program began. In 1957 Colonial Williamsburg, in collaboration with the AASLH and the National Trust for Historic Preservation, established an annual Seminar for Historical Administrators.[50]

It is profoundly ironic that in 1973 Timothy Donovan could write that "if anything has characterized the re-examination of the generation since 1945, it has been a concern with the function and scope of historians and history," and yet discuss only the work of scholars in the academy.[51] By the mid 1970s, a critical mass of professional historians worked outside academe, and a few widely scattered colleges and universities were responding to changes in the professional landscape by offering courses or requiring internships to develop specific skills. However, by and large, historians had become a disparate lot. The time, then, was ripe for a movement that would attempt to cohere dispersion in the professional ranks, reconcile the alienation between academic and nonacademic historians, and forge a new professional identity.

The Modern Public History Movement Emerges

The University of California at Santa Barbara (UCSB) provided the impetus that began to coalesce new academic training programs with professionally dispersed historians to create the public history movement. In the mid 1970s Robert Kelley began to ponder his own experiences as a historian called upon to offer expert testimony in court cases and similar instances among historians who had lent their expertise to public service in national planning, policymaking, or court proceedings. This recognition, heightened by the reality of a shrinking academic market for history Ph.D.'s and a commensurate decline in history graduate students, led Kelley and G. Wesley Johnson, a UCSB colleague, to design a graduate program in public historical studies. Their intent was to create a method whereby the discipline of history could demonstrate its full potential to inform public processes. "We concluded," Kelley explained, "that the best method was to begin training small groups of graduate students in public history skills, imbuing them with the idea of a *public* rather than an *academic* career, and sending them out, one by one, to demonstrate their value by their work."[52]

In so doing, Kelley and Johnson were not concerned about identifying precedents or previous models that would demonstrate the value of public history training as they conceived it; they simply opened their eyes to the range of positions historians were holding and the contributions they were making outside the academy. Their outlook, at this stage, was confidently idealistic and elitist, much as Benjamin Shambaugh's had been. They observed that "people in positions of responsibility do not think historically, though they like to think that they do. . . . If, by sending young people out to take up careers in public history we slowly change this situation, so that the historical method of analysis becomes an integral element in all decision-making, we shall have made a signal contribution to American life."[53] In short, Kelley and Johnson defined the UCSB public historical studies program as "generalist" in scope, and they set out to train historians for leadership in many aspects of public life. Backed with funding from the Rockefeller Foundation and the National Endowment for the Humanities, the UCSB program admitted its first graduate students in fall 1976.

History departments elsewhere also had begun to push the curricular boundaries toward public history in the 1970s, and a few of them preceded UCSB's well-publicized program. In 1967 the University of Wisconsin–Madison began a graduate program in archival administration. Auburn University added an archival training program in 1972. In 1973 the University of California at Riverside established a graduate program in historic resources management; a year later, Middle Tennessee State University established a graduate program in historic preservation. Wright State University initiated a master's degree program in archival and historical administration in 1975; the University of South Carolina launched a program in history and archives in 1976. By 1980, nearly fifty colleges and universities were offering degree programs or course concentrations that loosely fit the broad category of "public history." More than a dozen of the public history programs hastily established in the 1970s have survived the test of time.[54]

Responding more directly to the second job crisis for Ph.D.'s seeking faculty positions, in 1976 the AHA, the Organization of American Historians (OAH), and several other associations representing professional historians united forces and formed the National Coordinating Committee for the Promotion of History, which quickly became known by its shortened acronym, NCC. Under the leadership of its first executive director, Arnita Jones, the NCC generated several goals and initiatives that were geared to promote and guide the "expand[ing] use of historians in government, business and other areas."[55] As part of this effort, a special Federal Government Resource Group, chaired by Richard Hewlett of the DOE, compiled a directory of more than 125 federal historical offices and programs, convened a conference of federal historians in September 1977, and began to press for higher qualifications to define the job classification of "historian" in the federal government.[56] After Ronald Reagan became president in 1981, administration attempts to undermine federal agencies responsible for implementing historical and cultural policies and programs led the NCC board to reassess its mission. Within a few years, the NCC, now under the direction of Page Putnam Miller, changed course "to become the central advocacy office in Washington for the historical and archival professionals."[57]

Other historians, vastly separated by geography yet purposely search-ing for alternatives to teaching, began charting new paths in several parts of the country. In 1974 Alan Newell established a private consulting firm, Historical Research Associates, "to take advantage of a particular opportu-nity to contract historical/legal work for the Omaha District of the Corps of Engineers" and at the same time stay in Montana.[58] In 1975 Darlene Roth and six other people, "most of them professional historians—who were curious about the business potential of historical research, and who were committed to the idea that historical evidence is relevant to all as-pects of public affairs, commerce, and government," founded The History Group, Inc., a for-profit corporation based in Atlanta, Georgia.[59] A year later, in New York, more than seventy historians, most of them women, organized the Institute for Research in History as a not-for-profit corpora-tion. Their intent was to create an "independent community of scholars" operating from a common institutional base and organized internally into research groups focused on particular lines of inquiry. Some groups un-dertook research projects with outside funding, while others functioned as seminar or study groups.[60] On the West Coast, another band of histori-ans adopted the not-for-profit model and incorporated as the Institute for Historical Study, based in San Francisco.[61]

In the fall of 1978 the UCSB public historical studies program launched the *Public Historian* as a quarterly journal, a move that began to codify the term "public history." The UCSB then convened the first national confer-ence on public history in April 1979 at a historic retreat in the Montecito foothills above Santa Barbara. The Montecito conference, three days of high-energy roundtables and informal gatherings, hardly resembled a tra-ditional academic conference. More than eighty participants shared infor-mation about new and expanding opportunities for historians in the pub-lic and private sectors and new training programs for graduate and undergraduate students in universities across the country. Out of this con-ference came a steering committee with the self-appointed task of orga-nizing a second conference on public history and creating a national or-ganization to sustain the momentum generated at Montecito.[62]

Two extraordinary forces at work in the historical profession met in

Washington, D.C., on 13–14 September 1979: newly energized professional historians working in federal agencies and the public history steering committee formed at the Montecito conference. The federal historians met at the DOE's Forrestal Building on 13 September; the public history steering committee met at the National Archives on 14 September. Although the attendees at both meetings overlapped to a degree and common concerns drew them to Washington, there was enough difference of purpose to keep the two groups from merging. As a result, the Society for Historians in the Federal Government and the National Council on Public History emerged simultaneously.

The Society for Historians in the Federal Government was conceived, in part, as a reaction to governmental reorganization under the Richard Nixon and Jimmy Carter administrations, which threatened, in particular, to undermine the historical program established by the former AEC; as of 1978, the program began idling in Carter's new DOE. "Unintentionally," as Jack Holl explains, "our efforts to remain pertinent to the Department of Energy led us into the mainstream of the public history movement."[63] Litigation instigated by civilian victims of radiation exposure from nuclear weapons testing and the near-meltdown of a nuclear reactor at Three Mile Island in March 1979 suddenly transformed the DOE history office into the central repository for official records and the control center to handle requests for documentary information. In order to manage these added responsibilities, continue work on the history of the AEC, and undertake a new project to write the history of the Three Mile Island crisis, the DOE history office intensified its search for historians to work under contract. Responding to these emergencies brought DOE historians face-to-face with a number of harsh realities: there were few professional historians willing or prepared to work as contractors, and there were no agreed-upon professional standards for contract history. At the same time, DOE historians, along with David Trask at the State Department, were centrally involved in the effort to rally colleagues in other federal agencies. This led to an initial conference of federal historians in 1978 that especially drew younger historians in search of a cohesive professional identity and who were ready to organize. Two hundred federal historians unanimously endorsed a proposal to do so at the 13 September 1979 meeting, and the Society for History in the Federal Government was born.[64]

The next day, the public history steering committee met to discuss an appropriate form of organization for the diverse constituencies of the burgeoning public history movement: government historical offices, for-profit and not-for-profit historical research organizations, historical societies, museums, public and corporate archives, academic training programs, and hard-to-categorize professional niches such as those exemplified by Robert Pomeroy, an adviser for the Inter-American Bank, and Keith Berwick, a pioneer in history and media. The committee settled on a model analogous to the American Council of Learned Societies, an organizational form that lent itself to coordinating the activities of member constituencies with those of the major historical associations. Thus the National Council on Public History was born.[65]

In 1979 public history asserted itself boldly into the consciousness of the historical profession. The movement was brash, brim-full with optimism, and headed in several directions at once. Many people feared that a separate organization of federal historians would undermine the fragile public history movement by dividing energies and vision needed to sustain momentum and create direction. But that did not happen. "Indeed," as Jack Holl observed twenty years later, "we succeeded in mobilizing many young federal historians who had not previously been active in professional affairs. Rather than dividing the profession, our movement brought federal historians into the main-line of public history discourse."[66]

But the "main-line of public history discourse" often resembled cacophony more than orderly dialogue in the early years. The National Council on Public History soon evolved from a loosely defined council into a member organization as it became clear that individuals, more than constituent groups, were embracing the idea of public history. Despite an uncertain future for the National Council on Public History and for the dozens of public history programs that had sprung up by 1980, the public history movement received a measure of respect from one of the two major professional associations when in 1981 the OAH created a Committee on Public History. This development not only signaled recognition by a mainstream professional association, it also inaugurated a measure of cooperation among professional associations that has increased steadily over the years.[67]

Reflections on the Maturing Process

The public history movement of the last three decades has been, and remains, a complex phenomenon, the silhouette of which still seems amorphous. It is not the purpose of this chapter to weave the strands that give the movement breadth or to trace the contours of controversy and change. Rather, it is an attempt to understand the public history movement in relation to the changing identity of professional historians in the twentieth century and to assess Benjamin Shambaugh's particular role in that process. It seems clear that the movement has been an influential force in the discipline as a whole in at least two areas. First, the public history movement kindled a healthy debate on professionalism and professional ethics. Second, the movement has caused historians to reconsider the bounds of historical scholarship.

The for-profit organization of Historical Research Associates and The History Group, Inc. quickly proved to be an alluring prospect for historians with established credentials and aspiring newcomers who had one thing in common: an urge to chart a truly new professional path. The first *Directory of Historical Consultants*, published by the NCC in 1981, listed approximately thirty individuals or firms. Many more joined the stream of private consultants in the ensuing years, and most if not all were unprepared for the harsh realities of the business world. Nonetheless, the pioneering firms that were successful proved there was a real demand for professional historical services in the private sector. In addition to Historical Research Associates and The History Group, survivors of the first wave include History Associates Inc., founded in 1980 by Philip Cantelon, Richard Hewlett, Robert Williams, and Rodney Carlisle; Jackson Research Projects, founded in 1982 by W. Turrentine Jackson, a professor of history at the University of California at Davis, and two of his graduate students; and PHR Associates, founded in 1982 by three graduates of the UCSB public historical studies program.[68]

Although the directors of the UCSB program took pride in fostering a sense of entrepreneurship in their students, history-for-profit raised eyebrows in the historical profession as a whole. It challenged an implicit assumption, shared by many, that public history was somehow integrally linked to public service, public affairs, or public benefit. Many were uncomfortable with the implications of creating history work products for the marketplace. More than anything else, the emergence of private historical consulting firms forced a spirited debate on professional ethics. Private consultant Darlene Roth was among the first to raise the question of a code of ethics for public historians based on situations The History Group encountered during its first two years of business.[69]

The Oral History Association, the American Association of Museums, and the Society of American Archivists had struggled with questions of ethics long before "public history" entered the lexicon; by 1980, these groups had issued guidelines for ethical practices in, respectively, oral history, museums, and archives. Their guidelines certainly served to reinforce a sense of responsibility among professionals working in museums, archives, and larger, institution-based oral history programs. The fact that historians were working for clients, that is, practicing history outside familiar institutional settings, nonetheless raised fears that rogues and bumblers in the profession would compromise, if not undermine, the central canon of historical inquiry: objectivity, or the disinterested pursuit of knowledge. Thus, as Ted Karamanski has noted, the question of ethics quickly "blossomed into a critique of public history."[70]

Much of the debate over professional ethics took place in the pages of the *Public Historian*, although the journal was by no means the only forum.[71] Other developments raised the level of concern about ethics and advocacy during the early 1980s, most notably the publicity surrounding *Equal Employment Opportunity Commission v. Sears, Roebuck, & Co.*, an important affirmative action lawsuit that pitted well-known historians against one another as expert witnesses. However, historians engaged in private practice and employed by private companies, augmented by the growing number of historians working in government agencies, unwittingly became the catalyst that enjoined calls to redefine historical professionalism. Indeed, because public historians had a decided tendency to identify themselves as "professional" historians, academicians raised the question of whether history was a "profession" or a time-honored "learned discipline."[72]

Public historians by and large found this question irrelevant. They knew they were engaged in historical inquiry, using the same knowledge and methods as their academic counterparts; more often than they wanted, public historians were finding themselves in complicated situations that demanded professional standards of conduct to buttress their own personal codes of ethics. Very little in their graduate courses of study had prepared public historians for the ethical challenges they faced outside the halls of academe. Matters practical and immediate drove the California Committee for the Promotion of History (CCPH) to adopt "Standards of Professional Conduct" in October 1984, a document that was coupled with the CCPH Register of Professional Historians, a formal registry of historians who agreed in writing to abide by these standards. Later that same year, the Society for History in the Federal Government adopted its own "Principles and Standards for Federal Historical Programs." The following April, the National Council on Public History approved "Ethical Guidelines for the Historian," a succinct document that "established general principles to govern the conduct of researchers and professionals."[73] These formal statements did little to mollify critics who were convinced that public history was the slippery slope to professional prostitution, but they did signify that public historians were serious in their claim to professionalism.[74]

Another debate emerged about what constituted "public history," and the definition question has never been answered satisfactorily, although Karamanski has consistently insisted that "ethical service is at the heart of our [public historians'] definition of history as a profession."[75] Even so, it is this debate, which waxes and wanes, that echoes the difficulty Benjamin Shambaugh faced when he introduced the term "applied history." But more than this, the reality of a marketplace for history has complicated the definition question, something Shambaugh never faced.

The first sentence of the inaugural issue of the *Public Historian* invited debate by declaring that the historical profession had just witnessed "the birth of a new field" defined not by subject area but by training in team research and some intangibles that were vaguely set forth as entrepreneurship, pragmatism, and "professional competence . . . beyond the world of the educator."[76] In the same issue, Robert Kelley defined public history not as a new field but as "the employment of historians and the historical method outside of academia" and justified the "public" half of the term by asserting that "Public Historians are at work whenever, in their professional capacity, they are part of the public process."[77] Since the only concrete dimension of this initial, and uncoordinated, effort to define public history was the employment of historians in positions other than teaching, this aspect, coupled with the tight market for Ph.D.'s seeking faculty positions, helped to establish public history as little more than a timely solution to the discipline's second job crisis. For instance, in *The Past Before Us* (1980), an important summary of the state of historical scholarship at the time, "public history" is cross-referenced with "employment problems" in the index. Editor Michael Kammen remarked that "insofar as historians do make themselves useful to society and find employment outside of academe, they not only help to counteract the job crisis for new Ph.D.'s but help to demonstrate the imperative of historical perspective as well."[78]

The lack of a compelling definition clearly distinguishing public history within the discipline as a whole also opened the door to skepticism from the academic community; when greeted by a lack of professional deference, public historians responded defensively. As many have observed, a kind of status anxiety beset public historians. More important, the lack of a unifying definition led those who identified themselves as public historians to disagree among themselves about what the term signified. Some, like Joel Tarr, equated public history with applied history and insisted that both were here to stay, not because of the job crisis but "because of their intellectual nature as concepts." In words that would have had a familiar ring to Shambaugh, Tarr defined applied history as "an approach to using history" to address the problems of contemporary society. Tarr further defined applied history as a derivative of the new social history "in that it tries to use social science methodology, mainly in terms of approaching contemporary policy problems rather than investigating history generally."[79] Thus, just as Shambaugh had tried in 1910 to explain applied history as an extension of the New History associated with the progressive era, Tarr's updated concept linked applied history with the new social history that emerged in the 1960s.

Still others tried to define public history in terms of purpose, of which there could be more than one. For instance, one could define public history as history in the public arena for the purpose of policy- or decisionmaking. Alternatively, if public consumption was the purpose, one could define public history as interpreting history for the general public. Or if profit was the purpose, as in privately owned historical consulting firms, somehow the word "public" just did not seem to fit.[80] The latter, in particular, allowed critics to charge that "much of what went under the name of 'public history' was in fact 'private history'" and to dismiss almost as imposters those historians who worked "in the service of government agencies, businesses, or other organizations with very particularist agendas inconsistent with universalist norms of disinterested objectivity."[81]

Historians who considered themselves in the mainstream of the new social history movement challenged the narrow construction of public history as applied history by asking an important question: *who* constituted the public in public history?[82] This critique, advanced chiefly through the *Radical History Review*, broadened the link between public history and the new social history in terms of activism at the grassroots level.[83] The radical critique posited that the public also included the mass of ordinary people and compelled public historians to consider the purposes of history not just in terms of policy-making or public consumption or profit but also in terms of public good or social purpose and, more specifically, empowering ordinary people and communities to understand their roles in shaping the broad patterns of history. Among other things, this had the effect of introducing the critical aspect of *audience* into the definitional mix, but more than that, the radical critique raised questions, as Ronald Grele so eloquently phrased it, "that go to the heart of the uses of history in the culture and the processes by which historical consciousness is formed and expressed."[84] Several historians subsequently began to pursue a rich area of inquiry into the relationships between history and the process of memory as well as the relationships between scholarship and public discourse.[85] Beginning in the late 1980s, theoretical works in this vein influenced public history as practiced and as taught, but they did not produce an overwhelming desire to revisit the definition question.

Rather, the majority of public historians gravitated to a definitional gray area and stayed there. Ernest May once said that he saw "no earthly reason" to define public history by linking it to anything, noting "that for the pursuit of scholarship, research and publication, there are many places outside of academia that are better bases."[86] This was a liberating notion that enabled the movement to skirt the knotty problem of definition. But because public history is not a term that explains itself, a working definition of sorts developed whereby public history more or less became a big tent accommodating the pursuit or practice or use of history outside the academy for diverse purposes.

It would be easy to dismiss this lack of interest in definitions as reflective of public history's practical nature: after all, there were more important issues to draw concern and provide common rallying ground in the early years. However, the radical critique, for all of its intellectual probity, also exhibits an unmistakable disdain for historians who practice in the murky world of "economic interests" and has sought to assert that *people's history* is public history's highest calling. In addition, the job crisis lengthened into a perennial shortfall of academic positions to absorb history Ph.D.'s. This made it difficult in the eyes of many to define public history convincingly as anything but a rearguard action to rescue the historical profession from the brink of extinction. In 1980 Joan Hoff bluntly told academicians that in order to save the profession they needed to trim the training period for Ph.D.'s and emphasize technical skills, such as editing, quantitative analysis, and archival techniques, that would prepare doctoral graduates for nonacademic employment.[87]

Practically speaking, public history degree programs, as defined broadly, are the only history programs where professional training is an integral part of graduate study, but the job market has so far dictated an emphasis on training at the master's, not the doctoral, level. As a result, public historians generally have become viewed as the working class in the larger community of historians, a factor that perhaps contributes to the tendency among those who have graduated from public history programs to assume job classification titles as their primary identity: curator, education director, interpretive specialist, collections manager, and so forth.

Despite all the inroads public historians have made inside as well as outside the academy, the public history movement has not produced a unifying agenda or an agreed-upon definition. This is a serious concern because the shape and boundaries of public history remain unfathomed by members of the historical profession as a whole, not to mention the general public. As Arnita Jones observed in 1999, "Press most historians today for a definition of public history and you are much more likely to be given as an example the work of Barbara Fields, who advised Ken Burns on his film history of the Civil War, than cultural and environmental impact studies written under contract for the U.S. Army Corps of Engineers; more apt to hear about Eric Foner's work on *A House Divided* for the Chicago Historical Society than institutional histories written for the Department of Energy or AT&T." In short, many historians view the hard-to-characterize realm of public history much more narrowly as "public programming in history." [88]

Jones attributes the tendency to recast public history as "public programming in history" to four developments beginning in the 1960s that have changed society, the discipline of history, and institutions of higher learning. First, she notes a steadily increasing public demand for historical interpretation that is packaged, in varying degrees, as entertainment: film and video, living history interpretations, historical reenactments, and interactive exhibits. Growing demand has been matched, if not preceded, by increased funding for the humanities from public agencies, most notably the National Endowment for the Humanities, and from private foundations. Third, just as institutions of higher learning have pruned budgets and faculty in response to financial constraints that result from widespread fiscal and social conservatism, so, too, have they reoriented the mission of higher education to include a greater degree of outreach and public service. Finally, Jones argues that "public history programming has found a congenial companion in the now not-so-new social history, one of the key intellectual developments of American history" since the 1960s.[89]

At least two more factors must be considered. First, by failing to construct a compelling definition of public history at the outset, public historians have been left with no unifying identity other than "historian." This may seem like nothing more than a truism, but it has opened the way for academicians to recast public history as "public programming in history." Because public history has been defined inconsistently, it has been easier for academicians to ignore those who seem to them to be operating on the fringes, that is, those who practice history in the private sector and, even more so, those entrepreneurs who produce historical work products for clients. To come to the point, defining public history as "public programming in history" conveniently avoids sticky ethical issues that come with the joining of history and the marketplace. Avoidance is appealing because it allows history departments to ignore the need to incorporate professional ethics into graduate degree programs in a meaningful way. It also enables public historians to avoid an uncomfortable dialogue on the eviltwin issue of professional ethics: professional certification.[90] One can presume that historians who engage in public programming activities abide by the implicit canons of the profession. One can only hope that historians engaged in private enterprise abide by these canons.

Second, there is a long tradition of public service within the historical profession, although the tenure and promotion system has relegated service to the position of least value in the academy. Even so, since the turn of the twentieth century historians have been advocating the utility of history in society at large, although relatively few of them actually wrestled with the practicalities of transforming advocacy into action. Benjamin Shambaugh stands as an early example of one who consciously and repeatedly attempted to figure out just how history could be made useful to society at large. But if few progressive historians ventured beyond advocacy into the shaky ground of applied history during the early decades of the 1900s, academic tradition has always mandated that scholars contribute to the greater good of society through public service. This is professional territory with which historians, and humanists in general, are familiar; it is precisely this turf that public historians within the academy, that is, those who teach in public history programs, have groomed to establish greater credibility for public history, and themselves, among their academic colleagues. "Public historians," Ted Karamanski has asserted, "are the service arm of the history profession. Our work makes history complete as a field. Through public history, the moral goals of the profession are translated into social good."[91]

If the public history movement has not generated a sustained dialogue on ethics in the profession, it has contributed greatly to a reassessment of what constitutes historical scholarship.[92] Public historians within the academy have been a strong voice for expanding the research criterion of tenure and promotion guidelines to include many of the intellectual pursuits that tend to be relegated to the least-valued service criterion: museum exhibits, technical reports, documentary films and videos, and other tangible manifestations of historical research and analysis that can be subjected to peer review. Indeed, the admonishment that public historians must heed the canons of good scholarship has been met by a reciprocal demand that the academy take steps to reward faculty members for their public scholarship and to integrate public scholarship into historiography courses.[93]

Reassessing the nature of historical scholarship within the narrow confines of the academic reward system has had the effect of blurring the lines between research and service and, in the process, elevating "public programming in history" to a higher status. If it is still beneath the epitome of research codified in refereed scholarly journals and in books published by university presses, "public programming in history" nonetheless ranks higher than service on departmental and university committees or on the boards of historical organizations. In short, the notion of public history as "public programming in history" comfortably fulfills the imperative of utilizing history for social good. More to the point, it extends a reward benefit to every member of a history faculty, not just to the public historians among them. It also tends to ignore scholarship for which a historian has received payment, especially if it is from a private funding source. Despite assertions that "historians are professionals who *ought* to be paid for their expertise without prejudicing the merit of their work in the eyes of their colleagues," professional deference in the academy often does not extend this far.[94]

Patricia Mooney-Melvin has argued forcefully that it is the whole profession of history that needs redefinition, not just the nature of historical scholarship. She characterizes public history as a pioneer force leading the way: an "organizing principle" that has drawn together "those who were already employed as historians in nonacademic settings, historians who believed in the importance of communication with a broader public, [and] those individuals interested in pursuing history as a career but not inside the academy." The employment crisis of the 1970s, she notes, led historians seated in the academy to accept the practicality of public history because it provided a kind of legitimacy for alternative, or nonteaching, careers for their students. However, there has been steadfast reluctance to reconceptualize professional identity to incorporate the "dynamic combination of historical training, expansion of traditional notions of locale and audience, and service to society" that the public history movement has brought to the profession.[95] Mooney-Melvin stops short of offering her own concept of a new professional identity, but, like many, she has grown tired of the persistent artifice that divides "academic" and "public" historians as though they were two distinct races of the species.

After a century that witnessed a tremendous expansion of the professional practice of history—alongside a narrowing definition of the historical profession itself—it is clear that some sort of reassessment of professional identity is under way. The public history movement has at the very least proved the inadequacy of a professional identity that admits only those historians who increase knowledge through research and writing and who transmit knowledge through teaching and scholarly publication. In the footsteps of Benjamin Shambaugh, public historians have demonstrated that the methods and knowledge of history should, and can, be applied to serve society in multitudinous ways. But the public history movement has done more than advance Shambaugh's concepts of applied history and commonwealth history. The intellectual currents of the new social history have melded into public history an attitude that embraces a respect for audience, whether defined narrowly or broadly, and an awareness that historians outside the academy do not possess exclusive rights to interpret the past but share authority with the public in the process of doing so. In addition, problem-oriented and client-defined research has forced public historians to pursue an expansive range of research questions. The gray literature of public history defies easy categorization, and it cannot be equated with or contained in the same manner as scholarly monographs. Nonetheless, in the avalanche of work products that pour from public historical scholarship, there are significant contributions of knowledge and interpretation. Finally, the enterprising spirit of public history, the willingness of public historians to push the boundaries of historical scholarship into the marketplace, has fostered a new kind of pride in the value of history in society at large. All these elements must be forged into a professional identity that is inclusive. If I may return for a moment to this book's opening metaphor, it is time to get back on the floor, together, and dance.

Back to Benjamin

Benjamin Shambaugh would have felt at home in much of the modern public history movement. Indeed, his own career enfolded many of the elements we now associate with public history: policy analysis, heritage education, public programming, historic preservation and cultural resources management, archival collections and management, institutional history, and historical administration. In his own time, he was a leader in pushing the boundaries of historical inquiry and practice. Although he might be astonished by the changes that have taken place in the practice of history since World War II, Shambaugh most assuredly would be pleased that the boundaries of historical scholarship have been expanded beyond anything he envisioned and that the imperative he felt—an obligation to make history serve society—eventually assumed the proportions of a widespread movement in the historical profession.

There is also much in the modern public history movement that would seem foreign to him. He did not, like Carl Becker, possess an innate respect for "Everyman," and he might find troubling the concept of shared authority in the interpretive process. To Shambaugh, the historian pursued accuracy and objectivity and communicated history to an educated, or at least educable, audience. Shambaugh's own examination of the "processes by which historical consciousness is formed and expressed," to recapitulate Ronald Grele, appears to have led him to the conclusion, by the early 1930s, that he could serve society more effectively by focusing on the process of molding a humanistic consciousness in malleable students.

It was not until the 1930s, when the locus of historical activity outside academe shifted from the state to the federal level, that Shambaugh seems to have felt alienated from, or perhaps adrift in, the historical profession as a whole. Most assuredly, academicians turned away from state and local history and largely ignored historians practicing in the larger public arena. In this respect, the AHA, which by now spoke almost exclusively for academic historians, was unavailable to advocate on behalf of those who found jobs in federal agencies or to effectively coordinate federally funded historical programs with the loose network of professionals working in state and local history. Shambaugh's consternation with the disorganization and disinterest in scholarship that he found in the Federal Writers' Project mirrors the disintegration of the historical profession. He watched it happen, and he would understand completely the exasperation that public historians often express, or at least feel, with respect to their academic colleagues.

Above all, Shambaugh would undoubtedly find it amusing that the origin of public history is persistently ascribed to a so-called job crisis. At the same time, he might be surprised to find historians employed by private corporations, except perhaps in archival positions, and even more surprised to discover that "history business" is not a transposition. The idea of a marketplace for history would probably give him pause, and it is difficult to know how he would reconcile his strong attachment to the ideal of public service with the unpredictable demands of business clients. The best clue to how he might resolve this dilemma comes from the political maneuvers that drove him to invent applied history from the New History. This is to say that Shambaugh understood that if historians maintained professional control over the uses of history in society, they could assure that history did indeed serve society. In this respect, he probably would counsel professional historians, through the many organizations that now speak for them, to maintain a united front.

Given the thought that Shambaugh invested in crafting and defining "applied history," he would, I suspect, be fully engaged in the definition question. However, he might be troubled by the recurring debate on professional ethics; such a debate would have been unthinkable in his day. Like Karamanski, he believed ethical service to be at the heart of professionalism. Service was something that he did not take for granted or view as a minor requirement for tenure and promotion, but he considered it as an obligation to society. To be sure, he could be high-minded about the purposes of applied history, but he never allowed his dedication to serving the commonwealth assume the proportions of unquestioning nationalism or a disregard for professional standards.

The practice of history and the boundaries of historical inquiry expanded greatly in the twentieth century, and Shambaugh was a major contributor to that expansion for the first thirty years of it. However, for reasons that remain hard to fathom, the sense of professional identity cultivated by the major historical organizations did not reflect the changes that took place in the profession as a whole; in the process of excluding amateur historians, the arbiters of professionalism narrowed the bounds of professional identity so much that other colleagues were left sitting on the sidelines. If there is a benefit in the twisted evolution of the profession from Shambaugh's applied history to the present, it is that the modern public history movement has opened the way for historians to reassess the nature of historical scholarship and the definition of professional identity.

Abbreviations and Shortened References

AHA Annual Report	*Annual Report of the American Historical Association*
AHR	*American Historical Review*
AI	*Annals of Iowa*
APSR	*American Political Science Review*
IHR	*Iowa Historical Record*
IJHP	*Iowa Journal of History and Politics*
MVHR	*Mississippi Valley Historical Review*
PH	*Public Historian*
SHSI	State Historical Society of Iowa
SHSW	State Historical Society of Wisconsin
Shambaugh Correspondence	State Historical Society of Iowa Archives, Benjamin F. Shambaugh Correspondence, SHSI, Iowa City
Shambaugh Papers	Shambaugh Family Papers, University of Iowa Libraries, Special Collections, Iowa City
Thwaites Papers	Papers of Reuben Gold Thwaites, State Historical Society of Wisconsin, Madison

Notes

Foreword and Acknowledgments

1. Alan M. Schroder, "Applied History: An Early Form of Public History," *Public Works Historical Society Newsletter* 17 (March 1980), 3–4. Schroder has also written of Shambaugh's contributions to western history; see Alan M. Schroder, "Benjamin F. Shambaugh" in *Historians of the American Frontier*, ed. John R. Wunder (Westport, Conn.: Greenwood Press, 1988), 611–623.

2. Peter N. Stearns and Joel A. Tarr, "Applied History: New/Old Frontier for the Historical Discipline," *Institute News: Newsletter of the North Carolina Institute of Applied History* 1:3 (October 1982): 6–9.

3. Stanley R. Ridgeway, "Democratic Individualism, Expertise, and the Public Interest: The Legacy of the Commonwealth Conference," *AI* 50 (1990): 359–374.

4. Mary possesses an intimate knowledge of Bertha Horack Shambaugh's photographs and papers, and she has published two outstanding books on historical images and Iowa history; see Mary Bennett, *An Iowa Album: A Photographic History of Iowa, 1860–1920* (Iowa City: University of Iowa Press, 1990), and Mary Bennett and Paul C. Juhl, *Iowa Stereographs: Three-dimensional Visions of the Past* (Iowa City: University of Iowa Press, 1997).

5. Alan M. Schroder, *History, Analysis and Recommendations Concerning the Public Programs of the Iowa State Historical Department, Division of the State Historical Society* (Iowa City: SHSI, 1981).

6. Paper shortages during World War II would have delayed publication, in which case it also is possible that Swisher's effort was eclipsed by Nellie Slayton Aurner's brief work, *Benjamin Franklin Shambaugh* (Iowa City: University of Iowa Press, 1947), which the university published as part of its Centennial Memoirs.

7. Biographical data taken from "In Memory of Jacob Swisher," SHSI *News for Members* 29:3 (fall 1976): 3–4.

8. John Ely Briggs, "This Book," in *Benjamin Franklin Shambaugh As Iowa Remembers Him: In Memoriam,* [ed. John Ely Briggs] (Iowa City: SHSI, 1941), 5.

Prologue

1. Herbert B. Adams, "Report of the Proceedings of Thirteenth Annual Meeting of the American Historical Association," *AHA Annual Report for 1897*, 3–4.

2. Peter Novick, *That Noble Dream: The "Objectivity Question" and the American Historical Profession* (Cambridge: Cambridge University Press, 1988), 87–88.

3. Magali Sarfatti Larson, *The Rise of Professionalism: A Sociological Analysis* (Berkeley and Los Angeles: University of California Press, 1977).

4. Novick, *That Noble Dream*, 47–60.

5. Morey Rothberg, introduction to *John Franklin Jameson and the Development of Humanistic Scholarship in America, Volume One: Selected Essays*, ed. Morey Rothberg and Jacqueline Goggin (Athens: University of Georgia Press, 1993), xxvii–liii. See also Morey D. Rothberg, "The Brahmin as Bureaucrat: J. Franklin Jameson at the Carnegie Institution of Washington, 1905–1928," *PH* 8:4 (fall 1986): 47–60.

6. Laurence Veysey, "Plural Organized Worlds of the Humanities" in *The Organization of Knowledge in Modern America, 1860–1920*, ed. Alexandra Oleson and John Voss (Baltimore: Johns Hopkins University Press, 1979), 58, 61.

7. Veysey, "Plural Organized Worlds," 65–66.

8. John Higham, *History: Professional Scholarship in America* (Baltimore: Johns Hopkins University Press, 1965), 68–72.

9. Veysey, "Plural Organized Worlds," 76–78.

10. On memory and the politics of public history in the twentieth century, see Michael Kammen, *Mystic Chords of Memory* (New York: Knopf, 1991); David Glassberg, *American Historical Pageantry: The Uses of Tradition in the Early Twentieth Century* (Chapel Hill: University of North Carolina Press, 1990); John Bodnar, *Remaking America: Public Memory, Commemoration, and Patriotism in the Twentieth Century* (Princeton, N.J.: Princeton University Press, 1992); and John Gillis, ed., *Commemorations: The Politics of National Identity* (Princeton, N.J.: Princeton University Press, 1994).

11. Rothberg, introduction to *Jameson*, xxxvii.

12. See Michael C. Scardaville, "Looking Backward Toward the Future: An Assessment of the Public History Movement," *PH* 9:4 (fall 1987): 35–43, for an earlier assessment of the multidimensional origins of the historical profession and the subsequent narrowing of professional identity in the twentieth century.

13. Novick, *That Noble Dream*, 52.

14. Leland L. Sage notes that "few Midwestern states could match the Iowa story in one-party domination [Republican] over a forty-year period" stretching from 1892 to 1932. One-party domination might have squelched political activity in another era, but as Sage further notes, "the state took a prominent place, probably just behind Wisconsin, in the standpat-progressive conflicts which were the dominant feature of state and national politics in the early 1900s." Moreover, so

many Iowa Republicans held important posts in the presidential administrations of William McKinley and Theodore Roosevelt or controlled congressional committees that "it was commonly said to those who wanted something from the federal government, 'Ask Iowa!'" See Leland L. Sage, *A History of Iowa* (Ames: Iowa State University Press, 1974), 220, 222, and esp. 216–248.

15. Frank Friedel, "The Iowa Progressive Tradition and National Achievements," in *Three Progressives from Iowa: Gilbert N. Haugen, Herbert C. Hoover, Henry A. Wallace*, ed. John N. Schacht (Iowa City: Center for the Study of the Recent History of the United States, 1980), 66.

16. These biographical details appear in many obituaries and eulogies; see, for instance, *AHR* 45 (1940): 1007; *APSR* 34 (1941): 556–557; Ruth A. Gallaher, "Benjamin F. Shambaugh," *IJHP* 38 (1940): 227–233; and John Ely Briggs, "Benj. F. Shambaugh," *Palimpsest* 21 (1940): 133–139.

1. From the New History to Applied History

1. E[arle] W. Dow, "Features of the New History: Apropos of Lamprecht's 'Deutsche Geschichte,'" *AHR* 3 (1898): 431–448.

2. Eggleston was then in declining health and died two years later in 1902. Arthur M. Schlesinger noted that the self-educated Eggleston did not particularly identify with the scientific aspects of the New History, but he was passionately driven to understand the social and cultural history of America and to present his work with literary style. Eggleston, a prolific writer throughout his life, is best known for *The Beginnings of a Nation* (1896) and *The Transit of Civilization from England to America in the Seventeenth Century* (1900). See Arthur M. Schlesinger, introduction to *The Transit of Civilization from England to America in the Seventeenth Century*, by Edward Eggleston (1900; reprint, Gloucester, Mass.: Peter Smith, 1972), vii–xix.

3. Edward Eggleston, "The New History," *AHA Annual Report for 1900*, vol. 1, 37–47.

4. Ibid., 38–43, 47.

5. Higham, *History*, 108, 115–116; Novick, *That Noble Dream*, 21–46; Phyllis K. Leffler and Joseph Brent, *Public and Academic History: A Philosophy and Paradigm* (Malabar, Fla.: Krieger, 1990), 33–42; Joyce Appleby, Lynn Hunt, and Margaret Jacob, *Telling the Truth About History* (New York: W. W. Norton, 1994), 72–76.

6. Novick, *That Noble Dream*, 87–88; Higham, *History*, 112–113.

7. Frederick Jackson Turner, "The Significance of the Frontier in History," *AHA Annual Report for 1893*, 199–227.

8. Frederick Jackson Turner, "The Significance of History," in *Frontier and Section: Selected Essays of Frederick Jackson Turner*, ed. Ray Allen Billington (Englewood Cliffs, N.J.: Prentice-Hall, 1961), 13–14, 17.

9. Ibid., 18, 20–21.

10. See, for instance, Richard Etulain, ed., *Does the Frontier Make America Exceptional?* (Boston: Bedford/St. Martin's, 1999).

11. Turner, "The Significance of History," 21–22.

12. Novick, *That Noble Dream*, 92–107; Higham, *History*, 111–112.

13. James Harvey Robinson, *The New History* (New York: Macmillan, 1912), 21, 23–24.

14. Paul S. Reinsch, "The American Political Science Association," *IJHP* 2 (1904): 156–157; see also *AHA Annual Report for 1903*, 21–22.

15. *Proceedings of the Mississippi Valley Historical Association for the Year 1907–1908* (Cedar Rapids, Iowa: Torch Press, 1909), 8; see also "Twenty-fifth Anniversary Dinner of the Mississippi Valley Historical Association, Lincoln, Nebraska, April 29, 1932," typescript of Shambaugh's speech, Shambaugh Papers.

16. J. Franklin Jameson, "The American Historical Association, 1884–1909," *AHR* 15 (October 1909): 15–16.

17. The AHA annual reports for 1890, 1892, and 1895 contain A. P. C. Griffin's "Bibliography of the Historical Societies of the United States" in three installments.

18. J. Franklin Jameson, "The Functions of State and Local Historical Societies with Respect to Research and Publication," *AHA Annual Report for 1897*, 59.

19. "Report of the Public Archives Commission," *AHA Annual Report for 1901*, 5.

20. Ibid., 5–25.

21. "Report on the Public Archives of Iowa," *AHA Annual Report for 1900*, vol. 2, 39–46.

22. "Report of the Public Archives Commission," *AHA Annual Report for 1903*, 407–664.

23. Thomas McAdory Owen, "State Departments of Archives and History," *AHA Annual Report for 1904*, 237–253.

24. The Iowa legislature, for instance, established a state archives in 1892 as a branch of the state library, and during the late 1890s Shambaugh began campaigning, with others, to transform this arrangement into a separate state archives. However, it would be fifteen years before the Iowa State Department of History and Archives moved into the new Historical Memorial and Art Building constructed across the street from the state capitol in Des Moines. This story is detailed in chapter 3. The progress reports submitted to the AHA Public Archives Commission provide only scant detail of this protracted effort. See John C. Parish, "Some Points in Connection with the Public Archives of Iowa," in the "Third Report of the Conference of State and Local Historical Societies," *AHA Annual Report for 1906*, 145–149; and Shambaugh's report on the status of public archives in Iowa in Herman V. Ames, comp., "Resume of the Archives' Situations in the Several States in 1907," *AHA Annual Report for 1907*, 168–171.

25. "Report of the Public Archives Commission," *AHA Annual Report for 1903*, 409–414; Frontis W. Johnson, "The North Carolina Historical Commission, 1903–1978," in *Public History in North Carolina, 1903–1978*, ed. Jeffrey J. Crow (Raleigh: North Carolina Department of Cultural Resources, Division of Archives and History, 1979), 1–4. In North Carolina, the commissioners charged with the duty of collecting said materials were expected to serve without pay, and the legislature made no provision to house the documents that immediately began to accumulate.

26. "Report of the Public Archives Commission," *AHA Annual Report for 1904*, 483–484.

27. Owen, "State Departments of Archives and History," 241–242.

28. Rothberg, introduction to *Jameson*, xxxviii–xl. See also Jameson's remarks as reported in the *AHA Annual Report for 1905*, 30, 209.

29. Waldo Gifford Leland, "Recollections of the Man Who Rang the Bell," *American Archivist* 21 (1958): 56.

30. Ames, "Resume of the Archives' Situations," 163–187.

31. Herman V. Ames, "Conference of Archivists: Introductory Remarks by the Chairman," *AHA Annual Report for 1909*, 339–341 (as part of "Tenth Annual Report of the Public Archives Commission, Appendix A, Proceedings of the First Annual Conference of Archivists," 337–378).

32. William F. Birdsall, "The Two Sides of the Desk: The Archivist and the Historian, 1909–1935," *American Archivist* 38 (1975): 159–173.

33. Jameson, "The American Historical Association," 17. See A. P. C. Griffin, "Bibliography of the Historical Societies of the United States," which actually contains Canadian societies, too, in *AHA Annual Report for 1890*, 161–267; *AHA Annual Report for 1892*, 307–619; and *AHA Annual Report for 1895*, 675–1147, including index.

34. See Clifford L. Lord and Carl Ubbelohde, *Clio's Servant: The State Historical Society of Wisconsin, 1846–1954* (Madison: State Historical Society of Wisconsin, 1967), passim.

35. Julian P. Boyd, "State and Local Historical Societies in the United States," *AHR* 40 (1934): 24.

36. Reuben Gold Thwaites, "State-Supported Historical Societies and Their Functions," *AHA Annual Report for 1897*, 63–65.

37. Ibid., 66–67.

38. Ibid., 67–70.

39. Jameson, "The Functions of State and Local Historical Societies," 51–59.

40. Herbert B. Adams, "Report of the Proceedings of Fourteenth Annual Meeting of the American Historical Association," *AHA Annual Report for 1898*, 7.

41. Bourne to Thwaites, 15 September 1903, Thwaites Papers.

42. Thwaites to Bourne, 17 September 1903, Thwaites Papers.

43. Thwaites to Shambaugh, 3 January 1906, Shambaugh Correspondence.

44. Jameson to Thwaites, 17 August 1904; Thwaites to Jameson, 25 August 1904, Thwaites Papers.

45. Thwaites to Jameson, 8 October 1904; Jameson to Thwaites, 10 October 1904, Thwaites Papers.

46. Thwaites to Alcee Fortier, Tulane University, 20 September 1904; Fortier to Thwaites, 8 October 1904; Thwaites to Fortier, 13 October 1904; Bourne to Thwaites, 19 October 1904; Thwaites to Bourne, 26 October 1904; and Jameson to Thwaites, 21 October 1904, Thwaites Papers; Thwaites to Shambaugh, 11 October 1904; Shambaugh to Thwaites, 15 October 1904; and Thwaites to Shambaugh, 26 October 1904, Shambaugh Correspondence.

47. Henry E. Bourne, "The Work of American Historical Societies," *AHA Annual Report for 1904*, 117–119; Boyd, "State and Local Historical Societies," contains a summary of Bourne's 1904 report and subsequent events.

48. Bourne, "American Historical Societies," 120–123, 125–126.

49. Ibid., 117, 127.

50. Frederick Wightman Moore, "First Report of the Conference of State and Local Historical Societies," *AHA Annual Report for 1904*, 221, 233–234.

51. Ibid., 222–233.

52. Charles H. Haskins, corresponding secretary, AHA, to Thwaites, 11 January 1905, Thwaites Papers.

53. Haskins to Thwaites, 17 January 1905; Thwaites to Haskins, 23 January 1905; Shambaugh to Thwaites, 18 January 1905; Thwaites to Shambaugh, 2 March 1905; Shambaugh to Thwaites, 11 March 1905; Thwaites to Shambaugh, 13 March 1905; Bourne to Thwaites, 18 April 1905; Thwaites to Bourne, 21 April 1905; Shambaugh to Thwaites, 2 May 1905; and Thwaites to Shambaugh, 3 May 1905, Thwaites Papers; see also Thwaites to Shambaugh, 14 January 1905; Shambaugh to Riley, 15 March 1905; Riley to Shambaugh, 8 May 1905; and Riley to Shambaugh, 22 May 1905, Shambaugh Correspondence. The full text of the questionnaire appears in "Report of Committee on Methods of Organization and Work on the Part of State and Local Historical Societies," *AHA Annual Report for 1905*, vol. 1, 252–253.

54. "Rich Historical Treat Is Pledged: Reuben Gold Thwaites to Be Heard," *Iowa City Daily Press*, 16 May 1905; "Exposition of Lewis and Clark," *Iowa City Daily Press*, 17 May 1905.

55. Thwaites to Shambaugh, 28 March 1905; Shambaugh to Thwaites, 31 March 1905; and Shambaugh to Thwaites, 29 May 1905, Shambaugh Correspondence; "Report of the Committee on Methods of Organization," 269–270.

56. "Second Report of the Conference of State and Local Historical Societies," *AHA Annual Report for 1905*, vol. 1, 177–217; see also "Report of the Proceedings of the Twenty-first Annual Meeting of the American Historical Association," ibid., 27–30.

57. "Second Report of the Conference of State and Local Historical Societies," 181–183.

58. Ibid., 182–183.

59. Ibid., 184–188.

60. Ibid., 200–204.

61. Ibid., 205–209.

62. Unless otherwise noted, the information that follows is drawn from tables that appear on pp. 255–256 and 258–261 of the "Report of the Committee on Methods of Organization"; see also "Proceedings of the Twenty-first Annual Meeting of the American Historical Association," 27–28.

63. It is difficult to provide a similar comparison of local historical societies because so many of them did not report a date of organization. However, using the information available, the oldest local societies appear to be the New York Historical Society (1804); the New England Society of Charleston, South Carolina (1819); Essex Institute, Salem, Massachusetts (1821); Old Colony Historical Society, Taunton, Massachusetts (1853); the Chicago Historical Society (1855); the Phila-delphia Numismatic and Antiquarian Society (1858); and the Wyoming Historical and Geological Society of Wilkes-Barre, Pennsylvania (1858). Fifty-five local societies reported dates of organization between 1890 and 1906 (the 1905 proceedings were published in 1906). See also Boyd, "State and Local Historical Societies," for another useful accounting of the earliest historical organizations.

64. "Report of the Committee on Methods of Organization," 262.

65. Ibid., 264–269, 273–419.

66. "Third Report of the Conference of State and Local Historical Societies," *AHA Annual Report for 1906*, 129–159.

67. The commission published these reports, as received, in the AHA's annual reports beginning with the report of the 1900 meeting.

68. Beginning with Alabama in 1901, these states also included Mississippi, Pennsylvania, Illinois, Maryland, South Carolina, West Virginia, Kansas, Delaware, Arkansas, and Iowa.

69. "Third Report of the Conference of State and Local Historical Societies," 130–133. The annual report of the 1906 meeting also contains a state-by-state summary of legislation concerning the disposition of public records; see Robert T. Swan, "Summary of the Present State of Legislation of the States and Territories Relative to the Custody and Supervision of the Public Records," *AHA Annual Report for 1906*, 13–21.

70. "Third Report of the Conference of State and Local Historical Societies," 149–150. Bourne was least concerned about what sites deserved marking. In a statement that may have been made to disarm critics, he asserted that "whatever stimulates local interest sufficiently to give rise to an effective desire to place an inscription, or erect a monument, requires no further argument to commend it."

71. "Report of the Proceedings of the Twenty-second Annual Meeting of the American Historical Association," *AHA Annual Report for 1906*, 21.

72. "Report of Conference on the Work of State and Local Historical Societies," *AHA Annual Report for 1907*, 57–63; "Report of Conference on the Work of State and Local Historical Societies," *AHA Annual Report for 1908*, 149–153. The Committee of Seven was formed in response to a paper presented by Dunbar Rowland at the 1907 meeting.

73. See successive reports of the Conference of Historical Societies appearing in *AHA Annual Report for 1909*, 289–292; *AHA Annual Report for 1910*, 245–247; *AHA Annual Report for 1911*, 253–254; *AHA Annual Report for 1912*, 201–205; *AHA Annual Report for 1913*, 211–215; and *AHA Annual Report for 1914*, 301–304.

74. See Ray Allen Billington, "Tempest in Clio's Teapot: The American Historical Association Rebellion of 1915," *AHR* 78 (1978): 348–369; and Novick, *That Noble Dream*, 73 n. 15, 182–185, 202–204.

75. "Joint Conference of Historical Societies and the National Association of State War History Organizations," *AHA Annual Report for 1919*, 135; "Proceedings of the Sixteenth Annual Conference of Historical Societies," *AHA Annual Report for 1920*, 132–134.

76. "Proceedings of the Twelfth Annual Conference of Historical Societies," *AHA Annual Report for 1915*, 238–239; "Proceedings of the Thirteenth Annual Conference of Historical Societies," *AHA Annual Report for 1916*, 233–236. Through 1917, information gathered from the annual circulars was abstracted and appended to the published proceedings; they provide a convenient reference for tracing broad trends in the evolution of state and local historical societies, particularly in the U.S. but, to a lesser degree, also in Canada.

77. "Proceedings of the Thirteenth Annual Conference of Historical Societies," 233–236.

78. "Report of the Conference of Historical Societies," *AHA Annual Report for 1925*, 77–79.

79. Boyd, "State and Local Historical Societies," 29.

80. Ibid., 35–36.

81. Jameson, "The Functions of State and Local Historical Societies," 51–59.

82. Allan Nevins, "What's the Matter with History?" *Saturday Review of Literature* 19 (4 February 1939), 3–4, 16; see also Higham, *History*, 80–81.

83. See "The Conference of Historical Societies" reports for 1933, 1934, and 1935 in *AHA Annual Report for 1935*, 215–219; "Minutes of the Conference of State and Local Historical Societies, December 28, 1939," *AHA Annual Report for 1939*, 103–104; and "Minutes of the Conference of State and Local Historical Societies, December 27, 1940," *AHA Annual Report for 1940*, 95–109. See also George Rollie Adams, "Planning for the Future, AASLH Takes a Look at Its Past," *History News* 37:9 (September 1982): 12–18.

84. Benjamin F. Shambaugh, "Applied History," *Proceedings of the Mississippi Val-*

ley Historical Association for the Year 1908–1909 (Cedar Rapids, Iowa: Torch Press, 1910), 137–139.

85. Benjamin F. Shambaugh, "Editor's Introduction," *Applied History*, vol. 1 (Iowa City: SHSI, 1913), ix.

86. Ibid., viii–ix.

87. Ibid., vii–viii.

88. Novick, *That Noble Dream*, 93–94, n. 14.

2. A Gift of Fate

[Note: Unless otherwise noted, the correspondence cited in this chapter is located in the SHSI Archives in Iowa City. Citations that mention a "Ringfold Book" refer to a set of ring binders containing newspaper clippings, handwritten notes, and other ephemera that Bertha Shambaugh prepared to aid Swisher in writing Benjamin's biography. These are located in the Shambaugh Papers. A note in Ringfold Book 1 explains that "at the present time [June 1942] there are 4 ring-fold books [eventually the number totaled seven]. Because of overcrowding, some sections have been transferred from one book to another—which leaves them in no special order and contents incomplete." The Ringfold Books are not to be confused with the House Books that Bertha Shambaugh began keeping in 1902, thirty-six handwritten notebooks that record the special events and the life that took place in their home at 219 Clinton Street in Iowa City. The House Books are a separate series in the Shambaugh Papers.]

1. *Catalogue of the State University of Iowa* (1888–1889), 95.

2. *S.U.I. Quill*, 8 October 1892.

3. Stow Persons, *The University of Iowa in the Twentieth Century: An Institutional History* (Iowa City: University of Iowa Press, 1990), 1–14.

4. "Convocation Address, February 3, 1926," Shambaugh Papers.

5. Shambaugh Papers, Boxes 5, 6, and 7, contain Shambaugh's lecture notes of the courses he took at the University of Iowa, which included at least two courses in American history and one course each in English, Greek, and Roman history taken under W. R. Perkins.

6. "The West and the Pioneer." The manuscript was later published as "The History of the West and the Pioneers," *Proceedings of the State Historical Society of Wisconsin for 1910* (1911): 133–145.

7. Benjamin F. Shambaugh, *Iowa City: A Contribution to the Early History of Iowa* (Iowa City: SHSI, 1893), 4.

8. Shambaugh Papers.

9. Shambaugh to Robinson, 14 November 1903; Robinson to Shambaugh, 21 November 1903; Shambaugh to Robinson, 8 January 1904.

10. Persons, *The University of Iowa*, 14–15.

11. *Catalogue of the State University of Iowa* (1892–1893), 9–64. A letter from Loos to Schaeffer, 13 July 1894, is preserved in the University of Iowa Archives.

12. Minutes of the University of Iowa Board of Regents, March 1895.

13. Persons, *The University of Iowa*, 20; Macbride later served as president from 1914 to 1916.

14. Ibid., 26, 302 n. 18.

15. Brookings Institution, Institute for Government Research, *Report on a Survey of Administration in Iowa* (Des Moines: State of Iowa, 1933), 598; Ringfold Book 3:170a.

16. Margaret N. Keyes, *Old Capitol: Portrait of an Iowa Landmark* (Iowa City: University of Iowa Press, 1988), 22–45.

17. Construction began in 1840, and the state legislature began using the partially completed building in 1842. However, the building was not finished until sometime after 1857 when the state capital was redesignated as Des Moines, and the legislature deeded the old capitol building to the University of Iowa.

18. Shambaugh's private journal, 25 April 1905; Ringfold Book 5:210.

19. Keyes, *Old Capitol*, 46–72.

20. This quote is not attributed in Swisher's manuscript, so Swisher may have constructed it from his own memory of conversations with Shambaugh.

21. Persons, *The University of Iowa*, 19.

22. Persons intimates that Loos and Shambaugh differed philosophically on the question of whether political science and history belonged in the social sciences or in the liberal arts. In attempting to build an expansive interdisciplinary School of Political and Social Science, Loos introduced a four-year course in "commerce," which set in motion an evolutionary process that culminated in 1914 when the School of Political and Social Science became the School of Commerce. During the period of flux that Persons describes as the "era of creative anarchy," Shambaugh managed to keep his department, political science, seated in the College of Liberal Arts. See ibid., 84–85.

23. *Iowa Federated News*, March–April 1924, 3, 13.

24. SHSI, *Report of Curators*, 1883, 5; Ringfold Book 2:35.

25. [Benjamin F. Shambaugh], "A Brief History of the State Historical Society of Iowa, 1857–1907," in *Proceedings of the Fiftieth Anniversary of the Constitution of Iowa*, ed. Benjamin F. Shambaugh (Iowa City: SHSI, 1907), 411–423.

26. Benjamin F. Shambaugh, ed., *Fragments of Debates of the Iowa Constitutional Conventions of 1844 and 1846* (Iowa City: SHSI, 1900).

27. Minutes, SHSI Board of Curators, 14 April 1900, 12 May 1900.

28. Minutes, SHSI Board of Curators, 4 June 1900, 5 September 1900, 26 September 1901, 13 September 1902.

29. Bicknell to Shambaugh, 12 December 1900, 13 March 1901, 7 June 1901.

30. Bicknell to Shambaugh, 12 June 1901. See also Bicknell to Shambaugh, 21 March 1901, 11 June 1901.

31. Deemer to Shambaugh, 30 December 1902.

32. Rowe to Shambaugh, 6 and 9 January 1903.

33. Robinson to Shambaugh, 15 October 1902.

34. Hart to Shambaugh, 3 December 1903. Frederick Jackson Turner also received a complimentary copy, to which he responded less effusively: "The idea of the series is an excellent one, and it seems to me to have been very well worked out. Already I have found these speeches a useful mine of material on the history of the period which they cover. Indeed, I was quite surprised to find how much of early ideals and interests were reflected in these speeches." Turner to Shambaugh, 16 December 1903.

35. Hart to Shambaugh, 17 December 1904.

36. Lord and Ubbelohde, *Clio's Servant*, passim; David Kinnett, "Miss Kellogg's Quiet Passion," *Wisconsin Magazine of History* 62 (summer 1979): 275–276.

37. Shambaugh to Thwaites, 14 January 1904, SHSI; Thwaites to president of the State Historical Society of Iowa [Shambaugh], 18 January 1904, Thwaites Papers.

38. Owen to Shambaugh, 6 November 1906.

39. Editor's preface to Shambaugh, *Fiftieth Anniversary of the Constitution of Iowa*, v–vi.

40. See "Summary of Work of Historical Society" in a letter to Mrs. D. N. Heard, 2 September 1907, prepared for publication in the *Waterloo Reporter*.

41. Turner to Shambaugh, 29 January 1908.

42. Hart to Shambaugh, 6 and 11 May 1908.

3. The Politics of Public Institutions

[Note: The correspondence cited in this chapter is located in the Shambaugh Correspondence.]

1. "Report on the Public Archives of Iowa," *AHA Annual Report for 1900*, vol. 2, 39–46.

2. *Laws of Iowa*, 1892, ch. 56.

3. Charles Aldrich, "Origin of the Historical Department," *AI*, 3rd series, 1 (April 1893): 56–58.

4. See "Charles Aldrich: In Memoriam," *AI*, 3rd series, 8 (January 1909): 566.

5. Swisher cites only "Aldrich to Shambaugh" without listing a date, and the location of this correspondence remains unknown. The "1890–1896 A" folder in the Shambaugh Correspondence contains a few letters from Aldrich, but these typically ask Shambaugh to write something for the *AI*.

6. Aldrich to Shambaugh, 1 February 1895.

7. Aldrich to Shambaugh, 10, 14, and 17 January 1896, 23 April 1896.

8. Aldrich to Shambaugh, 23 April 1896.

9. Aldrich to Shambaugh, 2 May 1896.

10. Shambaugh to Aldrich, 11 May 1896.

11. Aldrich to Shambaugh, 13 May 1896.

12. See, for instance, Shambaugh's article, "The Preservation of Historical Material," *AI*, 3rd series, 3 (July 1897): 155–156.

13. *Laws of Iowa*, 1896, ch. 115.

14. The Executive Council was, and still is, an administrative unit comprising the governor, secretary of state, state auditor, state treasurer, and secretary of agriculture.

15. Swisher probably used the term "the program" to signify a general sense among citizens and legislators that the state should take an active role in promoting "cultural affairs," to use a contemporary phrase.

16. *AHA Annual Report for 1900*, vol. 2, 39–46.

17. "Report of the Public Archives Commission," *AHA Annual Report for 1900*, vol. 2, 14–15.

18. *AI*, 3rd series, 5 (April 1901): 66–68.

19. Shambaugh to Aldrich, 13 October 1903; Shambaugh to Deemer, 24 October 1903.

20. Shambaugh to Aldrich, 22 June 1905; Shambaugh to Deemer, 3, 10, and 15 July 1905.

21. *Laws of Iowa*, 1906, ch. 142.

22. Aldrich to Shambaugh, 23 April 1901, 27 January 1902, 23 April 1902.

23. Aldrich to Shambaugh, 21 June 1905; Shambaugh to Aldrich, 22 June 1905; Aldrich to Shambaugh, 2 January 1906.

24. See Shambaugh to Crossley, 18 January 1907; Aldrich to Shambaugh, 24 January 1906.

25. Aldrich to Shambaugh, 22 December 1906.

26. Shambaugh, for instance, was not among the ten authors whose eulogies to Aldrich, delivered at his memorial service in the Historical Building, were published in a special memorial issue of the *Annals of Iowa*. Rather, a very brief message from Shambaugh appears among a collection of like remembrances included as a "Tribute from Absent Friends." See *AI*, 3rd series, 8 (January 1909): 606.

27. Aldrich to Shambaugh, 3 November 1904; Shambaugh to Aldrich, 4 November 1904, 9 November 1904; Aldrich to Shambaugh, 26 April 1906.

28. About three months before Aldrich died, Shambaugh wrote him an uncustomary New Year's greeting that, in retrospect, can only be read as a private eulogy: "Some of the most enjoyable hours of the last six or eight years have been spent in talking with you about the historical interests of our Commonwealth. Those of us who belong to the younger generation get much from you, from your ideals, your

industry, your perseverance and your patience." Shambaugh to Aldrich, 7 January 1908.

29. Shambaugh to Aldrich, 16 May 1906, 11 June 1906.

30. Letters between Shambaugh and Owen appear at more or less regular intervals in the Shambaugh Correspondence from 1903 through at least 1919. They established a long-standing custom of exchanging publications (and commenting on same), so much of the correspondence consists of cover letters or short messages to confirm receipt of some item. However, they also exchanged information about administrative matters, regular program activities, special projects, state legislation, and appropriations. The length of their correspondence, in years, suggests the importance of this professional relationship to both men.

31. *AI*, 3rd series, 7 (January 1907): 561–591; *Des Moines Register and Leader*, 4 November 1906.

32. "Some Unpublished Books," *(Des Moines) Mail and Times*, 17 November 1906 (interleaved with Frank W. Bicknell's correspondence in the Shambaugh Correspondence).

33. Frank Horack also followed his brother-in-law's career path. After taking his bachelor's and master's degrees at the University of Iowa, he pursued graduate studies at the University of Chicago, Halle, and Berlin and then at the University of Pennsylvania, where he earned his doctorate. In 1902 he joined the political science faculty at the University of Iowa. He also authored many studies for the SHSI, including several that appeared in the Applied History Series.

34. "Governor's Message to the Senate and House of Representatives of the Thirty-second General Assembly," *Iowa Documents*, vol. 1 (1907): 13.

35. Shambaugh to Senator J. J. Crossley, 18 January 1907; Shambaugh to Deemer, 29 January 1907.

36. Shambaugh to Cummins, 11 February 1907.

37. *Laws of Iowa*, 1907, ch. 157.

38. Shambaugh to Deemer, 10 April 1907.

39. "Mr. Berryhill Brings Charges," *Des Moines Register and Leader*, 11 May 1908.

40. Neidig to Shambaugh, 15 and 28 June 1907.

41. Neidig to Shambaugh, 28 June 1907, 4 July 1907.

42. Neidig to Shambaugh, 8 August 1907.

43. Shambaugh to Bicknell, 18 July 1907.

44. Shambaugh to Bicknell, 8 November 1907.

45. Shambaugh to Bicknell, 14 November 1907.

46. Shambaugh to Deemer, 11 September 1908.

47. Shambaugh to W. I. Babb, 29 December 1908.

48. Shambaugh to Pickard, 30 December 1908.

49. House File No. 266, *Iowa House Journal*, 1909, 435, 1383–1384.

50. Shambaugh to Carroll, 10 April 1909.

51. Shambaugh to Brindley, 12 October 1908.

52. Brindley's manuscript subsequently was published; see John Brindley, "The Legislative Reference Movement," *IJHP* 7 (1909): 132–141.

53. Ibid., 136–138, 140–141.

54. Brindley to Shambaugh, 2 November 1908.

55. Shambaugh to Brindley, 9 November 1908; Brindley to Shambaugh, 10 November 1908, 14 November 1908, the latter including Brigham's "independent department bill" and Brindley's substitute language.

56. Shambaugh to Brindley, 16 November 1908.

57. Shambaugh to Brigham, 30 November 1908, 5 December 1908.

58. Shambaugh to Brindley, 6 December 1908. Shambaugh also announced this plan in his annual report; see Benjamin F. Shambaugh, "Historical Research," *Twenty-seventh Biennial Report of the Board of Curators of the State Historical Society of Iowa to the Governor of the State* (1908), 20–21.

59. In a confidential letter of 28 November 1908, Shambaugh asked Brigham to "please assure Mr. Harlan [the newly hired assistant curator] that there is no 'French Revolution' impending."

60. Shambaugh to Brindley, 16 February 1909, including draft bill to establish a "legislative reference research bureau."

61. Shambaugh to Brindley, 16 February 1909.

62. Shambaugh to Brindley, 24 March 1909.

63. Brindley to Shambaugh, 24 March 1909; Shambaugh to Brindley, 25 March 1909.

64. Shambaugh to Brindley, 12 April 1909; Shambaugh to Brigham, 14 April 1909.

65. Bicknell to Shambaugh, 18 May 1909; Shambaugh to Bicknell, 29 June 1909.

66. Shambaugh to Clarke, 15 April 1909.

67. Shambaugh to Cummins, 10 April 1909.

68. Shambaugh to Bicknell, 29 June 1909.

69. Ames, "Introductory Remarks," 339–341.

4. A Deliberate Course

[Note: Correspondence cited in this chapter is located in the SHSI Archives, Iowa City.]

1. Schroder, *History*, 32–33.

2. A[ndrew] C. McLaughlin, "A Bureau of Historical Research," *IJHP* 2 (1904): 303–305. By 1905, the bureau had been renamed the Department of Historical Research, as it was known under J. Franklin Jameson's directorship.

3. *Historical Research in the State Historical Society of Iowa* (Iowa City: SHSI, 1908), 5–7; copy in the SHSI Archives, Iowa City.

4. Schroder, *History*, 33.

5. Benjamin F. Shambaugh, "The Iowa School of Research Historians," *Proceedings of the Mississippi Valley Historical Association for 1910–1911* (Cedar Rapids: Torch Press, 1912), 152; see also "The Spirit and Method of Research in Iowa," typescript of remarks delivered in abbreviated reform at the 1910 MVHA meeting, Shambaugh Papers; see also Shambaugh to F. W. Beckman, Experiment Station, Iowa State College, 29 July 1911.

6. As early as 1905 Shambaugh reported that "during the past year ten (10) students have been doing original work in Iowa History under the direction of the head of the Department of Political Science. It is believed that this is the largest number of students doing special research work in local history in any college or university in the United States." Shambaugh to the president and Board of Regents of the State University of Iowa, 23 May 1905.

7. Report of the SHSI Board of Curators, 1912, 29–31.

8. John F. Sly, review of *Municipal Government and Administration in Iowa*, vols. 5 and 6 in the Applied History Series, *APSR* 25 (1931): 189–190.

9. *Des Moines Register*, 8 September 1912.

10. Ibid.

11. Shambaugh to Parish, 15 June 1912. Parish earned his doctorate in 1908 under Shambaugh and served as assistant editor at the SHSI from 1907 to 1910, during which time he conducted research in archives in France and Spain as part of the AHA's documents project. During the next several years, Parish returned to the SHSI from time to time to conduct research while he was teaching at Colorado College, then finally moved back to Iowa City. From 1919 to 1922 he held three positions: associate editor of the SHSI, editor of the *Palimpsest*, and secretary of the Conference of Historical Societies. In 1922 he left the SHSI to accept a position on the UCLA history faculty, where he spent the remainder of his career.

12. Schroder, *History*, 44.

13. Handwritten roster compiled by Schroder; see his research notes for *History*, SHSI Archives.

14. Biographical information taken from volumes in *Who's Who in America* and *Who's Who in Iowa* (Iowa Press Association, 1940); see also Ethyl Martin to Howard H. Preston, 12 December 1945.

15. In Gallaher's case, she achieved a professional status matched or exceeded by few women scholars of her generation. Although many women undertook graduate study, few earned doctoral degrees and even fewer held academic positions. The professionalization of historical societies thus created more career opportunities for women with doctorates in history or political science, although

these opportunities were still limited and a top post in a state historical society still virtually unthinkable. Louise Phelps Kellogg, Gallaher's counterpart at the State Historical Society of Wisconsin (SHSW), wrote prolifically and was widely recognized for her scholarship, was the first woman to serve as president of the Mississippi Valley Historical Association, and was a fellow of the Royal Historical Society of Britain. Still, the University of Wisconsin never offered her a tenured faculty position, and the SHSW never considered her for the directorship. As she wrote to a friend in 1918, "The curators would never consider a woman for the headship, at least not in your and my generation, although the next generation of women are going to have much greater chances." See Kinnett, "Miss Kellogg's Quiet Passion," 267–299, quote 284. Similarly, Grace Lee Nute served as curator of manuscripts at the Minnesota State Historical Society from 1921 to 1946 and as research associate from 1946 to 1957. Nute, however, also taught at Hamline University for ten years and at the University of Minnesota as associate professor of history from 1937 to 1940 and as full professor beginning in 1940. See Robert Burchfield, "The Career of Ethyl Martin: Superintendent of the State Historical Society of Iowa, 1940–1947," 4–5. On file, SHSI.

16. See, for instance, Senator F. F. Jones to Shambaugh, 24 February 1913, in which he writes, "In support of the Applied History Series being a benefit to legislation, I am inclined to think Prof. [John] Brindley's History of Road Legislation aided greatly in preparing the legislators to accept the road legislation now proposed, and I think these results would have been impossible without the preliminary work and suggestions offered by the book mentioned." See also Brindley to Shambaugh, 18 January 1913, in which he writes, "The Applied History Series has . . . reduced to a minimum, the necessity of doing this class of work [lobbying] for any of the important measures which have been comprehensively treated on a comparative and historical basis. . . . The historical essays have done the work much more effectively than any amount of what is generally called 'lobbying' could possibly do." Thus, in "The Activities of the State Historical Society of Iowa," *History Teacher's Magazine* 6 (March 1915): 75–81, Louis B. Schmidt had some basis for stating that highway legislation enacted by the Iowa legislature in 1913 was "in all its essential features . . . an embodiment of Brindley's findings and recommendations," which were published as "Road Legislation in Iowa" in *Applied History*, vol. 1 (1912).

17. "Editor's Introduction," *Applied History*, vol. 1 (Iowa City: SHSI, 1912), vi, vii, x.

18. Ibid., xii–xiii.

19. Ibid., xiii.

20. Beard to Shambaugh, 16 October 1913, 20 January 1915; Pound to Shambaugh, 21 January 1915.

21. "Our States and Their History," *Nation*, 20 May 1915, 555.

22. "Editor's Introduction," viii–ix.

23. Edward A. Fitzpatrick, review of *Applied History*, vol. 2, *AHR* 20 (1914–1915): 896–897.

24. Ibid.

25. In 1912 excerpts from this work appeared under the title "Tax Administration" in *Applied History*, vol. 1.

26. Schroder, *History*, 42–43, 48; *AHA Annual Report for 1910*, 257.

27. William I. Atkinson, Speaker of the House, Thirty-sixth General Assembly, to Shambaugh, 13 April 1915.

28. There are many references in the Ringfold Books to the Foskett Bill, S.F. 356; see Ringfold Book 5: 17, 20, 21, 29, 90; see also Shambaugh correspondence with C. K. Patton.

29. Shambaugh to Louis Pelzer, 10 April 1909.

30. Boyd, "State and Local Historical Societies," 31.

31. "Proceedings of the Fourteenth Annual Conference of Historical Societies," *AHA Annual Report for 1917*, 179–180.

32. Ibid., 194.

33. Schroder, *History*, 59.

34. Novick, *That Noble Dream*, 116–117.

35. "Statement Respecting the Work of the National Board for Historical Service," *AHA Annual Report for 1918*, 62–63; Novick, *That Noble Dream*, 118–128.

36. "Statement Respecting the Work of the National Board for Historical Service," 63.

37. Report of Conference of Historical Societies," *AHA Annual Report for 1917*, 179–181; "Report of Conference of Historical Societies," *AHA Annual Report for 1919*, 123–136; "Report of Conference of Historical Societies," *AHA Annual Report for 1920*, 131–152.

38. "Joint Conference of Historical Societies," 123–136; Franklin F. Holbrook, "The Collection of State War Service Records," *AHR* 25 (October 1919): 72–78.

39. See, for instance, the form letter of 20 May 1919 sent to county chairs of Victory Boys, Victory Girls, the United War Work Campaign, Publicity, the Speakers' Bureau, Women's Work, and the YMCA Campaign, asking them to provide specific kinds of information and documentary material relating to various facets of wartime activities.

40. "Collection and Preservation of the Materials of War History: A Patriotic Service for Public Libraries, Local Historical Societies, and Local Historians," *Bulletin of Information*, no. 8 (SHSI, 1919); see also Shambaugh to Clarence W. Alvord, 3 October 1918.

41. "Shall the Story of Iowa's Part in the War be Preserved?" *Iowa and War* (Iowa City: SHSI, January 1919); press release, "Iowa and the War," TS, 4 January 1919; Minutes, SHSI Board of Curators, 6 May 1919.

42. Holbrook, "War Service Records," notes that Iowa, Minnesota, Indiana, Mississippi, New Jersey, New York, and North Carolina had plans or proposals to publish "comprehensive state war histories"; other states were planning to publish rosters of those who served in the military or histories of specific military units.

43. Albert E. McKinley, "Progress in the Collection of War History Records by State War History Organizations," in "Proceedings of the Sixteenth Annual Conference of Historical Societies," *AHA Annual Report for 1920*, 145–150; see also Newton D. Mereness, director of research for NASWHO, to Shambaugh, 20 January 1920, requesting information and the corresponding response in the form of a typescript report, "Historical Activities in Iowa Resulting from the World War."

44. Schroder, *History*, 59–60; see also Shambaugh to O. A. Byington, Iowa Senate, 12 April 1919.

45. Schroder, *History*, 61–62. At the May 1919 Board of Curators meeting, the members "informally agreed" that plans for publishing a comprehensive history of Iowa's part in the war should go forward; see Minutes, SHSI Board of Curators, 6 May 1919.

46. Shambaugh to Quick, 1 August 1923.

47. *AI*, 3rd series, which in 1893 resumed publication of the original periodical that began in 1863, was now published by the historical department in Des Moines; it continued as the venue for publishing the work of amateur historians.

48. Augustus H. Shearer, "American Historical Periodicals," *AHA Annual Report for 1916*, 471.

49. Ibid., 474–475.

50. Ibid., 474, 476, 480–481.

51. Schroder, *History*, 62.

52. The *Palimpsest* was published continuously from 1920 to 1996, when the name changed to *Iowa Heritage Illustrated*. Old hands like me protested the name change, but editor Ginalie Swaim forced us to accept it, explaining that the archaic term now made the cover "a locked door with a secret password." The new title reflects modern vocabulary as well as the magazine's evolution from a five-by-seven-inch booklet with no illustrations to a glossy seven-by-ten-inch magazine with full-color illustrations; Ginalie Swaim, "An Old Friend with a New Name," *Palimpsest* 76 (1995): 146–147.

53. Schroder, *History*, 85, notes that from 1925 to 1940 membership dues averaged about $3,000 per year. The number of members peaked at about 1,400 in 1926, declined slightly to 1,350 by 1932, then dropped to fewer than 1,000 in 1934–1935. Membership campaigns in the late 1930s succeeded in raising the membership to about 1,200 by 1940.

54. Ibid., 65.

55. Ibid., 92–96.

56. Merle Curti, review of *In Cabins and Sod-Houses* by Thomas Macbride, *AHR* 34 (April 1929): 656–657. It is not clear in what sense Curti used the term "pioneer" in reference to Macbride, a botanist at the University of Iowa (and president 1914–1916) who is chiefly remembered in Iowa for his leadership in the conservation movement. Born in Tennessee, he came to Iowa in 1854 with his family when he was six years old, so Macbride grew up during Iowa's "pioneer days," but he was hardly the "old settler" type.

57. Harlow Lindley, review of *In Cabins and Sod-Houses* by Thomas Macbride, *MVHR* 16 (June 1929): 137.

58. Maurice C. Latta, review of *Josiah Bushnell Grinnell* by Charles E. Payne, *MVHR* 26 (June 1939): 103–104; J. L. Sellers, review of *Robert Gordon Cousins* by Jacob A. Swisher, *MVHR* 26 (September 1939): 273; Philip D. Jordan, review of *The Old Stone Capitol Remembers* by Benjamin F. Shambaugh, *MVHR* 26 (December 1939): 437–438; H. C. Nixon, review of *The Old Stone Capitol Remembers* by Benjamin F. Shambaugh, *AHR* 45 (April 1940): 728.

59. Shambaugh, *Fiftieth Anniversary of the Constitution of Iowa*; see especially 253–257.

60. "Proceedings of the Conference of Local Historical Societies of Iowa Held at Iowa City on Wednesday, May 25, 1910," *IJHP* 8 (1910): 522. In a speech that Shambaugh prepared for but did not deliver at the 1910 MVHA meeting, he stated that his research group, the Iowa School of Research Historians, was "studying our history from the bottom up instead of from the top down." However, he did not mean the kind of grassroots social history that took hold in the 1960s. While the rhetoric might suggest a kinship of thought, the published works that emanated from the SHSI in the 1910s were, to a large degree, policy research studies. See "The Spirit and Method of Research in Iowa History," undated TS [c. 1910], Shambaugh Papers.

61. "An Iowa Program for Study Clubs," *Bulletin of Information*, no. 2 (SHSI, 1904), 2.

62. "Suggestions to Public Libraries and Local Historical Societies in Iowa Relative to Collecting and Preserving the Materials of Local History," *Bulletin of Information*, no. 3 (SHSI, 1904): 2–5.

63. Press release on official depository program, undated TS.

64. Martin to Kenneth E. Colton, director, Manuscripts and Publications, Iowa State Department of History and Archives, 25 March 1941; Colton to Martin, 26 March 1941; Colton to John E. Briggs, SHSI, 28 April 1941; "The Iowa Conference on Local History," *AI*, 3rd series, 23 (July 1941): 57–68; "Iowa Association of Local Historical Societies," TS, undated minutes of the organizational meeting of 11 October 1941.

65. Schroder, *History*, 78.

66. Ibid., 78–80, 102–104. The January, February, or March issue of the *Palimp-*

sest typically carried the Iowa History Week topic for each year; from 1926 through 1938 the topics were, in chronological order: Iowa, The Pioneers, Indians of Iowa, The Past at Play, Iowa and the Nation, Ioway to Iowa, Black Hawk and the Treaty of 1832, The Settlers Came: 1833, The Establishment of Civil Government in Iowa, A Century Ago: 1835, Wisconsin Territory: 1836, Iowa in 1837, and Iowa in 1838; see "Topics for Iowa History Week," in William J. Petersen, *Iowa History Reference Guide* (Iowa City: SHSI, 1952). See also the Iowa History Week Collection, SHSI, which contains correspondence, programs, and radio transcripts.

67. Schroder, *History*, 104–106.

68. Bennett, *An Iowa Album*, 4–17.

69. Lynn M. Alex, *Iowa's Archaeological Past* (Iowa City: University of Iowa Press, 2000), 20–23; Schroder, *History*, 70–74.

70. Schroder, *History*, 91–92.

71. Brookings Institution, *Survey of Administration in Iowa*, 213.

5. The Commonwealth Conference

[Note: Unless otherwise noted, the citations in this chapter refer to materials contained in the Commonwealth Conference Collection.]

1. Turner, "The Significance of History," 21–22; Robinson, *The New History*, 21.

2. *Iowa City Daily Press*, 29 June 1925.

3. [Shambaugh], "First Annual Commonwealth Conference on the Public Welfare in Iowa; held at Iowa City on May sixth, seventh, eighth, 1913, under the auspices of the State University of Iowa, Extension Division," four-page MS.

4. Shambaugh, "The History of the West and the Pioneers," 143.

5. *Mason City Gazette*, 10 July 1928.

6. Shambaugh to Wade, 21 November 1922.

7. Wade to Shambaugh, 22 November 1922.

8. "The Second Commonwealth Conference," *University of Iowa Service Bulletin* 8:11 (15 March 1924): 5.

9. *Iowa City Press Citizen*, 30 June 1924; handwritten copy with additional text is located in the Commonwealth Conference Collection.

10. Garner to Shambaugh, 12 July 1924.

11. Shepard to Shambaugh, 11 July 1924; Ray to Shambaugh, 13 July 1924.

12. Kerner to Shambaugh, 9 July 1924.

13. Conard to Shambaugh, 30 July 1924. Laetitia Moon Conard ran for governor of Iowa on the Socialist Party ticket in 1932. She was the highly educated but professionally frustrated wife of Henry Conard, a long-time professor of botany at Grinnell College who also was active in resource conservation affairs.

14. *Iowa City Daily Press*, 29 June 1925.

15. TS press releases for the Third Commonwealth Conference, June 29–July 1, 1925; see also various newspaper clippings, for example, "An Introspective Conference," *New York Times*, 13 June 1925; "Pitfalls Await President of a State College: Glenn Frank Sees Politics Crippling Science," *Chicago Daily Tribune*, 1 July 1925; "Political Scientists Meet for Annual Conference" and "Newspaper Men Cover Conference," *Daily Iowan*, 30 June 1925.

16. Program, Third Commonwealth Conference, 3.

17. Program, Third Commonwealth Conference, "The Costs of Government," 29 June–1 July 1925.

18. Program, Fourth Commonwealth Conference, "Local Self-Government," 28–30 June 1926.

19. See Harper Leech, "View Dry Law as Mistaken Zeal of the Crusader," *Chicago Daily Tribune*, 30 June 1926; Harlan Miller, "Advocates an Armed Revolt on Dry Laws," *Des Moines Register*, 30 June 1926.

20. Shambaugh to Hall, 6 July 1926.

21. See "America in Iowa," *Chicago Daily Tribune*, 22 June 1926; "Experts Discuss Self-Government," *New York Times*, 30 June 1926; "Civic Problems Under Analysis," *Christian Science Monitor*, 28 June 1926; Harper Leech, "City Government Savant's Theme at Round Table," *Chicago Daily Tribune*, 28 June 1926; Harper Leech, "Cities Diagnosed Politically Fit by Scientists," *Chicago Daily Tribune*, 1 July 1926; Harper Leech, "Finds Political Science Now Is Really Science," *Chicago Daily Tribune*, 2 July 1926.

22. Leech, "View Dry Law as Mistaken Zeal."

23. Hall to Shambaugh, 14 July 1926.

24. Shambaugh to Hall, 21, 22, and 26 July 1926; Hall to Shambaugh, 24 and 29 July 1926.

25. "Tentative Working Outlines for Researches in Municipal Government and Administration in Iowa, for Consideration at the Fourth Commonwealth Conference."

26. Sly, review of *Municipal Government*, 189–190.

27. Program, Fifth Commonwealth Conference, "Municipal Government and Administration," 27–29 June 1927; "Radio Program on the Fifth Commonwealth Conference, to Be Given June 20–25 [1927] from Station WSUI, Iowa City, Iowa," TS.

28. Anderson to Shambaugh, 1 July 1926.

29. Maphis to Shambaugh, 26 May 1927.

30. Shambaugh to Maphis, 2 June 1927; mailing list for the Fifth Commonwealth Conference.

31. Kendrick A. Clements notes that Hoover's management of relief efforts for the federal government during the great Mississippi River flood of 1927 "catapulted him to the forefront among Republicans." See Kendrick A. Clements,

Hoover, Conservation, and Consumerism: Engineering the Good Life (Lawrence: University Press of Kansas, 2000), 111.

32. Program, Sixth Commonwealth Conference, 9–11 July 1928.

33. *New Republic*, 6 June 1928.

34. Kirk H. Porter, "Brief Report on My Trip to the East in re Sixth Commonwealth Conference," 15 December 1927, TS. Quotes that follow are extracted from this nine-page report.

35. "Giant power" and "superpower" were shorthand terms for interconnected, regional transmission systems of electric power produced at centralized generating plants, which were only in the proposal stages at that time. As Secretary of Commerce, Hoover supported giant power; see Clements, *Hoover*, 87–89.

36. "Instructions to Researchers in re Commonwealth Conference, Issues of 1928," TS.

37. Anonymous postcard to Shambaugh, 9 July 1928.

38. Program, Sixth Commonwealth Conference.

39. "Feature Stories for *The Iowan* in re Commonwealth Conference," TS; "Opinions of the Conference and Its Program," TS.

40. *Iowa City Press Citizen*, 11 July 1928.

41. There may have been no conference in 1929 because considerable staff time was then being devoted to producing the two-volume *Municipal Government and Administration in Iowa*, which appeared in 1930, but this is speculation on my part. Nothing in the files of the Commonwealth Conference Collection indicates why there was no conference in 1929.

42. Hoover to Shambaugh, telegram, 19 June 1930, SHSI Archives.

43. Program, Seventh Commonwealth Conference, 30 June–2 July 1930.

44. President Hoover set up the Commission on Law Observance and Enforcement, of which Loesch, an attorney specializing in corporate law, was a member. Loesch was a senior member of the Chicago law firm of Loesch, Scofield, Loesch, and Richards. In addition to holding office in a number of law-related professional organizations, Loesch also was a trustee of the Chicago Historical Society.

45. Ruth Bryan attended the University of Nebraska before marrying Major Reginald Altham Owen of the British army. She was a member of the executive committee of the American Women's War Relief Fund in London, and she served as a war nurse in the Egypt-Palestine campaign from 1915 to 1918. After her husband died, she settled in Florida. From 1926 to 1929 she served as vice president of the Board of Regents and member of the faculty of the University of Miami. She was elected to Congress in 1928.

46. Gruening, trained in medicine at Harvard, chose instead to make his career in journalism. By 1930, he had served on the editorial staffs of several Boston newspapers, as managing editor of the *New York Tribune*, as general manager of *La Prensa*, and as managing editor of the *Nation*, before establishing his own news-

paper, the *Portland Evening News*, in 1927. He also had written *Mexico and Its Heritage* (1928).

47. Ridgeway, "Democratic Individualism," 373; Boyd, "State and Local Historical Societies," 35. Since the late 1960s, the University of Iowa Department of Political Science has sponsored, on an occasional basis, Shambaugh Conferences on various legislative and government topics.

48. Charles Beard (1874–1948) received his doctorate from Columbia University in 1904 and taught there from 1907 to 1917; he authored, coauthored (several with his wife, Mary), or edited more than thirty books on American and European history and politics. Charles E. Merriam (1874–1953) received his bachelor's degree from the University of Iowa in 1895 and his doctorate from Columbia University in 1900. He taught at the University of Chicago from 1900 until his retirement; he authored, coauthored, or edited nearly twenty-five books on American politics and political ideas, the history of political theories, and the sociology of political behavior. William B. Munro (1875–1957), a native of Ontario, Canada, received his doctorate from Harvard in 1900. He taught history and politics at Williams College (1901–1904), Harvard University (1904–1925), and the California Institute of Technology (1925–1945); he wrote more than fifteen books on American, European, and Canadian government and politics.

49. Before going to Columbia University, Moley had been a member of the faculties of Western Reserve University and the University of Chicago. By 1930, he had also conducted research for crime commissions in Ohio, New York, Illinois, and Pennsylvania. Isador Lubin had served as a consultant for the War Industries Board in 1918. He taught at the University of Michigan and the University of Missouri before joining the faculty of the Robert Brookings Graduate School of Economics and Government. In 1929 he served as an assistant to the U.S. Senate Committee on Education and Labor. By 1930, he also had published *The Absorption of the Unemployed by American Industry*.

6. A New Deal in the Game of Life

[Note: Unless otherwise noted, the citations in this chapter refer to materials in the Works Progress Administration Collection and the Iowa State Planning Board Collection at the SHSI, Iowa City.]

1. Joseph Mayer, chairman, Commission on National Archives Survey, Joint Committee on Materials for Research, to Verne E. Chatelain, historian, National Park Service, memorandum of 12 February 1934; Sub-Committee on Inventory of the Joint Committee on Materials for Research, "Library Projects Under the Civil Works Administration (CWA), Circular No. 5, Memorandum on a Proposed National Survey of Local Archives," [c. February 1934].

2. Schroder, *History*, 98–99; quote from Shambaugh to Francis S. Philbrick,

University of Pennsylvania Law School, 23 January 1934, in response to Philbrick's letter of 13 January 1934. Charles H. Brown, librarian, Iowa State College, tried to persuade Shambaugh to change his mind but to no avail; see Brown to Shambaugh, 18 October 1934.

3. Schroder, *History*, 100; Jay Du Von, state director, Federal Writers' Projects, to Shambaugh, 19 February 1936. The survey of local public records was a project separate from the Survey of Federal Archives until 1937, when both were incorporated into the WPA Historical Records Survey; see Donald R. McCoy, *The National Archives: America's Ministry of Documents, 1934–1968* (Chapel Hill: University of North Carolina Press, 1978) 64–66.

4. Luther Evans, national director, Historical Records Survey, to Field Supervisors, 11 January 1936, memorandum concerning "Iowa-Historical Records Survey" enclosed with Du Von letter of 19 February 1936; Don Farran, state director, Historical Records Survey to Shambaugh, 27 July 1937; Shambaugh to Farran, 31 July 1937. In a 1975 article, Don Farran notes enigmatically that "there had been some malfunctions in that project" before he was appointed state director in the summer of 1937 but does not elaborate; see Don Farran, "The Historical Records Survey in Iowa, 1936–1942," *AI* 42 (1975): 599.

5. Stiles to Shambaugh, 23 March 1936; Shambaugh to Stiles, 25 March 1936.

6. Stiles to Shambaugh, 30 March 1936; undated three-page description of the society's collections obviously written in response to Stiles's request.

7. See correspondence between Shambaugh and Farran, 4 and 5 June 1937, 27 and 31 July 1937, 4 August 1937.

8. Farran to Shambaugh, 5 October 1937; Shambaugh to Farran, 6 October 1937; Farran to Evans, 11 October 1937; Farran to Shambaugh, 12 October 1937.

9. Farran to Shambaugh, 21 September 1937; Shambaugh to Farran, 9 October 1937.

10. Farran, "The Historical Records Survey," 606.

11. Ibid., 605; Farran to Shambaugh, 19 January 1938; Shambaugh to Farran, 20 January 1938.

12. The foreword appears in the form of a letter from Shambaugh following the title page to Federal Writers' Project, *Iowa: A Guide to the Hawkeye State* (New York: Viking Press, 1938).

13. Du Von to Gallahauer [*sic*], 17 March 1936; Gallaher to Du Von, 19 March 1936.

14. Kresensky to Shambaugh, 17 March 1936.

15. Shambaugh to Kresensky, 18 March 1936.

16. Shambaugh to Kresensky, 27 March 1936.

17. Kresensky to Gallaher, 20 February 1937.

18. Kresensky to Gallaher, 5 April 1937.

19. Kresensky to Gallaher, 1 February 1937.

20. Shambaugh to Kresensky, 23 August 1938; Kresensky to Shambaugh, 24 August 1938; Kresensky to Shambaugh, 19 September 1938, containing a transcript of Catton's review, "They Bring You Iowa's Story," dated 7 September 1938, which appeared in the nationally syndicated newspaper column "About Books."

21. See *The Complete Poems of Raymond Kresensky* (1986).

22. Kresensky to Gallaher, 9 April 1936.

23. Kresensky to Gallaher, 9 and 14 April 1936, 1 May 1936; Gallaher to Kresensky, 11 and 18 April 1936, 7 May 1936. The pragmatic questions that Gallaher raised about folkways—"Why, I wonder, are these social customs all credited to farmers? What about bank nights, giving cars to the holder of a lucky number, and goodwill tours of members of Chambers of Commerce?"—received notice beyond the Iowa office. On 4 June 1936 Kresensky informed her that the essay on folkways "with your changes incorporated was chosen by the Washington office as material for supplementary instructions and sent out to all the projects in the country."

24. Schroder, *History*, 101.

25. Ibid., 82; Persons, *The University of Iowa*, 99–100.

26. Du Von to Shambaugh, 28 January 1937; Du Von to Gallaher, 29 January 1937.

27. Shambaugh to Keller, 20 April 1937.

28. Undated "Memoranda" outlining project tasks and sponsor requirements and containing six sets of figures obviously prepared for discussions concerning the SHSI 1937 appropriation.

29. Shambaugh to Du Von, 4 May 1937.

30. Shambaugh to Kresensky, 11 November 1937, 15 December 1937.

31. Kresensky to Shambaugh, 23 December 1937.

32. Gallaher to Kresensky, 11 January 1938; Kresensky to Gallaher, 12 January 1938.

33. Kresensky to Henry G. Alsberg, director, Federal Writers' Project, 13 October 1937; Kresensky to Shambaugh, 18 October 1937; Shambaugh to Alsberg, 21 October 1937; Alsberg to Shambaugh, 27 October 1937; Shambaugh to Alsberg, 1 November 1937.

34. See Kresensky to Shambaugh, 18 October 1937, 3 and 12 November 1937, 23 December 1937; Shambaugh to Alsberg, 13 November 1937.

35. Alsberg to Shambaugh, 5 March 1938.

36. Shambaugh to Alsberg, telegram, 7 March 1938.

37. Shambaugh to Alsberg, telegram, 9 March 1938; Shambaugh to Alsberg, 10 March 1938.

38. Shambaugh to Alsberg, 15 March 1938, 27 June 1938.

39. Shambaugh to Kresensky, 11 October 1938.

40. Kresensky to Shambaugh, 18 November 1938; Shambaugh to Kresensky, 19 November 1938.

41. Schroder, *History*, 101–102.

42. Robert Cantwell, "America and the Writers' Project," *New Republic*, 26 April 1939, 325.

43. Ibid., 323–325 passim.

44. Jacob L. Crane Jr. and George Wheeler Olcott, *Iowa Twenty-five Year Conservation Plan* (Des Moines: Meredith, 1933); P. H. Elwood, "Iowa State Planning Board: Project and Fiscal Procedure," 15 May 1934.

45. Rebecca Conard, *Places of Quiet Beauty: Parks, Preserves and Environmentalism* (Iowa City: University of Iowa Press, 1997), 136–137.

46. P. H. Elwood to [State Planning] Board Members and Technical Advisors, memorandum of 28 May 1934 with a revised list of project committees; see also Iowa State Planning Board, *The Second Report* (n.p., 1935), 148–152.

47. Elwood to Board Members and Technical Advisors, 28 May 1934; Herring to Shambaugh, 2 May 1934; Shambaugh to Herring, 4 May 1934; Conard, *Places of Quiet Beauty*, 135.

48. Rapp to Shambaugh, 8 May 1934; Rapp to members of the Scenic and Historical Committee, 17 May 1934.

49. Jacob A. Swisher, "Some Historic Sites in Iowa," *IJHP* 32 (1934): 195–259; reprinted and bound as a separate monograph under the same title.

50. Shambaugh to Rapp, 9 June 1934, 26 July 1934.

51. Swisher, "Some Historic Sites," 244–245; Federal Writers' Project, *Iowa* 486; see also Sage, *A History of Iowa*, 139–140.

52. A notice in *IJHP* 33 (1935): 186–187 indicates there were six planned projects in 1934—restoring the John Brown House; constructing a replica of Iowa's first schoolhouse in Lee County; restoring a stone mill in Clayton County; purchasing the former home of Ansel Briggs near Winterset, also associated with the Underground Railroad; and purchasing a historic flour mill at Decorah. Only two of these projects ever went beyond the discussion stage.

53. Rapp, "Progress Report of the Historic Scenic Com.," contained in 3 September 1934 letter to committee members and technical advisers.

54. Rapp to Shambaugh, 19 September 1934; Shambaugh to Rapp, 24 September, 1934; Fitzsimmons to Rapp, 8 November 1934; Rapp to Shambaugh, 9 November 1934; Shambaugh to Fitzsimmons, 30 November 1934; Shambaugh to Rapp, 30 November 1934.

55. Fitzsimmons to Shambaugh, 24 January 1935.

56. Rapp to Shambaugh, 16 October 1934; Shambaugh to Rapp, 18 October 1934; Fitzsimmons to Shambaugh, 24 January 1935; Shambaugh to Fitzsimmons, 25 January 1935; Fitzsimmons to Shambaugh, 26 January 1935.

57. Orville Francis Grahame, "The First Iowa School," *Palimpsest* 5 (1924): 401–407; Jacob Swisher, *Some Historic Sites in Iowa* (Iowa City: SHSI, n.d.), 45–46.

58. See Shambaugh to Rapp, 18 October 1934.

59. Fitzsimmons to Shambaugh, 9 February 1935; Shambaugh to Fitzsimmons, 13 February 1935.

60. Rapp to Shambaugh, 12 September 1934.

61. Shambaugh to Rapp, 18 September 1934.

62. Shambaugh to C. B. Murtagh, State Comptroller, 23 October 1934.

63. Conard, *Places of Quiet Beauty*, 170–179.

64. Fitzsimmons to Shambaugh, 7 March 1936; Shambaugh to Fitzsimmons, 9 March 1936.

65. Fitzsimmons to Shambaugh, 20 May 1936; Shambaugh to Fitzsimmons, 22 May 1936; Fitzsimmons to Shambaugh, 23 May 1936; Fitzsimmons to E. R. Morgan, WPA engineer, 27 May 1936; Shambaugh to Fitzsimmons, 10 June 1936; Ethyl Martin to Fitzsimmons, 13 October 1936; Shambaugh to Fitzsimmons, 21 October 1936, 5 November 1936; Fitzsimmons to Shambaugh, 21 June 1937; Shambaugh to Fitzsimmons, 16 July 1937; Fitzsimmons to Shambaugh, 8 November 1937; Shambaugh to Fitzsimmons, 9 November 1937; Fitzsimmons to Shambaugh, 27 November 1937; Shambaugh to Margaret Marnette Hart, Council Bluffs, Iowa, 16 April 1938. See also the notice in *IJHP* 36 (1938): 110.

66. Shambaugh to Jim Berry, Marquette, Iowa, 3 September 1937.

67. See the notice in *IJHP* 39 (1941): 108.

68. See Kammen, *Mystic Chords*, especially part three, "Circa 1915 to 1945."

69. See William Stott, *Documentary Expression and Thirties America* (New York: Oxford University Press, 1973).

70. Peter T. Harstad and Michael D. Gibson, "An Iowa-Born Historian and the American Revolution: Carl Becker and 'The Spirit of '76,'" *Palimpsest* 75 (1976): 174–192.

71. Carl L. Becker, "Everyman His Own Historian," *AHR* 397 (1932): 229–231.

72. Charles Beard, "Written History As an Act of Faith," *AHR* 39 (1934): 219–231.

73. Novick, *That Noble Dream*, 268.

74. Persons, *The University of Iowa*, 160.

75. Bertha Shambaugh, "Notes made on June 28, 1945 on rereading the first draft of the ms," Shambaugh Papers.

76. Campus Course file, Shambaugh Papers.

77. Shambaugh's remarks are preserved in the typescript of his speech, "The More Than in University Education," Shambaugh Papers; see also *APSR* 25 (1931): 176.

78. "Address to Freshman, 1926," TS, Shambaugh Papers.

79. "Social Hygiene," undated TS, Shambaugh Papers.

80. "The Campus Course," author unidentified, but probably Ethan Allan judging by the greater specificity concerning teaching method, Shambaugh Papers.

81. Ibid.

82. Shambaugh to Robinson, 22 January 1932, 22 July 1932; Robinson to Shambaugh, 16 July 1932, Shambaugh Correspondence.

83. "The Campus Course," version that appears with the Swisher manuscript at both the SHSI and at the University of Iowa.

84. This two-word summation also is the title of a separate chapter in the Swisher manuscript.

85. "New S.U.I. Course Will Boil Down All Learning to Gain Insight Into Life," *Des Moines Sunday Register*, 22 May 1932.

86. Ibid.

87. Bertha Shambaugh, "Notes made on June 28, 1945."

88. During Martin's seven-year tenure, she demonstrated an administrative style that reflected her many years of working at Shambaugh's side. Despite paper shortages during the war, she saw to it that the SHSI continued publishing the *IJHP* and the *Palimpsest*, although book reviews were dropped from the *IJHP*, and that the SHSI continued to publish at least some books, although the Centennial Series was cut short. Martin also steered the society in some new directions: improving the library, working with the Association of Local Historical Societies, and working with the Iowa Centennial Committee. Moreover, in 1947 when Governor Robert Blue proposed consolidating the SHSI with the Department of Archives in Des Moines, she mounted a strong opposition campaign similar to those Shambaugh had waged in earlier years. She managed to keep the consolidation bills from emerging out of committee and in the process even secured an increased appropriation for the SHSI. See Burchfield, "The Career of Ethyl Martin."

89. Schroder, *History*, 127–140.

7. The Emergence of the Modern Public History Movement

1. James B. Rhoads, "The North Carolina State Archives," in *Public History in North Carolina, 1903–1978*, ed. Jeffrey J. Crow (Raleigh: North Carolina Department of Cultural Resources, Division of Archives and History, 1979), 17–22; McCoy, *The National Archives*, 13–26, 113–117.

2. Veysey, "Plural Organized Worlds," 71; Novick, *That Noble Dream*, 49. See also Scardaville, "Looking Backward Toward the Future," 35–43, for an assessment of the multidimensional origins of the historical profession in the late nineteenth century and the subsequent narrowing of professional identity via the AHA.

3. Patricia Mooney-Melvin, "Professional Historians and the Challenge of Redefinition," in *Public History: Essays from the Field*, ed. James B. Gardner and Peter S. LaPaglia (Malabar, Fla.: Krieger, 1999), 10–12. This essay is a revised version of

Mooney-Melvin's presidential address at the 1995 meeting of the National Council of Public Historians, subsequently published as "Professional Historians and 'Destiny's Gate,'" *PH* 17:3 (summer 1995): 9–24.

4. Benjamin Franklin Cooling, "History Programs in the Department of Defense," *PH* 12:4 (fall 1990): 45–48; William S. Dudley, "World War I and Federal Military History," *PH* 12:4 (fall 1990): 23–31; "Proceedings of the Conference on Military History," *AHA Annual Report for 1912*, 159–197; see also Martin Reuss, "Public History in the Federal Government," in *Public History: An Introduction*, ed. Barbara J. Howe and Emory L. Kemp, rev. ed. (Malabar, Fla.: Krieger, 1988), 294.

5. Cooling, "History Programs," 45, 48–49, 52–53; Dudley, "World War I," 31–35, 37–38, 40; Reuss, "Public History," 295; Thomas P. Ofcansky, "The History of the United States Air Force History Program," in Howe and Kemp, *Public History*, 310–311.

6. Elizabeth B. Drewry, "Historical Units of Agencies of the First World War," *Bulletins of the National Archives* 4 (July 1942): 3–5.

7. Ibid., 21–31.

8. Arnita A. Jones and Wayne D. Rasmussen, "Wayne Rasmussen and the Development of Policy History at the United States Department of Agriculture," *PH* 14:1 (winter 1992): 13, 17–18; see also Reuss, "Public History," 294–295.

9. McCoy, *The National Archives*, 40–44.

10. Charles B. Hosmer Jr., *Preservation Comes of Age: From Williamsburg to the National Trust, 1926–1949*, vol. 1 (Charlottesville: University Press of Virginia, 1981), 513–521; Harlan D. Unrau and G. Frank Williss, "To Preserve the Nation's Past: The Growth of Historic Preservation in the National Park Service during the 1930s," *PH* 9:2 (spring 1987): 21–23; Barry Mackintosh, "The National Park Service Moves into Historical Interpretation," *PH* 9:2 (spring 1987): 53–54; Charles B. Hosmer Jr., "Verne E. Chatelain and the Development of the Branch of History of the National Park Service," *PH* 16:1 (winter 1994): 26–27.

11. Hosmer, "Verne E. Chatelain," 36–37.

12. Mackintosh, "The National Park Service," 53–55; see also Barry Mackintosh, *The Historic Sites Survey and National Historic Landmarks Program: A History* (Washington, D.C.: National Park Service, History Division, 1985), 11.

13. Hosmer, "Verne E. Chatelain," 26. Chatelain went on to serve as director of the St. Augustine Restoration Program for the Carnegie Institution, out of which experience came *The Defenses of Spanish Florida, 1565 to 1763* (1941). Eventually, his career would lead to a faculty position at the University of Maryland.

14. Unrau and Williss, "To Preserve the Nation's Past," 28–49; Hosmer, *Preservation Comes of Age*, vol. 1, 562–576, and vol. 2, 926–950; Mackintosh, "The National Park Service," 55–63; Mackintosh, *The Historic Sites Survey*, 12–26.

15. Hosmer, *Preservation Comes of Age*, vol. 1, 11–74; Michael Wallace, "Visiting the Past: History Museums in the United States," in *Presenting the Past: Essays on*

History and the Public, ed. Susan Porter Benson, Stephen Brier, and Roy Rosenzweig (Philadelphia: Temple University Press, 1986), 144, 146–147. See also Cary Carson, "Colonial Williamsburg and the Practice of Interpretive Planning in American History Museums," *PH* 20:3 (summer 1998): 13–16.

16. Wallace, "Visiting the Past," 149–150.

17. Becker, "Everyman," 228.

18. McCoy, *The National Archives*, 134–145; see also John J. Rumbarger, "The War Production Board and Historical Research: Some Observations on Writing Public History," *PH* 6:2 (spring 1984): 5–19.

19. Cooling, "History Programs," 46; Reuss, "Public History," 296–297; William R. McClintock, "Clio Mobilizes: Naval Reserve Historians during the Second World War," *PH* 13:1 (winter 1991): 25–46.

20. Jamie W. Moore, "History, the Historian, and the Corps of Engineers," *PH* 3:1 (winter 1981): 64–66.

21. Cooling, "History Programs," 49–50, 55, 58; Ofcansky, "Air Force History Program," 312–313.

22. Maurice Matloff, "Government and Public History: The Army," *PH* 2:3 (spring 1980): 43–44.

23. Ibid., 45.

24. Forrest C. Pogue and Holly C. Shulman, "Forrest C. Pogue and the Birth of Public History in the Army," *PH* 15:1 (winter 1993): 27–46.

25. Ibid., 40.

26. Matloff, "Government," 46.

27. Cooling, "History Programs," 58–60.

28. Ibid., 46–47, 50–51, 55–57; Ofcansky, "Air Force History Program," 315–321.

29. Reuss, "Public History," 298–299.

30. Hosmer, *Preservation Comes of Age*, vol. 2, 810.

31. Ibid., 813–865.

32. See Conrad Wirth, *Parks, Politics, and the People* (Norman: University of Oklahoma Press, 1980), chapter 9; and Dwight F. Rettie, *Our National Park System: Caring for America's Greatest Natural and Historic Treasures* (Urbana and Chicago: University of Illinois Press, 1995), 7, 116, 121 n. 6, 185 n. 15, 210, for contrasting views on MISSION 66. See also Edwin C. Bearss, "The National Park Service and Its History Program: 1864–1986—An Overview," *PH* 9:2 (spring 1987): 10–18.

33. Jerry L. Rogers, "The National Register of Historic Places: A Personal Perspective on the First Twenty Years," *PH* 9:2 (spring 1987): 92–93; Beth Grosvenor Boland, "Federal Programs in Historic Preservation," in Howe and Kemp, *Public History*, 133–135.

34. Richard G. Hewlett and Jo Anne McCormick Quatannens, "Richard G. Hewlett: Federal Historian," *PH* 19 (winter 1997): 53–83.

35. George T. Mazuzan, "Countering 'Doublethink': Doing History at the Nuclear Regulatory Commission," *PH* 7:3 (summer 1985): 35–42.

36. Jones and Rasmussen, "Wayne Rasmussen," 16–17.

37. James B. Gardner and David F. Trask, "Serving Time in the Trenches: David F. Trask, Public Historian and Federal Historian," *PH* 22:2 (spring 2000): 8–28, quote 13.

38. Roger Trask, "Small Federal History Offices in the Nation's Capital," *PH* 13:1 (winter 1991): 47–60; Reuss, "Public History," 297–298; Dennis Roth, "History in the U.S. Forest Service," *PH* 11:1 (winter 1989): 49–56; Steven Lubar, "Public History in a Federal Museum: The Smithsonian's National Museum of American History" in Howe and Kemp, *Public History*, 219.

39. Jack M. Holl, "The New Washington Monument: History in the Federal Government," *PH* 7 (fall 1985): 14–15; see Reuss, "Public History," 302–306, for a more detailed summary of federal historians based on data compiled by the Society of Federal Historians in 1981.

40. Among other things, Firestone produced synthetic rubber, which was crucial to the war effort.

41. William D. Overman, "The Firestone Archives and Library," *American Archivist* 16 (October 1953): 305–309; Philip F. Mooney, "The Practice of History in Corporate America: Business Archives in the United States," in Howe and Kemp, *Public History*, 427–428; Elizabeth W. Adkins, "The Development of Business Archives in the United States: An Overview and a Personal Perspective," *American Archivist* 60 (winter 1997): 9–11.

42. Overman, "The Firestone Archives," 307.

43. Mooney, "History in Corporate America," 429.

44. Adkins, "The Development of Business Archives," 10–11. Adkins goes on to note on p. 15 that, at some as-yet-undetermined date, the Firestone archive was abandoned (Bridgestone Corporation acquired Firestone in 1988), underscoring the point that corporate archives, unlike their institutional counterparts, are less permanent in nature.

45. Helen L. Davidson, "A Tentative Survey of Business Archives," *American Archivist* 24 (1961): 323–327; Gary P. Saretzky, "North American Business Archives: Results of a Survey," *American Archivist* 40 (1977): 413–419; David R. Smith, "A Historical Look at Business Archives," *American Archivist* 45 (1982): 273–278; see also Mooney, "History in Corporate America," 428. The 1960 survey polled a cross section of 113 business organizations, including manufacturing, wholesale, food-processing, mail-order, and insurance companies; banks; and not-for-profit organizations. Thus the 51 respondents represent 45 percent of those polled, indicating that the number of business firms consciously preserving records as of 1960 may actually have been higher.

46. Adkins, "The Development of Business Archives," 13.

47. William T. Alderson Jr., "The American Association for State and Local History," *Western Historical Quarterly* 1 (1970): 177–178; Adams, "Planning for the Future," 15.

48. Adams, "Planning for the Future," 16.

49. Ibid., 16–17; Alderson, "The American Association," 175–182.

50. Constance B. Schulz, "Becoming a Public Historian," in Gardner and LaPaglia, *Public History*, 23–40, provides a useful overview of the role of professional associations in establishing specialized training programs for professional work in museums and archives.

51. Timothy Paul Donovan, *Historical Thought in America: Postwar Patterns* (Norman: University of Oklahoma Press, 1973).

52. Robert Kelley, "Public History: Its Origins, Nature, and Prospects," *PH* 1:1 (fall 1978): 19.

53. Ibid., 20.

54. "First National Symposium on Public History: A Report," *PH* 2:1 (fall 1979): 9–10, 22–40, 84–116; Schulz, "Becoming a Public Historian," notes that of fifty-seven programs listed in the National Council on Public History (NCPH) *Guide to Graduate Programs in Public History*, fourteen trace their origins to the 1970s.

55. Arnita Jones, "The National Coordinating Committee: Programs and Possibilities," *PH* 1:1 (fall 1978): 49–60.

56. Richard G. Hewlett, "The Washington Scene: 1977–1981," *PH* 21:3 (summer 1999): 39–42.

57. Page Putnam Miller, "Advocacy on Behalf of History: Reflections on the Past Twenty Years," *PH* 22:2 (spring 2000): 40.

58. Alan Newell to author, e-mail, 16 January 2000.

59. Darlene Roth, in "News and Notes," *PH* 1:1 (fall 1978): 90; Darlene Roth, "The Mechanics of a History Business," *PH* 1:3 (spring 1979): 26–40.

60. Nina Kressner Cobb, "Necessity Was the Mother: The Institute for Research in History," *PH* 2:3 (spring 1980): 77–85; see also "News and Notes," *PH* 1:1 (fall 1978): 92.

61. Paula Gillett, "History in a New Key," *PH* 2:3 (spring 1980): 86–90; "The Institute for Research in History—After Three Years," *AHA Newsletter* 17:1 (January 1979): 11–12.

62. "First National Symposium on Public History: A Report," passim.

63. Jack M. Holl, "Getting on Track: Coupling the Society for History in the Federal Government to the Public History Train," *PH* 21:3 (summer 1999): 43–55, quote 46; much of the information that follows in this paragraph is extracted from the entire article.

64. In addition to Holl's article, see also Philip L. Cantelon, "The Business of Professional History," *PH* 21:3 (summer 1999): 17; Hewlett, "The Washington Scene," 41–42; and Gardner and Trask, "Serving Time in the Trenches," 21–23.

65. G. Wesley Johnson, "Editor's Preface," *PH* 1:4 (summer 1979): 6–9; "National Council on Public History," *AHA Newsletter* 17:9 (December 1979): 8.

66. Holl, "Getting on Track," 55. There are those who still believe, however, that the NCPH took a wrong turn when it became a membership organization. David Trask, for instance, asserts that "instead of being a medium for uniting and improving the profession as a whole, the National Council is kind of a PR operation for the public historians." See Gardner and Trask, "Serving Time in the Trenches," 20–21.

67. For example, in 1986 the NCPH and OAH began meeting jointly on an occasional basis. Additionally, newsletters and journals of both the OAH and AHA incorporate articles on public history, and in 1988 the *JAH* began reviewing museum exhibits. The 1987 AHA "Statement on Standards of Professional Conduct" recognizes that "the historical profession is diverse, composed of people who work in a variety of institutional settings and also as independent professionals."

68. See W. Turrentine Jackson and David E. Russell, "Practicing Public History: A Conversation with W. Turrentine Jackson," *PH* 20:1 (winter 1998): 21–48; Hewlett and McCormick Quatannens, "Richard G. Hewlett," 78; Philip L. Cantelon, "As a Business: Hired, Not Bought," in Gardner and LaPaglia, *Public History*, 385–395; Jannelle Warren-Findley, "Contract Historians and Consultants," in Gardner and LaPaglia, *Public History*, 75–86. The founders of PHR Associates— Shelley Bookspan, Greg King, and myself—were influenced by Darlene Roth's success. PHR Environmental split off from PHR Associates in 1988 and continues business in Santa Barbara. The History Group, Inc., is now Darlene Roth and Associates. Jackson Research Projects became JRP Inc. in 1991. Historical Research Associates incorporated in 1978.

69. Roth, "History Business," 36–38.

70. Theodore J. Karamanski, "Introduction: Ethics and the Use of History," in *Ethics and Public History: An Anthology* (Malabar, Fla.: Krieger, 1990), 1.

71. See Terrence O'Donnell, "Pitfalls Along the Path of Public History," *PH* 4:1 (winter 1982): 65–72; J. Morgan Kousser, "Are Expert Witnesses Whores? Reflections on Objectivity in Scholarship and Expert Witnessing," *PH* 6:12 (winter 1984): 5–19; Stanley M. Hordes, "Does He Who Pays the Piper Call the Tune? Historians, Ethics, and the Community," *PH* 8:1 (winter 1986): 53–56; Albert L. Hurtado, "Historians and Their Employers: A Perspective on Professional Ethics," *PH* 8:1 (winter 1986): 47–52; Roy H. Lopata, "Ethics in Public History: Clio Meets Ulasewicz," *PH* 8:1 (winter 1986): 39–46; Martin Reuss, "Federal Historians: Ethics and Responsibility in the Bureaucracy," *PH* 8:1 (winter 1986): 13–20; Carl Ryant, "The Public Historian and Business History: A Question of Ethics," *PH* 8:1 (winter 1986): 31–38; Ronald C. Tobey, "The Public Historian as Advocate: Is Special Attention to Professional Ethics Necessary?" *PH* 8:1 (winter 1986): 21–30; James C. Williams, "Standards of Professional Conduct in California," *PH* 8:1 (winter 1986):

57–59. Most of the articles appearing in the special winter 1986 issue of the *PH* were reprinted in Karamanski, *Ethics and Public History*.

72. Novick, *That Noble Dream*, 512–521.

73. "Roundtable Appendix" to "Roundtable: Ethics and Public History," *PH* 8:1 (winter 1986): 60–68; Karamanski, "Introduction," 3.

74. Many public historians, like Alan Newell, have acquired a seasoned perspective on the question of ethics. "I won't say that in 26 years we haven't faced any ethical questions with clients," he writes, "but, there have been remarkably few and none that have kept me awake at night for very long. Frankly, most clients expect professionalism, know what it is, and respect it, even if it causes them problems on a project. How often do attorneys, accountants, engineers really face 'gut-wrenching' ethical questions? Why should historians expect to confront anything different? There are 'social conscience' questions that I think historians must face and, sometimes, we confuse this with 'ethics.' . . . If anything, public history has, I think, brought a measure of maturity, level-headedness, and practicality to the questions of ethics. I am not a relativist in any sense of the word. But, I believe that, in the final analysis, one's professional ethics are rooted in personal ethics and the declination of one's own moral compass." Newell to author, e-mail, 16 January 2000.

75. Theodore J. Karamanski, "Reflections on Ethics and the Historical Profession," *PH* 21:3 (summer 1999): 127–133, quote 133.

76. G. Wesley Johnson, "Editor's Preface," *PH* 1:1 (fall 1978): 4, 7–8.

77. Kelley, "Public History," 16.

78. Michael Kammen, ed. *The Past Before Us: Contemporary Historical Writing in the United States* (Ithaca, N.Y.: Cornell University Press, 1980), 44.

79. Remarks of Joel Tarr as reported in "First National Symposium," 9–10.

80. Remarks of Martin Sullivan as reported in "First National Symposium," 16–17.

81. Novick, *That Noble Dream*, 513.

82. Ronald J. Grele, "Whose Public? Whose History? What Is the Goal of a Public Historian?" *PH* 3:1 (winter 1981): 40–48.

83. The October 1981 issue of the *Radical History Review* (vol. 25) was devoted entirely to articles and reviews on "Presenting the Past: History and the Public," which the editors subsequently turned into a book of essays; see Benson, Brier, and Rosenzweig, *Presenting the Past*. Since 1987, "Public History" has appeared as a section in the *Radical History Review*; typically, the articles in this section are review essays of films, museum exhibits, or other examples of "public programming in history."

84. Grele, "Whose Public?," 40.

85. See especially Benson, Brier, and Rosenzweig, *Presenting the Past*.

86. Remarks of Ernest May as reported in "First National Symposium," 14.

87. Joan Hoff Wilson, "Is the Historical Profession an 'Endangered Species?'" *PH* 2:2 (winter 1980): 4–21.

88. Arnita A. Jones, "Public History Now and Then," *PH* 21:3 (summer 1999): 25–26.

89. Ibid., 26–27.

90. Those who support some type of certification or credential for public historians typically are seeking to raise the level of professionalism in historical organizations and among contractors by excluding amateurs and avocationalists. See, for instance, Michael J. Devine, "Administators: Students of History and Practitioners of the Art of Management," in Gardner and LaPaglia, *Public History*, 45–56; Michael J. Devine, "Public History Beyond the Classroom," *OAH Council of Chairs Newsletter* 45 (June 1995): 2–4. This strategy troubles others because it is inherently elitist and still others because where there is certification, litigation is sure to follow.

91. Theodore J. Karamanski, "Making History Whole: Public Service, Public History, and the Profession," *PH* 12:3 (summer 1990): 96.

92. See Leffler and Brent, *Public and Academic History*; Ernest Boyer, *Scholarship Reconsidered: Priorities Reconsidered for the Professoriate* (Menlo Park, Calif.: Carnegie Foundation for the Advancement of Teaching, 1990; reprint, San Francisco: Jossey-Bass, 1997); Louis R. Harlan, "The Future of the American Historical Association," *AHR* 95 (February 1990): 1–8; Ralph D. Gray, "Reaching Out: An Agenda for Academic Historians in the 1990s," *OAH Newsletter* 18:3 (August 1990): 8, 19; "Redefining Historical Scholarship: Report of the American Historical Association *Ad Hoc* Committee on Redefining Scholarly Work," *AHA Perspectives* 32:3 (March 1994): 19–23, subsequently published as a separate pamphlet; "Redefining Historical Scholarship," *OAH Newsletter* 22:4 (November 1994): 13–14; "A Continuing Conversation on Redefining Historical Scholarship," *OAH Newsletter* 23:1 (February 1995): 1, 5–7; James B. Gardner, "The Redefinition of Historical Scholarship: Calling a Tail a Leg?" *PH* 20:4 (fall 1998): 43–57; Noel J. Stowe, "Public Historians as Faculty: Roles and Rewards," *PH* 21:2 (spring 1999): 84–87.

93. "A Roundtable: Promotion and Tenure Criteria for Faculty in Applied History," *PH* 6 (spring 1984): 51–66; Kendrick A. Clements, "Promotion and Tenure for Public Historians," *OAH Council of Chairs Newsletter* 2:1 (April 1988): 6–8; Philip V. Scarpino, "Some Thoughts on Defining, Evaluating, and Rewarding Public Scholarship," *PH* 15:2 (spring 1993): 55–61; Constance B. Schulz and Kendrick Clements, "Revisiting a History Department's Tenure and Promotion Guidelines: A Response to James B. Gardner," *PH* 21:2 (spring 1999): 89–93.

94. Scarpino, "Some Thoughts," 59.

95. Mooney-Melvin, "Professional Historians," 14–15.

Collected Works of Benjamin F. Shambaugh, 1893–1940

The following bibliography represents the scope of publications that were either authored or edited by Benjamin F. Shambaugh, the earliest being 1893, or that emanated from the State Historical Society of Iowa from the time he took over as editor of the *Iowa Historical Record* in 1900 until his death in 1940. It synthesizes information found in Ruth Gallaher's tribute, "Benjamin Shambaugh," in the *Iowa Journal of History and Politics* 38 (1940); an undated typescript located with Shambaugh's papers at the State Historical Society of Iowa, titled "Benjamin Franklin Shambaugh," possibly compiled by Ruth Gallaher and Francis O. Wilcox; and a 1980 bibliography compiled by Mary Bennett for the inventory of the Shambaugh Family Papers at the University of Iowa. Discrepancies between and among these compilations and the actual holdings of the State Historical Society preclude any claim to this being a definitive bibliography; however, it fairly represents the body of work associated with Shambaugh's professional career. Matthew Schaefer and David Hudson graciously assisted with crosschecking and provided emendations. Unless noted otherwise, the publisher is the State Historical Society of Iowa.

Edited Series, SHSI
Applied History Series

Applied History [topics in municipal government in Iowa]. Vol. 1, 1912.
Applied History [topics in state government in Iowa]. Vol. 2, 1914.
County Government and Administration in Iowa. Vol. 4, 1925.
Municipal Government and Administration in Iowa. Vols. 5–6, 1930.
Statute Law-Making in Iowa. Vol. 3, 1916.

Biographical Series

Briggs, John E. *William Peters Hepburn*. 1919.
Brigham, Johnson. *James Harlan*. 1913.
Clark, Dan E. *Samuel Jordan Kirkwood*. 1917.

Cole, Cyrenus. *I Am a Man—The Indian Black Hawk*. 1938.

————. *I Remember, I Remember*. 1936.

Gregory, Charles Noble. *Samuel Freeman Miller*. 1907.

Haynes, Fred Emory. *James Baird Weaver*. 1919.

Johnson, Jack T. *Peter Anthony Dey: Integrity in Public Service*. 1939.

Parish, John C. *George Wallace Jones*. 1912.

————. *John Chambers*. 1909.

————. *Robert Lucas*. 1907.

Payne, Charles E. *Josiah Bushnell Grinnell*. 1938.

Pelzer, Louis. *Augustus Caesar Dodge*. 1908.

Reid, Harvey. *Thomas Cox*. 1909.

Swisher, Jacob A. *Leonard F. Parker*. 1927.

————. *Robert Gordon Cousins*. 1939.

Bulletins of Information, Nos. 1–7 (1904–1915)

Centennial History Series

Cole, Cyrenus. *Iowa through the Years*. 1940.

Parker, George F. *Iowa Pioneer Foundations*. 2 vols. 1940.

Swisher, Jacob. *Iowa: Land of Many Mills*. 1940.

Economic History Series

Brindley, John E. *History of Road Legislation in Iowa*. 1912.

————. *History of Taxation in Iowa*. 2 vols. 1911.

Downey, E. H. *History of Labor Legislation in Iowa*. 1910.

————. *History of Work Accident Indemnity in Iowa*. 1912.

Hopkins, John A., Jr. *Economic History of the Production of Beef Cattle in Iowa*. 1928.

Pollock, Ivan L. *History of Economic Legislation in Iowa*. 1918.

Preston, Howard H. *History of Banking in Iowa*. 1922.

Iowa and War Series, 24 booklets (1917–1919)

Iowa Chronicles of the World War Series

Fullbrook, Earl. *The Red Cross in Iowa*. 2 vols. 1922.

Hansen, Marcus L. *Welfare Campaigns in Iowa*. 1920

————. *Welfare Work in Iowa*. 1921.

Pollock, Ivan L. *The Food Administration in Iowa*. 2 vols. 1923.

Whitney, Nathaniel. *The Sale of War Bonds in Iowa*. 1923.

Iowa Historical Record (IHR), Vols. 17–18 (1900–1902)

Iowa Journal of History and Politics (IJHP). Vols. 1–38 (1903–1940)

Iowa Monograph Series

Allen, Ethan P. *Invalidation of Municipal Ordinances by the Supreme Court of Iowa.* 1933.

Swisher, Jacob A. *The Legislation of the Forty-third General Assembly of Iowa.* 1929.

———. *The Legislation of the Forty-fourth General Assembly of Iowa.* 1932.

———. *The Legislation of the Forty-fifth General Assembly of Iowa (Extra Session).* 1934.

Swisher, Jacob A., and Ruth Gallaher. *The Legislation of the Forty-fifth General Assembly of Iowa (Regular Session).* 1933.

Wilcox, Francis O. *Some Aspects of the Financial Administration of Johnson County, Iowa.* 1934.

Iowa Social History Series

Briggs, John E. *History of Social Legislation in Iowa.* 1915.

Gillin, John L. *History of Poor Relief Legislation in Iowa.* 1914.

Miscellaneous Publications

Aurner, Clarence. *History of Education in Iowa.* 5 vols. (1914–1920).

———. *History of Township Government in Iowa.* 1914.

Black Hawk. *Life of Black Hawk, Ma-ka-tai-me-she-kia-kiak.* Translated by Antoine LeClaire; prepared for publication by J. B. Patterson. 1932.

Chambers, John. *Autobiography of John Chambers.* 1908.

Clark, Dan E. *History of Senatorial Elections in Iowa.* 1912.

Cook, Herbert Clare. *The Administrative Functions of the Department of Public Instruction in Iowa.* 1929.

Gallaher, Ruth. *Legal and Political Status of Women in Iowa.* 1918.

Gingerich, Melvin. *The Mennonites in Iowa.* 1939.

Hansen, Marcus Lee. *Old Fort Snelling, 1819–1858.* 1918.

Haynes, Fred E. *Child Labor Legislation in Iowa.* 1914.

———. *History of Third Party Movements since the Civil War, with Special Reference to Iowa.* 1916.

Jones, Louis T. *The Quakers of Iowa.* 1914.

Lea, Albert M. *The Book That Gave Iowa Its Name.* 1935. Reprint, *Notes on the Wisconsin Territory: Particularly with Reference to the Iowa District, or Black Hawk Purchase,* 1836. Also reprinted in *Annals of Iowa,* 3rd series, 11 (1913): 115–167.

Macbride, Thomas Huston. *In Cabins and Sod-houses.* 1928.

Mahan, Bruce E. *Old Fort Crawford and the Frontier.* 1926.

———. *State and Local History in the High School.* 1924.

McCarty, Dwight G. *Early Social and Religious Experiments in Iowa.* 1902.

———. *The Territorial Governors of the Old Northwest.* 1910.

Patton, O. K. *Removal of Public Officials in Iowa.* 1914.

Pelzer, Louis. *Marches of the Dragoons in the Mississippi Valley.* 1917.

Rich, Joseph W. *The Battle of Shiloh.* 1911.

Richman, Irving Berdine. *Ioway to Iowa*. 1931.

Robeson, George F. *Governments of Special Charter Cities in Iowa*. 1923.

Shambaugh, Bertha Horack. *Amana: The Community of True Inspiration*. 1908.

———. *Amana That Was and Amana That Is*. 1932.

Swisher, Jacob A. *American Legion in Iowa, 1919–1929*. 1929.

———. *The Iowa Department of the Grand Army of the Republic*. 1936.

Taber, John H. *The Story of the 168th Infantry*. 1925.

Teakle, Thomas. *Spirit Lake Massacre*. 1918.

Thwaites, Reuben Gold. *The Romance of Mississippi Valley History*. 1907.

Van der Zee, Jacob. *The Black Hawk War*. 1918.

———. *The British in Iowa*. 1922.

———. *The Hollanders of Iowa*. 1912.

———. *The Mormon Trails in Iowa*. 1914.

Weld, Laenas Gifford. *On the Way to Iowa*. 1910.

Wright, Henry H. *A History of the Sixth Iowa Infantry*. 1923.

Public Archives Series (edited by Benjamin F. Shambaugh)

Documentary Material Relating to the History of Iowa. 3 vols. 1897–1901.

Executive Journal of Iowa 1838–1841 [Robert Lucas]. 1906.

Messages and Proclamations of the Governors of Iowa. 7 vols. 1903–1905.

Shambaugh, Benjamin F.

Articles, Encyclopedia Entries, and Reviews

"Anarchism." In *Current Encyclopedia*. Vol. 1. Chicago: Modern Research Society, 1901.

"Applied History." In *Proceedings of the Mississippi Valley Historical Association for the Year 1908–1909*. Vol. 2, 137–139. Cedar Rapids, Iowa: Torch Press, 1910.

"Assembly Districting and Apportionment in Iowa." *IJHP* 2 (1904): 520–603. Reprinted as booklet, 1904.

"Available Law Books in the Territory of Iowa." Editorial. *AI*, 3rd series, 4 (January 1901): 631, 632.

"The Beginnings of a Western Commonwealth." In B. F. Gue, *Progressive Men of Iowa*. Vol. 2, 2–72. Des Moines: Conaway and Shaw Publishing, 1899.

"The Boundaries of Iowa." *AI*, 3rd series, 4 (1899): 70–71.

"A Brief History of the State Historical Society of Iowa." *IJHP* 1 (1903): 139–152. Reprinted as a pamphlet, 1907; as an article in *Proceedings of the Fiftieth Anniversary of the Constitution of Iowa*, 1907; and as an article in *Journal of History* 1 (1908): 208–220.

"The Case of Mr. Lorin(g) Wheeler: His Appointment and Resignation as Chief Justice of the County Court of Dubuque." *AI*, 3rd series, 3 (April 1898): 454–458.

"Claim Associations." In *Cyclopedia of American Government*. Vol. 1. 1914.

"Collection and Preservation of the Materials of War History." *Iowa Library Quarterly* 8 (1918): 81–83.

"Commission Government in Iowa: The Des Moines Plan." *Annals of the American Academy of Political and Social Science* 38 (1911): 698–718. Reprinted as *Commission Government: The Des Moines Plan*, 1912.

"The Commission Plan of Government." *Papers and Proceedings of the Minnesota Academy of Social Sciences* 3 (1910): 150–165.

"Constable." In *Cyclopedia of American Government*. Vol. 1. 1914.

"The Constitution of Cuba." In *Current Encyclopedia*. Vol. 2. Chicago: Current Encyclopedia Co., 1902.

"Constitutional Disfranchisement of the Negro." In *Current Encyclopedia*. Vol. 1. Chicago: Modern Research Society, 1901.

"Constitutional Law." *Progress* 4 (August 1900).

"The Creation of a Commonwealth." *Palimpsest* 15 (1934): 81–126. Extracted from *The Constitutions of Iowa*.

"The Des Moines Plan of City Government." *Proceedings of the American Political Science Association* 4 (1907): 189–192.

"Documentary Material Relating to the History of Iowa." *IHR* 14 (1898): 216–221, 257.

"Documentary Study of Western History." *Dial* 22 (16 June 1897): 353.

"Documents Relating to Governor Lucas." *IHR* 16 (1900): 56–73.

"Early Iowa." *Journal of History* 16 (1923): 117–119. Reprint of the introduction to *The Constitutions of Iowa*.

Early Iowa and the Pioneers. Privately published, n.d.

"The Founding of Iowa City." *Palimpsest* 20 (1939): 137–176.

"From the Standpoint of a Pioneer." Edited reminiscences of Hawkins Taylor. *IHR* 14 (1898): 310–318.

"Frontier Land Clubs or Claim Associations." In *Annual Report of the American Historical Association for 1900*. Vol. 1, 69–84.

"An Historical Journal." *IHR* 18 (1902): 460–462.

"Historical Research." In *Twenty-seventh Biennial Report of the Board of Curators of the State Historical Society of Iowa to the Governor of the State* (1908), 20–21.

Historical Research in the State Historical Society of Iowa. 1908.

"History of the University of Iowa." *IHR* 15 (1899): 521–523.

"The History of the West and the Pioneers." In *Proceedings of the State Historical Society of Wisconsin for 1910*, pp. 133–145. Madison, 1911.

"An Important Manuscript." *IHR* 9 (1893): 414–420.

"Injunctions: The Law Thereof and Its Recent Application in Labor Disputes." In *Current Encyclopedia*. Vol. 1. Chicago: Modern Research Society, 1901.

"Iowa History from 1699–1821: A History of Governments." *IHR* 16 (1900): 29–46.

"The Iowa Pioneers." *Palimpsest* 8 (1927): 1–4. Reprinted in *Palimpsest* 32 (1951): 1–4.

"The Iowa School of Research Historians." In *Proceedings of the Mississippi Valley Historical Association for 1910–1911*, 152. Cedar Rapids, Iowa: Torch Press, 1912.

"Law-making Powers of the Legislature in Iowa." In *Applied History*. Vol. 3 (1916), 137–158.

"The Laws of Iowa, 1838–1839." Editorial. *AI*, 3rd series, 4 (January 1901): 632, 633.

"Letters of J. W. Denison" [ed.]. *IJHP* 31 (1933): 87–126, 274–304.

"Maps Illustrative of the Boundary History of Iowa." *IJHP* 2 (1904): 369–380. Reprinted as a pamphlet, 1914.

"The Naming of Iowa." *Palimpsest* 5 (1924): 370–372. Reprinted in *Palimpsest* 7 (1926) Special Iowa No. 18–20, and in *Palimpsest* 16 (1935): 81–86.

"The New Consitution of Alabama." In *Current Encyclopedia*. Vol. 1. Chicago: Modern Research Society, 1901.

"Notes on the Early Church History of Iowa." *IHR* 15 (1899): 564–573.

"Original Manuscript Copies of the Constitutions of Iowa." *AI*, 3rd series, 2 (October 1896): 557–558.

"The Origin of the Name Iowa." *AI*, 3rd series, 3 (January 1899): 641–644.

"Overseers of the Poor." In *Cyclopedia of American Government*. Vol. 2. 1914.

"The Parish." In *Cyclopedia of American Government*. Vol. 2. 1914.

"The Pioneer." In *Proceedings of the Old Settlers of Johnson County, August 17, 1899*, 4–14. Iowa City, Iowa: Republican Print, 1899.

"The Preservation of Historical Material." *AI*, 3rd series, 3 (July 1897): 155–156.

"The Public Archives." *AI*, 3rd series, 7 (April 1906): 385–386.

"Recent Important Judicial Decisions." *American Political Science Review* 1 (1907): 333–336.

"Recent Publications in Iowa History." *IHR* 16 (1900): 197–200.

"Report of the Committee on Methods of Organization and Work on the Part of State and Local Historical Societies." In *Annual Report of the American Historical Association for 1905*. Vol. 1, 249–325.

"A Report on the Public Archives." *AI*, 3rd series, 7 (January 1907): 561–591. Reprinted as *A First Report on the Public Archives*, 1907.

"Report on the Public Archives of Iowa." In *Annual Report of the American Historical Association for 1900*. Vol. 2, 39–46.

Review of Alden's *New Governments West of the Alleghanies*. Annals of the American Academy of Political and Social Science 11 (1898).

Review of Bowman's *The Administration of Iowa: A Study in Centralization. IJHP* 2 (1904).

Review of Burgess's *Reconstruction and the Constitution. Annals of the American Academy of Political and Social Science* 20 (1902).

Review of Graham's *English Political Philosophy from Hobbes to Maine*. *Annals of the American Academy of Political and Social Science* 15 (1900).

Review of Hart's *Actual Government as Applied under American Conditions*. *IJHP* 1 (1903).

Review of Hart's *The American Nation: A History*. *IJHP* 3 (1905).

Review of MacDonald's *Select Statutes and Other Documents Illustrative of the History of the United States, 1861–1898*. *IJHP* 2 (1904).

Review of Merriam's *History of the Theory of Sovereignty since Rousseau*. *Annals of the American Academy of Political and Social Science* 16 (1901).

Review of Ostrogorski's *Democracy and the Organization of Political Parties*. *IJHP* 1 (1903).

Review of Richman's *Rhode Island: A Study in Separatism*. *IJHP* 4 (1906).

Review of Salter's *Iowa: The First Free State in the Louisiana Purchase*. *IJHP* 3 (1905).

Review of Thorpe's *The Constitutional History of the United States*. *IJHP* 1 (1903).

Review of Thorpe's *William Pepper, M.D., LL.D., Provost of the University of Pennsylvania*. *IJHP* 2 (1904).

Review of Willoughby's *The Political Theories of the Ancient World*. *IJHP* 2 (1904).

"Samuel J. Kirkwood." *Iowa Magazine*, 4 October 1923, 650.

"School District." In *Cyclopedia of American Government*. Vol. 3. 1914.

Scientific Law-making. 1914.

"Selectmen." In *Cyclopedia of American Government*. Vol. 3. 1914.

"Shall the Story of Iowa's Part in the War be Preserved?" *Iowa and War* 19 (1919): 1–21.

Some Comments upon J. W. Rich's Discussion of the Battle of Shiloh. 1914.

"Some Interesting Facts About the Early History of Iowa City and the Old Capitol Building." In *Year Book of the Old Settlers' Association, Johnson County, Iowa, 1921–1922*, 3–21. Iowa City, Iowa, n.p., 1922.

"The State Historical Society of Iowa in War Times." *Iowa and War* 18 (1918): 1–21.

"Statutory Adoption of the Common Law in the West." *AI*, 3rd series, 2 (April 1896): 372–375.

"Supreme Court Decisions in the Insular Cases." In *Current Encyclopedia*. Vol. 1. Chicago: Modern Research Society, 1901.

"Town Clerk." In *Cyclopedia of American Government*. Vol. 3. 1914.

"Towns and Townships." In *Cyclopedia of American Government*. Vol. 3. 1914.

"Township." In *Cyclopedia of American Government*. Vol. 3. 1914.

"Township Board." In *Cyclopedia of American Government*. Vol. 3. 1914.

"Treasurer in Local Government." In *Cyclopedia of American Government*. Vol. 3. 1914.

"Trustees of Township." In *Cyclopedia of American Government*. Vol. 3. 1914.

"The Vision." Editorial. *Palimpsest* 1 (1920): 1.

"The Work of the State Historical Society of Iowa." *Quarterly of the Iowa Library Commission* 4 (1904): 1–5.

Books

A History of the Constitutions of Iowa. 1902. Revised and expanded as *The Constitutions of Iowa*, 1934. Based on his 1895 doctoral dissertation.
Iowa City: A Contribution to the Early History of Iowa. 1893. An expanded version of his 1893 master's thesis.
The Old Stone Capitol Remembers. 1939.

Edited Works

Constitution and Records of the Claim Association of Johnson County, Iowa. 1894.
The Constitution of the State of Iowa with an Historical Introduction. 1902. Reprinted with revisions, 1907, 1914, 1922.
Debates of the Constitutional Conventions of 1844 and 1846. 1900.
First Census of the Original Counties of Dubuque and Demoine. 1897.
Fragments of Debates of the Iowa Constitutional Conventions of 1844 and 1846. 1900.
Iowa Manual of Legislative Procedure. 1917.
Proceedings of the Fiftieth Anniversary of the Constitution of Iowa. 1907.
A Second Report on the Public Archives. 1907.
True Tales of the Great Valley: The Man with the Iron Hand. Houghton Mifflin, 1913.

Other Editorial Positions

Editor. *Proceedings of the Mississippi Valley Historical Association*. Vols. 1–7 (1909–1914).
Member, Board of Editors. *APSR*, 1906–1914.
Member, Board of Editors. *MVHR*, 1914–1916.

Bibliography

Manuscript Collections

State Historical Society of Iowa Archives, Iowa City

Alan Schroder's research notes for the SHSI 1978–1979 institutional self-study
Benjamin F. Shambaugh Correspondence, 1896–1940
Commonwealth Conference Collection
Ethyl Martin Correspondence, 1940–1947
Iowa History Week Collection
Iowa State Planning Board Collection
Works Progress Administration Collection

State Historical Society of Wisconsin, Madison

Papers of Reuben Gold Thwaites

University of Iowa Special Collections, Iowa City

Shambaugh Family Papers

Official Reports and Documents

Annual Report of the American Historical Association, 1890–1940.
Biennial Report of the Board of Curators of the State Historical Society to the Governor and General Assembly. Des Moines, Iowa.
Brookings Institution, Institute for Government Research. *Report on a Survey of Administration in Iowa*. Des Moines: State of Iowa, 1933.
Crane, Jacob L., Jr., and George Wheeler Olcott. *Iowa Twenty-five Year Conservation Plan*. Des Moines: Meredith, 1933.
Iowa Documents.
Iowa House Journal.

Iowa State Planning Board. *The Second Report*. n.p., 1935.

Laws of Iowa.

Proceedings of the Mississippi Valley Historical Association. Cedar Rapids, Iowa: Torch Press.

Schroder, Alan M. *History, Analysis and Recommendations Concerning the Public Programs of the Iowa State Historical Department, Division of the State Historical Society*. Iowa City: SHSI, 1981.

State Historical Society of Iowa. Minutes of the Board of Curators.

———. Reports of the Board of Curators.

State University of Iowa Board of Regents.

Miscellaneous Sources

Aldrich, Charles. "Origin of the Historical Department." *AI*, 3rd series, 1 (April 1893): 56–58.

———. Untitled editorial in *AI*, 3rd series, 5 (April 1901): 66–68.

Briggs, John Ely. "Benj. F. Shambaugh." *Palimpsest* 21 (1940): 113–139.

Burchfield, Robert. "The Career of Ethyl Martin: Superintendent of the State Historical Society of Iowa, 1940–1947." On file, *SHSI*.

Cantwell, Robert. "America and the Writers' Project." *New Republic*, 26 April 1939, 323–325.

Catalogue of the State University of Iowa, 1888–1889, 1892–1893.

"Charles Aldrich: In Memoriam." *AI*, 3rd series, 8 (January 1909).

Clements, Kendrick A. "Promotion and Tenure for Public Historians." *OAH Council of Chairs Newsletter* 2:1 (April 1988): 6–8.

"Collection and Preservation of the Materials of War History: A Patriotic Service for Public Libraries, Local Historical Societies, and Local Historians." *Bulletin of Information*, no. 8 (SHSI, 1919).

"A Continuing Conversation on Redefining Historical Scholarship." *OAH Newsletter* 23:1 (February 1995): 1, 5–7.

Curti, Merle. Review of *In Cabins and Sod-Houses* by Thomas Macbride. *AHR* 34 (April 1929): 656–657.

Devine, Michael J. "Public History Beyond the Classroom." *OAH Council of Chairs Newsletter* 45 (June 1995): 2–4.

Fitzpatrick, Edward A. Review of *Applied History*, vol. 2. *AHR* 20 (1914–1915): 896–897.

Gallaher, Ruth A. "Benjamin F. Shambaugh." *IJHP* 38 (1940): 227–233.

Gray, Ralph D. "Reaching Out: An Agenda for Academic Historians in the 1990s." *OAH Newsletter* 18:3 (August 1990): 8, 19.

"In Memory of Jacob Swisher." SHSI *News for Members* 29:3 (fall 1976): 3–4.

"The Institute for Research in History—After Three Years." *AHA Newsletter* 17:1 (January 1979): 11–12.

"The Iowa Conference on Local History." *AI*, 3rd series, 23 (July 1941): 57–68.

Jordan, Philip D. Review of *The Old Stone Capitol Remembers* by Benjamin F. Shambaugh. *MVHR* 26 (December 1939): 437–438.

Latta, Maurice C. Review of *Josiah Bushnell Grinnell* by Charles E. Payne. *MVHR* 26 (June 1939): 103–104.

Lindley, Harlow. Review of *In Cabins and Sod-Houses* by Thomas Macbride. *MVHR* 16 (June 1929): 137.

"National Council on Public History." *AHA Newsletter* 17:9 (December 1979): 8.

Nevins, Allan. "What's the Matter with History?" *Saturday Review of Literature* 19 (4 February 1939): 3–4, 16.

Nixon, H. C. Review of *The Old Stone Capitol Remembers* by Benjamin F. Shambaugh. *AHR* 45 (April 1940): 728.

"Obituary, Benjamin F. Shambaugh." *AHR* 45 (1940): 1007.

"Obituary, Benjamin F. Shambaugh." *APSR* 34 (1941): 556–557.

"Our States and Their History." *Nation*, 20 May 1915, 555.

"Proceedings of the Conference of Local Historical Societies of Iowa Held at Iowa City on Wednesday, May 25, 1910." *IJHP* 8 (1910): 522 ff.

"Redefining Historical Scholarship." *OAH Newsletter* 22:4 (November 1994): 13–14.

"Redefining Historical Scholarship: Report of the American Historical Association *Ad Hoc* Committee on Redefining Scholarly Work." *AHA Perspectives* 32:3 (March 1994): 19–23.

Roth, Darlene. In "News and Notes." *PH* 1:1 (fall 1978): 90.

"The Second Commonwealth Conference." *University of Iowa Service Bulletin* 8:11 (15 March 1924): 5.

Sellers, J. L. Review of *Robert Gordon Cousins* by Jacob A. Swisher. *MVHR* 26 (September 1939): 273.

Sly, John F. Review of *Municipal Government and Administration in Iowa*, vols. 5 and 6 in the Applied History Series. *APSR* 25 (1931): 189–190.

"Suggestions to Public Libraries and Local Historical Societies in Iowa Relative to Collecting and Preserving the Materials of Local History." *Bulletin of Information*, no. 3 (SHSI, 1904).

Books and Monographs

Alex, Lynn M. *Iowa's Archaeological Past*. Iowa City: University of Iowa Press, 2000.

Appleby, Joyce, Lynn Hunt, and Margaret Jacob. *Telling the Truth About History*. New York: W. W. Norton, 1994.

Aurner, Nellie Slayton. *Benjamin Franklin Shambaugh*. Iowa City: University of Iowa Press, 1947.

Bennett, Mary. *An Iowa Album: A Photographic History, 1860–1920*. Iowa City: University of Iowa Press, 1990.

Benson, Susan Porter, Stephen Brier, and Roy Rosenzweig, eds. *Presenting the Past: Essays on History and the Public*. Philadelphia: Temple University Press, 1986.

Bodnar, John. *Remaking America: Public Memory, Commemoration, and Patriotism in the Twentieth Century*. Princeton, N.J.: Princeton University Press, 1992.

Boyer, Ernest. *Scholarship Reconsidered: Priorities Reconsidered for the Professorate*. Menlo Park, Calif.: Carnegie Foundation for the Advancement of Teaching, 1990. Reprint, San Francisco: Jossey-Bass, 1997.

[Briggs, John Ely, ed.]. *Benjamin Franklin Shambaugh As Iowa Remembers Him: In Memoriam*. Iowa City: SHSI, 1941.

Clements, Kendrick A. *Hoover, Conservation, and Consumerism: Engineering the Good Life*. Lawrence: University Press of Kansas, 2000.

Conard, Rebecca. *Places of Quiet Beauty: Parks, Preserves and Environmentalism*. Iowa City: University of Iowa Press, 1997.

Crow, Jeffrey J., ed. *Public History in North Carolina, 1903–1978*. Raleigh: North Carolina Department of Cultural Resources, Division of Archives and History, 1979.

Donovan, Timothy Paul. *Historical Thought in America: Postwar Patterns*. Norman: University of Oklahoma Press, 1973.

Etulain, Richard, ed. *Does the Frontier Make America Exceptional?* Boston: Bedford/St. Martin's, 1999.

Federal Writers' Project. *Iowa: A Guide to the Hawkeye State*. New York: Viking Press, 1938.

Frisch, Michael. *A Shared Authority: Essays on the Craft and Meaning of Oral and Public History*. Albany: State University of New York, 1990.

Gardner, James B., and Peter S. LaPaglia, eds. *Public History: Essays from the Field*. Malabar, Fla.: Krieger, 1999.

Gillis, John, ed. *Commemorations: The Politics of National Identity*. Princeton, N.J.: Princeton University Press, 1994.

Glassberg, David. *American Historical Pageantry: The Uses of Tradition in the Early Twentieth Century*. Chapel Hill: University of North Carolina Press, 1990.

Higham, John. *History: Professional Scholarship in America*. Baltimore: Johns Hopkins University Press, 1965.

Hosmer, Charles B., Jr. *Preservation Comes of Age: From Williamsburg to the National Trust, 1926–1949*. 2 vols. Charlottesville: University Press of Virginia, 1981.

Howe, Barbara J., and Emory L. Kemp, eds. *Public History: An Introduction*. Rev. ed. Malabar, Fla.: Krieger, 1988.

Kammen, Michael. *Mystic Chords of Memory*. New York: Knopf, 1991.

———. *The Past Before Us: Contemporary Historical Writing in the United States.* Ithaca, N.Y.: Cornell University Press, 1980.

Karamanski, Theodore J., ed. *Ethics and Public History: An Anthology.* Malabar, Fla.: Krieger, 1990.

Keyes, Margaret N. *Old Capitol: Portrait of an Iowa Landmark.* Iowa City: University of Iowa Press, 1988.

Larson, Magali Sarfatti. *The Rise of Professionalism: A Sociological Analysis.* Berkeley and Los Angeles: University of California Press, 1977.

Leffler, Phyllis K., and Joseph Brent. *Public and Academic History: A Philosophy and Paradigm.* Malabar, Fla.: Krieger, 1990.

Lord, Clifford L., and Carl Ubbelohde. *Clio's Servant: The State Historical Society of Wisconsin, 1846–1954.* Madison: State Historical Society of Wisconsin, 1967.

Mackintosh, Barry. *The Historic Sites Survey and National Historic Landmarks Program: A History.* Washington, D.C.: National Park Service, History Division, 1985.

McCoy, Donald R. *The National Archives: America's Ministry of Documents, 1934–1968.* Chapel Hill: University of North Carolina Press, 1978.

Novick, Peter. *That Noble Dream: The "Objectivity Question" and the American Historical Profession.* Cambridge: Cambridge University Press, 1988.

Persons, Stow. *The University of Iowa in the Twentieth Century: An Institutional History.* Iowa City: University of Iowa Press, 1990.

Petersen, William J. *Iowa History Reference Guide.* Iowa City: SHSI, 1952.

Rettie, Dwight F. *Our National Park System: Caring for America's Greatest Natural and Historic Treasures.* Urbana and Chicago: University of Illinois Press, 1995.

Robinson, James Harvey. *The New History.* New York: Macmillan, 1912.

Rothberg, Morey, and Jacqueline Goggin, eds. *John Franklin Jameson and the Development of Humanistic Scholarship in America, Volume One: Selected Essays.* Athens: University of Georgia Press, 1993.

Sage, Leland. *A History of Iowa.* Ames: Iowa State University Press, 1974.

Stott, William. *Documentary Expression and Thirties America.* New York: Oxford University Press, 1973.

Swisher, Jacob. *Some Historic Sites in Iowa.* Iowa City: SHSI, n.d.

Wirth, Conrad. *Parks, Politics, and the People.* Norman: University of Oklahoma Press, 1980.

Articles and Book Chapters

Adams, George Rollie. "Planning for the Future, AASLH Takes a Look at Its Past." *History News* 37:9 (September 1982): 12–18.

Adkins, Elizabeth W. "The Development of Business Archives in the United States: An Overview and a Personal Perspective." *American Archivist* 60 (winter 1997): 8–21.

Alderson, William T., Jr. "The American Association for State and Local History." *Western Historical Quarterly* 1 (1970): 175–182.

Beard, Charles. "Written History As an Act of Faith." *AHR* 39 (1934): 219–231.

Bearss, Edwin C. "The National Park Service and Its History Program: 1864–1986—An Overview." *PH* 9:2 (spring 1987): 10–18.

Becker, Carl L. "Everyman His Own Historian." *AHR* 37 (1932): 221–236.

Billington, Ray Allen. "Tempest in Clio's Teapot: The American Historical Association Rebellion of 1915." *AHR* 78 (1978): 348–369.

Birdsall, William F. "The Two Sides of the Desk: The Archivist and the Historian, 1909–1935." *American Archivist* 38 (1975): 159–173.

Boland, Beth Grosvenor. "Federal Programs in Historic Preservation." In Howe and Kemp, *Public History*.

Bourne, Henry E. "The Work of American Historical Societies." *AHA Annual Report for 1904*, 117–127.

———. "The Work of American Historical Societies." *IJHP* 3 (1905): 271–285.

Boyd, Julian P. "State and Local Historical Societies in the United States." *AHR* 40 (1934): 10–37.

Brindley, John. "The Legislative Reference Movement." *IJHP* 7 (1909): 132–141.

Cantelon, Philip L. "As a Business: Hired, Not Bought." In Gardner and LaPaglia, *Public History*.

———. "The Business of Professional History." *PH* 21:3 (summer 1999): 15–19.

Carson, Cary. "Colonial Williamsburg and the Practice of Interpretive Planning in American History Museums." *PH* 20:3 (summer 1998): 11–51.

Cobb, Nina Kressner. "Necessity Was the Mother: The Institute for Research in History." *PH* 2:3 (spring 1980): 77–85.

Cooling, Benjamin Franklin. "History Programs in the Department of Defense." *PH* 12:4 (fall 1990): 43–63.

Davidson, Helen L. "A Tentative Survey of Business Archives." *American Archivist* 24 (1961): 323–327.

Devine, Michael J. "Administators: Students of History and Practitioners of the Art of Management." In Gardner and LaPaglia, *Public History*.

Dow, E[arle] W. "Features of the New History: Apropos of Lamprecht's 'Deutsche Geschichte.'" *AHR* 3 (1898): 431–448.

Drewry, Elizabeth B. "Historical Units of Agencies of the First World War." *Bulletins of the National Archives* 4 (July 1942): 3–31.

Dudley, William S. "World War I and Federal Military History." *PH* 12:4 (fall 1990): 23–41.

Eggleston, Edward. "The New History." In *AHA Annual Report for 1900*, vol. 1, 37–47.

Farran, Don. "The Historical Records Survey in Iowa, 1936-1942." *AI* 42 (1975): 597–608.

"First National Symposium on Public History: A Report." *PH* 2:1 (fall 1979): 7–83.

Friedel, Frank. "The Iowa Progressive Tradition and National Achievements." In *Three Progressives from Iowa: Gilbert N. Haugen, Herbert C. Hoover, Henry A. Wallace*, ed. John N. Schacht. Iowa City: Center for the Study of the Recent History of the United States, 1980.

Gardner, James B. "The Redefinition of Historical Scholarship: Calling a Tail a Leg?" *PH* 20:4 (fall 1998): 43–57.

Gardner, James B., and David F. Trask. "Serving Time in the Trenches: David F. Trask, Public Historian and Federal Historian." *PH* 22:2 (spring 2000): 8–28.

Gillett, Paula. "History in a New Key." *PH* 2:3 (spring 1980): 86–90.

Grahame, Orville Francis. "The First Iowa School." *Palimpsest* 5 (1924): 401–407.

Grele, Ronald J. "Whose Public? Whose History? What Is the Goal of a Public Historian?" *PH* 3:1 (winter 1981): 40–48.

Griffin, A. P. C. "Bibliography of the Historical Societies of the United States." In *AHA Annual Report for 1890*, 161–267; *AHA Annual Report for 1892*, 307–619; and *AHA Annual Report for 1895*, 675–1147.

Harlan, Louis R. "The Future of the American Historical Association." *AHR* 95 (February 1990): 1–8.

Harstad, Peter T., and Michael D. Gibson. "An Iowa-Born Historian and the American Revolution: Carl Becker and 'The Spirit of '76.'" *Palimpsest* 75 (1976): 174–192.

Hewlett, Richard G. "The Washington Scene: 1977–1981." *PH* 21:3 (summer 1999): 39–42.

Hewlett, Richard G., and Jo Anne McCormick Quatannens. "Richard G. Hewlett: Federal Historian." *PH* 19:1 (winter 1997): 53–83.

Holbrook, Franklin F. "The Collection of State War Service Records." *AHR* 25 (October 1919): 72–78.

Holl, Jack M. "Getting on Track: Coupling the Society for History in the Federal Government to the Public History Train." *PH* 21:3 (summer 1999): 43–55.

———. "The New Washington Monument: History in the Federal Government." *PH* 7 (fall 1985): 9–20.

Hordes, Stanley M. "Does He Who Pays the Piper Call the Tune? Historians, Ethics, and the Community." *PH* 8:1 (winter 1986): 53–56.

Hosmer, Charles B., Jr. "Verne E. Chatelain and the Development of the Branch of History of the National Park Service." *PH* 16:1 (winter 1994): 25–38.

Hurtado, Albert L. "Historians and Their Employers: A Perspective on Professional Ethics." *PH* 8:1 (winter 1986): 47–52.

Jackson, W. Turrentine, and David E. Russell. "Practicing Public History: A Conversation with W. Turrentine Jackson." *PH* 20:1 (winter 1998): 21–48.

Jameson, J. Franklin. "The American Historical Association, 1884–1909." *AHR* 15 (October 1909): 1–20.

———. "The Functions of State and Local Historical Societies with Respect to Research and Publication." *AHA Annual Report for 1897*, 53–59.

Johnson, Frontis W. "The North Carolina Historical Commission, 1903–1978." In Crow, *Public History in North Carolina*.

Johnson, G. Wesley. "Editor's Preface." *PH* 1:1 (fall 1978): 4–10.

———. "Editor's Preface." *PH* 1:4 (summer 1979): 6–9.

Jones, Arnita A. "The National Coordinating Committee: Programs and Possibilities." *PH* 1:1 (fall 1978): 49–60.

———. "Public History Now and Then." *PH* 21:3 (summer 1999): 25–26.

Jones, Arnita A., and Wayne D. Rasmussen. "Wayne Rasmussen and the Development of Policy History at the United States Department of Agriculture." *PH* 14:1 (winter 1992): 11–29.

Karamanski, Theodore J. "Introduction: Ethics and the Use of Public History." In Karamanski, *Ethics and Public History*.

———. "Making History Whole: Public Service, Public History, and the Profession." *PH* 12:3 (summer 1990): 91–101.

———. "Reflections on Ethics and the Historical Profession." *PH* 21:3 (summer 1999): 127–133.

Kelley, Robert. "Public History: Its Origins, Nature, and Prospects." *PH* 1:1 (fall 1978): 16–28.

Kinnett, David. "Miss Kellogg's Quiet Passion." *Wisconsin Magazine of History* 62 (summer 1979): 267–299.

Kousser, J. Morgan. "Are Expert Witnesses Whores? Reflections on Objectivity in Scholarship and Expert Witnessing." *PH* 6:12 (winter 1984): 5–19.

Leland, Waldo Gifford. "Recollections of the Man Who Rang the Bell." *American Archivist* 21 (1958): 55–57.

Lopata, Roy H. "Ethics in Public History: Clio Meets Ulasewicz." *PH* 8:1 (winter 1986): 39–46.

Lubar, Steven. "Public History in a Federal Museum: The Smithsonian's National Museum of American History." In Howe and Kemp, *Public History*.

Mackintosh, Barry. "The National Park Service Moves into Historical Interpretation." *PH* 9:2 (spring 1987): 51–63.

Matloff, Maurice. "Government and Public History: The Army." *PH* 2:3 (spring 1980): 43–51.

Mazuzan, George T. "Countering 'Doublethink': Doing History at the Nuclear Regulatory Commission." *PH* 7:3 (summer 1985): 35–42.

McClintock, William R. "Clio Mobilizes: Naval Reserve Historians during the Second World War." *PH* 13:1 (winter 1991): 25–46.

McLaughlin, A[ndrew] C. "A Bureau of Historical Research." *IJHP* 2 (1904): 303–305.

Miller, Page Putnam. "Advocacy on Behalf of History: Reflections on the Past Twenty Years." *PH* 22:2 (spring 2000): 39–49.

Mooney, Philip F. "The Practice of History in Corporate America: Business Archives in the United States." In Howe and Kemp, *Public History*.

Mooney-Melvin, Patricia. "Professional Historians and the Challenge of Redefinition." In Gardner and LaPaglia, *Public History*.

Moore, Jamie W. "History, the Historian, and the Corps of Engineers." *PH* 3:1 (winter 1981): 64–74.

O'Donnell, Terrence. "Pitfalls Along the Path of Public History." *PH* 4:1 (winter 1982): 65–72.

Ofcansky, Thomas P. "The History of the United States Air Force History Program." In Howe and Kemp, *Public History*.

Overman, William D. "The Firestone Archives and Library." *American Archivist* 16 (October 1953): 305–309.

Owen, Thomas McAdory. "State Departments of Archives and History." *AHA Annual Report for 1904*, 237–253.

Pogue, Forrest C., and Holly C. Shulman. "Forrest C. Pogue and the Birth of Public History in the Army." *PH* 15:1 (winter 1993): 27–46.

"Presenting the Past: History and the Public." *Radical History Review* 25 (October 1981).

Reinsch, Paul S. "The American Political Science Association." *IJHP* 2 (1904): 156–157.

Reuss, Martin. "Federal Historians: Ethics and Responsibility in the Bureaucracy." *PH* 8:1 (winter 1986): 13–20.

———. "Public History in the Federal Government." In Howe and Kemp, *Public History*.

Rhoads, James B. "The North Carolina State Archives." In Crow, *Public History in North Carolina*.

Ridgeway, Stanley R. "Democratic Individualism, Expertise, and the Public Interest: The Legacy of the Commonwealth Conference." *AI* 50 (1990): 359–374.

Rogers, Jerry L. "The National Register of Historic Places: A Personal Perspective on the First Twenty Years." *PH* 9:2 (spring 1987): 91–104.

Roth, Darlene. "The Mechanics of a History Business." *PH* 1:3 (spring 1979): 26–40.

Roth, Dennis. "History in the U.S. Forest Service." *PH* 11:1 (winter 1989): 49–56.

Rothberg, Morey D. "The Brahmin as Bureaucrat: J. Franklin Jameson at the Carnegie Institution of Washington, 1905-1928." *PH* 8:4 (fall 1986): 47–60.

"Roundtable Appendix" to "Roundtable: Ethics and Public History." *PH* 8:1 (winter 1986): 60–68.

"A Roundtable: Promotion and Tenure Criteria for Faculty in Applied History." *PH* 6 (spring 1984): 51–66.

Rumbarger, John J. "The War Production Board and Historical Research: Some Observations on Writing Public History." *PH* 6:2 (spring 1984): 5–19.

Ryant, Carl. "The Public Historian and Business History: A Question of Ethics." *PH* 8:1 (winter 1986): 31–38.

Saretzky, Gary P. "North American Business Archives: Results of a Survey." *American Archivist* 40 (1977): 413–419.

Scardaville, Michael C. "Looking Backward Toward the Future: An Assessment of the Public History Movement." *PH* 9:4 (fall 1987): 35–43.

Scarpino, Philip V. "Some Thoughts on Defining, Evaluating, and Rewarding Public Scholarship." *PH* 15:2 (spring 1993): 55–61.

Schlesinger, Arthur M. Introduction to *The Transit of Civilization from England to America in the Seventeenth Century*, by Edward Eggleston. 1900. Reprint, Gloucester, Mass.: Peter Smith, 1972.

Schmidt, Louis B. "The Activities of the State Historical Society of Iowa." *History Teacher's Magazine* 6 (March 1915): 75–81.

Schroder, Alan M. "Applied History: An Early Form of Public History." *Public Works Historical Society Newsletter* 17 (March 1980): 3–4.

———. "Benjamin F. Shambaugh." In *Historians of the American Frontier*, ed. John R. Wunder. Westport, Conn.: Greenwood Press, 1988.

Schulz, Constance B. "Becoming a Public Historian." In Gardner and LaPaglia, *Public History*.

Schulz, Constance B., and Kendrick Clements. "Revisiting a History Department's Tenure and Promotion Guidelines: A Response to James B. Gardner." *PH* 21:2 (spring 1999): 89–93.

Smith, David R. "A Historical Look at Business Archives." *American Archivist* 45 (1982): 273–278.

Stearns, Peter N., and Joel A. Tarr. "Applied History: New/Old Frontier for the Historical Discipline." *Institute News: Newsletter of the North Carolina Institute of Applied History* 1:3 (October 1982): 6–9.

Stowe, Noel J. "Public Historians as Faculty: Roles and Rewards." *PH* 21:2 (spring 1999): 84–87.

Swisher, Jacob A. "Some Historic Sites in Iowa." *IJHP* 32 (1934): 195–259.

Swisher, Jacob A., and Dorothy Schaffter. "The Legislation of the Forty-second General Assembly." *IJHP* 25 (1927): 499–630.

Thwaites, Reuben Gold. "State-Supported Historical Societies and Their Functions." *AHA Annual Report for 1897*, 63–71.

Tobey, Ronald C. "The Public Historian as Advocate: Is Special Attention to Professional Ethics Necessary?" *PH* 8:1 (winter 1986): 21–30.

Trask, Roger. "Small Federal History Offices in the Nation's Capital." *PH* 13:1 (winter 1991): 47–60.

Turner, Frederick Jackson. "The Significance of History." In *Frontier and Section: Selected Essays of Frederick Jackson Turner*, ed. Ray Allen Billington. Englewood Cliffs, N.J.: Prentice-Hall, 1961.

————. "The Significance of the Frontier in History." In *AHA Annual Report for 1893*, 199–227.

Unrau, Harlan D., and G. Frank Williss. "To Preserve the Nation's Past: The Growth of Historic Preservation in the National Park Service during the 1930s." *PH* 9:2 (spring 1987): 19–49.

Veysey, Laurence. "Plural Organized Worlds of the Humanities." In *The Organization of Knowledge in Modern America, 1860–1920*, ed. Alexandra Oleson and John Voss. Baltimore: Johns Hopkins University Press, 1979.

Wallace, Michael. "Visiting the Past: History Museums in the United States." In Benson, Brier, and Rosenzweig, *Presenting the Past*.

Warren-Findley, Jannelle. "Contract Historians and Consultants." In Gardner and LaPaglia, *Public History*.

Williams, James C. "Standards of Professional Conduct in California." *PH* 8:1 (winter 1986): 57–59.

Wilson, Joan Hoff. "Is the Historical Profession an 'Endangered Species?'" *PH* 2:2 (winter 1980): 4–21.

Index

Adams, George Rollie, 162
Adams, Herbert Baxter, 1
Advisory Committee on War History, 154
Agricultural History Society, 151, 159
Alabama, 20
Alabama Department of Archives and History, 13, 22, 64, 76, 152
Albright, Horace M., 157
Alderson, William T., 163
Aldrich, Charles, 56–64, 69–70, 74–75, 194 n. 26, 194 n. 28
Allen, Ethan P., 138, 140, 143
Alsberg, Henry, 130
American Association for State and Local History, 20, 33, 97, 148, 162–63. *See also* American Historical Association Conference of Historical Societies
American Association of Museums, 161, 163, 169
American Council of Learned Societies, 121, 154, 168
American Dry League, 111
American Economic Association, 1, 11
American Guide Series. *See* Federal Writers' Project
American Heritage, 162
American Historical Association: Conference of Archivists, 15, 76, 148; Conference of Historical Societies (*aka* Conference of State and Local Historical Societies), 6, 11, 13, 15–33, 49, 55, 64, 89–90, 95, 97, 148; 1897 meeting, 1–2; Historical Manuscripts Commission, 2, 12, 15, 29, 51; and National Coordinating Committee, 165; and New History, 7–8; and professionalization of history, 1–4, 148–49, 178–79; Public Archives Commission, 2, 6, 11–15, 27–28, 29, 49, 51, 55, 61, 64, 76, 121; and World War I, 89–90, 149–50; and World War II, 154. *See also* American Association for State and Local History; Society of American Archivists
American Historical Review, 2, 7, 29–30, 84
American Political Science Association, 5–6, 10–11, 49, 107, 109, 112–13, 116–17, 139, 146, 154
American Political Science Review, 5–6
American Relief Administration, 150
American Scenic and Historic Preservation Society, 157
American Society of Public Administration, 154
American University, 163
Ames, Herman V., 15, 28, 76
Anderson, William, 113
Anti-Saloon League, 111
applied history. *See* Benjamin Shambaugh

239

Membership (p 86, 200 (fn 53)

1910 - 375
1922 - 1,200
1926 - 1,400
1932 - 1,350
1934/35 - under 1,000
1940 - 1,200